This study of the nineteenth-century French realist novel focuses on the difference, and fundamental incompatibility, between the narrative and the descriptive modes of discourse. James Reid shows how major novelists including Balzac, Flaubert, and Zola, like some of their twentieth-century successors, grappled with their belief or fear that their stories lied in their representation of time and history, or that their descriptions forgot (rather than remembered) the reality of their socio-historical world. He questions recent critical approaches which have tended to reduce the realist novel to individual or historically determined narratives or speech acts, demonstrating instead the writers' use of irony and allegory in struggling against the deceitfulness and forgetfulness of their own texts.

Cambridge Studies in French 44

NARRATION AND DESCRIPTION IN THE FRENCH REALIST NOVEL

CAMBRIDGE STUDIES IN FRENCH

Recent titles in this series include

33. Lawrence D. Kritzman
The Rhetoric of Sexuality and the Literature of the French Renaissance
34. Jerry C. Nash
The Love Aesthetics of Maurice Scève: Poetry and Struggle
35. Peter France
Politeness and its Discontents: Problems in French Classical Culture
36. Mitchell Greenberg
Subjectivity and Subjugation in Seventeenth-Century Drama and Prose: The Family Romance of French Classicism
37. Tom Conley
The Graphic Unconscious in Early Modern French Writing
38. Margery Evans
Baudelaire and Intertextuality: Poetry at the Crossroads
39. Judith Still
Justice and Difference in the Works of Rousseau: *bienfaisance* and *pudeur*
40. Christopher Johnson
System and Writing in the Philosophy of Jacques Derrida
41. Carol A. Mossman
Politics and Narratives of Birth: Gynocolonization from Rousseau to Zola
42. Daniel Brewer
The Discourse of Enlightenment in Eighteenth-Century France: Diderot and the Art of Philosophizing
43. Roberta L. Krueger
Women Readers and the Ideology of Gender in Old French Verse Romance

A complete list of books in the series is given at the end of the volume.

NARRATION AND DESCRIPTION IN THE FRENCH REALIST NOVEL

The temporality of lying and forgetting

JAMES H. REID

Associate Professor, Department of Foreign Languages,
Illinois State University

Published by the Press Syndicate of the University of Cambridge
The Pitt Building, Trumpington Street, Cambridge CB2 1RP
40 West 20th Street, New York, NY 10011-4211, USA
10 Stamford Road, Oakleigh, Melbourne 3166, Australia

First published 1993

Printed in Great Britain at the University Press, Cambridge

A catalogue record for this book is available from the British Library

Library of Congress cataloguing in publication data

Reid, James H.
Narrative and Description in the French Realist Novel: the temporality of lying and forgetting / James H. Reid.
p. cm. – (Cambridge Studies in French; 44)
Includes bibliographical references and index.
ISBN 0-521-42092-X
1. French fiction – 19th century – History and criticism. 2. Truthfulness and falsehood in literature. 3. Description (Rhetoric) 4. Realism in literature. 5. Memory in literature. 6. Narration (Rhetoric) 7. Time in literature. 8. Allegory.
I Title. II Series.
PQ663.R4 1993
843'.70912 – dc20 92-39126 CIP

ISBN 0 521 42092 x hardback

TAG

For all who
made this book possible

Contents

Preface

During the last thirty-five years or so, literary criticism has repeatedly questioned the historical significance of the French realist novel. Rejecting the illusion that it passively mirrors nineteenth-century reality, critics have redefined realist discourse as a repetition of contemporary discourses on what society thought to be real, and as the production of a realistic effect.[1] This discursive repetition and production efface any necessary link to the real, yet they take on the appearance of objective representation. Realist discourse forgets and lies, but it appears to forget its own forgetting, and to lie to itself about its own lying. Rather than an historical step towards scientific objectivity, the realist novel seems to constitute a falling away from an eighteenth-century awareness into a nineteenth-century blindness to discourse's forgetting and deceit.[2]

However, criticism has increasingly come to believe that realist novelists were not so blind to the forgetfulness and deceptiveness of their words as their third-person narrators' omniscience or some of their statements make them appear to be.[3] A subtle meditation on realist discourse takes as its object not the narrators', but the characters', use of words.[4] This meditation crystallizes around the realist characters' struggle with and against the power of words to lie or forget. It produces, in narrators and characters, a critical awareness of how the characters' words deceitfully produce or efface meaning, a consciousness that complicates any attempt to situate the realist novel historically in relation to seemingly less blind eighteenth- or twentieth-century French novels.

A major obstacle to interpreting this nineteenth-century

meditation on lying or forgetting is the tendency to conceive of words as an inside, and of reality as an outside. When we say that words forget or lie about the real, we cannot help but distinguish between their fictional contents, their inside, and the reality they forget or misrepresent, their outside. But any reduction of words to the inside/outside polarity inevitably leads to a dead-end. It produces either the naive assertion that discourse's inside passively mirrors a real outside or the logically self-contradictory assertion that the reality of discourse is that it necessarily misrepresents the real.

The inside/outside polarity of realist discourse, I will argue, derives from the purely linguistic distinction between language's two temporal aspects: the perfective aspect of complete duration and the imperfective aspect of incomplete duration. The perfective/imperfective distinction, in other words, is the means by which discourse produces the notions of a misrepresented or forgotten outside, and a misrepresenting or effacing inside. This aspectual distinction, I will suggest, is at the heart of the novelistic distinction between the descriptive and the narrative. A central topic of this book will be the ways in which major nineteenth-century French realist novels used descriptive and narrative discourses to construct reality in temporal terms, both as a temporalized inside – words or consciousness in time – and as a temporalized outside – society in historical time. The goal will be to foreground the rhetorical means by which realist discourse went "beyond" the themes of lying and forgetting: its ways of disclosing that any identification of discourse with lying or forgetting misrepresents or effaces the reality of words.

The introduction provides a brief explanation of the relationship between the themes of lying and forgetting, the perfective and imperfective temporal aspects, and narrative and descriptive discourses. Those who read only a chapter on one author may wish to consult the introduction for a discussion of the terminology and theory that inform each chapter's argument. Those interested in the debates that this theory presupposes might also consult the notes, many of which relate its principal arguments to a number of contemporary theories. The three chapters on Balzac, Flaubert, and Zola, respectively, build on each other in an attempt to sketch out a process of change and repetition that structured, at least in part, the history of the nineteenth-century French realist novel.[5]

Throughout the text, the repetition of certain key words, such as "the descriptive," and of arguments, like the distinction between the perfective and imperfective aspects, is part of a deliberate strategy. My hope is that this repetition will encourage readers to rethink the theoretical basis of the widespread presupposition that the novel is primarily a "narrative" recounted by a "narrator."

Acknowledgments

I wish to express my gratitude and dedicate this book to all those whose support and/or critical comments have made its writing and publication possible, in particular, Katharina Brett, Peter Haidu, Carol Hofmann, Lawrence Kritzman, Barbara Kurtz, Gillian Maude, Sara Melzer, Herbert Morris, Gerald Prince, Lorna Reid, Rainer Warning, and Robert White. I would also like to thank Malcolm Bowie for his sensitive suggestions and incisive comments concerning the revision of the manuscript. I will be forever indebted to the writings, thought, and encouragement of Eric Gans, Ross Chambers, and Paul de Man.

A section of chapter 2 has been adapted from "The Novel as Parody of Narrative Discourse: Flaubert and Balzac." *Michigan Romance Studies* (1990): 119–27.

Introduction

> Truths are illusions which we have forgotten are illusions ... [O]ur truth drive rests upon a foundation of lies.
>
> (Friedrich Nietzsche)[1]

> To-day, forgetting has perhaps become more of a puzzle than remembering, ever since we have learnt from the study of dreams and pathological phenomena that even something we thought had been forgotten long ago may suddenly re-emerge in consciousness. (Sigmund Freud)[2]

Lying and forgetting have become privileged, but rival, themes in modern critical discourse on writing and reading. "[E]verything that can be *taken* as a sign," Umberto Eco posits, should be defined as "*everything which can be used in order to lie.*"[3] Writing and reading are acts of producing meaning, regardless of whether this meaning is true or false.[4] But writing (and implicitly reading), Jacques Derrida writes, is also an "effacement ... de sa propre présence," a forgetting of what discourse is or is not doing.[5] If, on the one hand, writing and reading lie, then discourse remembers the act of producing meaning. If, on the other hand, they forget what if anything they are or are not doing, then discourse cannot know whether it produces anything at all.

Lying and forgetting play a critical role in the meditation upon writing and reading in the modern French novel. In Proust's *A la recherche du temps perdu*, the first-person narrator confesses that he is lying about his past: "Oui, j'ai été forcé d'amincir la chose et d'être mensonger."[6] In another passage he laments that he forgets his past: "[L]e souvenir d'une certaine image n'est que le regret d'un certain instant; et les maisons, les routes, les avenues, sont fugitives, hélas! comme les années."[7] The statements of Proust's first-person narrator on lying and forgetting can be traced back to a similar meditation on the lying and forgetting of characters in nineteenth-century French realist novels. In the first half of the nineteenth century, not only do Balzac's characters come to believe that they must lie in society ("[S]i vous avez un sentiment vrai, cachez-le comme un trésor");[8] historical discourse, indeed discourse itself, becomes, like Balzac's "auguste mensonge,"[9] the *Comédie humaine*, an "Histoire officielle, menteuse."[10] Near the end of the century, discourse develops into an historically determined process of forgetting signs of reality that makes Zola's impressionist painter "oubli[er] les premiers éléments du dessin."[11]

The fates of lying and forgetting in the fictional world of their characters are the means by which many nineteenth-century realist novels questioned whether their own writing and reading produced or erased signs of reality. Lying and forgetting are locked in an apparent struggle for domination. In Balzac the power to lie is increased by memory, and decreased by forgetting. Lying achieves power by eliminating forgetting. By contrast, in Flaubert and Zola, lying and forgetting struggle to subordinate each other. Liars forget what they believe they are doing in order to lie more powerfully. Forgetters lie to others and to themselves in order to better forget the very need to act.

The subordination of forgetting to lying, and lying to forgetting, leads to divergent notions of writing and reading the realist novel. When forgetting is subordinated to lying, discourse takes on the temporality of an irreversible, linear transformation. This irreversibility is illustrated by Nietzsche's discussion of lying and forgetting in his essays, "On Truth and Lies in a Nonmoral Sense," and "On the Uses and Disadvantages of History for Life," both published in the 1870s.[12] According to Nietzsche, "it is originally *language* which works on the construction of concepts."[13] This construction is not motivated by truth, but rather by the "drive toward the formation of metaphors" which takes the form of a deceit.[14] For society, "to be truthful means to employ the usual metaphors... to lie."

Society lies "according to a fixed convention" in order to deceive itself into believing that it is truthful.[15] These lies, however, change nothing. Art, on the other hand, acts as if it were truthful, it lies, purely in order to "[bring] forward new transferences, metaphors, and metonymies."[16] Rather than create the belief that it signifies a truth, rather than deceive, art's lie shatters the "immense framework and planking of concepts" and "puts it back together in an ironic fashion," "refashion[ing] the world which presents itself to waking man."[17] Art ironically demystifies its feint of being truthful, therefore, in order to make a change. For Nietzsche, the power to perform irreversible speech acts of transformation may be increased, as Balzac's characters imagine, by remembering society's old and deceitful metaphors, truths, and knowledge. But remembering often obstructs performance. Forgetting gives the most powerful support to art's ironic lie: "As he who acts is, in Goethe's words, always without a conscience, so is he also always without knowledge; he forgets most things so as to do one thing."[18]

Although Nietzsche's artistic liar subordinates remembering and forgetting to the act of transforming old into new metaphors, he presupposes that art remembers one thing, the act of lying itself: "Art works through deception – yet one which does not deceive us?"[19] In contrast, Freud posits a forgetting that undercuts even the memory of action, including Nietzsche's ironical lies. Indeed, lying in Freud often becomes a mere symptom of the forgetting he calls repression. Repression is an incomplete forgetting, a forgetting by consciousness only: "Since we overcame the error of supposing that the forgetting we are familiar with signified a destruction of the memory-trace – that is, its annihilation – we have been inclined to take the opposite view, that in mental life nothing which has once been formed can perish – that everything is somehow preserved and that in suitable circumstances ... it can once more be brought to light."[20] Repression is not simply the name that Freud gives to a specific mode of neurotic defence. It is a constitutive part of the mental processes of all human beings: "the ego's turning away from the Oedipus complex," and the mind's "constitution of the unconscious."[21]

In *Civilization and its Discontents*, Freud foregrounds the threat that forgetting poses. He suggests that history may consist in the ever greater power of forgetting over remembering. Repression, he argues, is the means by which civilization tries to master the guilt produced by its prohibition of incestuous and aggressive desires. Since this prohibition of love and hate increases aggression, civilization's laws are the paradoxical "cause of the hostility against which all civilizations have to struggle."[22] In other words, laws heighten the aggressive feelings they prohibit. As a result, civilization has been able to establish order only by sending aggression "back to where it came from."[23] Its laws have turned humanity's violence away from others and back towards the aggressive feelings themselves, towards the aggressive self. This aggression against aggression has created humanity's "sense of guilt," its "need for punishment."[24] Guilt has increased as civilization's laws have multiplied: "If civilization is a necessary course of development from the family to humanity as a whole, then ... there is inextricably bound up with it an increase of the sense of guilt, which will perhaps reach heights that the individual finds hard to tolerate."[25] "[P]ossibly the whole of mankind ... [may] have become 'neurotic.'"[26] Humanity's only means of dealing with its growing feelings of guilt, its repression of aggression, is to repress guilt as well: "the sense of guilt produced by civilization is not perceived as such."[27] Humans increasingly forget not only their growing aggressive desires, but also their forgetting. Forgetting its forgetting, civilization blindly augments the power of forgetting over the primary tool of the psychoanalytic cure, remembering.

Whereas Nietzsche's subordination of forgetting to lying constitutes writing and reading as an irreversible act of transforming the old into the new, Freud's subordination of lying to forgetting renders such a transformation reversible. It effaces change, action.[28] Symptoms of repression, he states in his paper on repression, are "not permitted to impinge upon the external world." They "must not be transformed into action."[29] If they appear to forget the old and create the new (a symptom), they do so purely in order to remember, albeit indirectly, the old: "[The] compulsion to repeat ... is [the patient's] way of remembering."[30] The resulting interplay between forgetting and remembering produces what Jacques Derrida calls a "réversibilité de temps et d'espace" which structures the hidden temporality of the unconscious in general.[31] Civilization's growing order, its "compulsion to repeat," gives life an increasingly reversible temporality that is "inconciliable avec le déroulement apparemment linéaire, unilinéaire, des pures représentations verbales," irreconcilable with Nietzsche's irreversible lies.[32]

Freud's reversible forgetting is clearly not entirely compatible with Nietzsche's irreversible artistic lies. Indeed, Freud questions temporal irreversibility when he proposes that the irreversibility of the conscious mind may always already be subordinated to the reversibility of the unconscious. In "A Note upon the 'Mystic Writing Pad'," he structures the mind as a "flickering-up and passing-away of consciousness," a reversible process that may be "at the bottom of the origin of the concept of time."[33] Unconscious reversibility makes the mind alternate between producing and effacing memory traces, remembering and forgetting. The seemingly irreversible memories that make consciousness possible are only deceptive moments within the overall unconscious process which produces then erases, constructs then deconstructs them. A memory is a mere "symptom of 'being conscious.'"[34] If consciousness is only a reversible symptom of the unconscious, then all discursive memory, Derrida concludes, is "constituée par la menace ou l'angoisse de sa disparition irrémédiable." Forgetting questions the very possibility of an irreversible transformation, whether it be called a Nietzschean artistic lie or a psychoanalytic cure.[35]

The purpose of this introduction is not to reduce Nietzsche's writings to passages that treat discourse as an irreversible lie or to limit Freud's writings to passages where discursive forgetting appears to reverse all remembering and action. Despite his glorification of the power to lie, Nietzsche also questions the centrality of action and the irreversibility of time. Despite his apocalyptic fear of historically or unconsciously determined forgetting, Freud also reaffirms the irreversibility of the psychoanalytic cure and thus of time.[36] The purpose here is rather to suggest that certain frequent (if not necessarily dominant) meditations on lying and forgetting in Nietzsche and Freud foreground the discursive and temporal implications of the characters' lying and forgetting in the novels of Balzac, Flaubert, and Zola. These meditations show that the themes of lying and forgetting presuppose a distinction between temporal irreversibility and reversibility which is at the heart of the linguistic category that makes the representation of time possible: temporal aspect. And temporal aspect, I will propose, is at the root of the distinction between the novelistic discourses with which realist narrators construct time: the narrative and the descriptive.

Temporal aspects have been defined as "'different ways of viewing the internal temporal constituency of a situation.'"[37] The fundamental aspects in the construction of time are the perfective and the imperfective. The perfective aspect "views" a situation as "complete ... with beginning, middle, and end."[38] By positing an observable difference between a fixed beginning and end, it constructs the (fiction of the) temporal situation that produced this difference: an irreversible act of differentiation or transformation.[39] A familiar grammatical sign of the perfective aspect is the French *passé simple* tense, which constructs past events as irreversible acts of change. Although perfectivity characterizes the *passé simple* tense, it is not limited to verb tenses; it also characterizes a number of grammatical and lexical signs. Moreover, specific signs of perfectivity depend upon the discursive context in which they are embedded. A context can reinforce or negate the connotation of irreversible change that specific signs of perfectivity produce.[40]

The perfective aspect makes possible the category of narrative. A. J. Greimas defines narrative discourse as a "trajectory leading from an initial state to a final state." It is an irreversible transformation with a perfective aspect.[41] Nietzsche's ironical lies are minimal narratives which are momentary and illogical. For Greimas, in contrast, individual transformations are always embedded within the duration of a narrative deep structure that renders them logical. But, whether narrative transformations be illogical and punctual as Nietzsche's writings suggest or logical and durative as Greimas argues, they presuppose the perfective aspect of irreversibility and change.[42] In the novel, the perfective aspect creates a bridge between the momentary Nietzschean lies of individual characters and the overall duration of a realist narrator's (logical or illogical) narrative.

Whereas Nietzsche's lie and Greimas's narrative presuppose the perfective aspect, Freud's incomplete forgetting and descriptive discourse entail the imperfective aspect. The imperfective aspect views a temporal "situation from within" as incomplete.[43] By deferring marks of beginning or end – signs of the perfective aspect – it constructs the (fiction of the) temporal situation that produced this deferral: an ongoing state, a duration, whether of change or non-change. Precisely because the imperfective aspect puts off completion, the ongoing duration it constructs is always potentially reversible. The imperfective aspect is not limited to verb tenses like the French imperfect tense; rather it characterizes a number of grammatical and lexical signs. It, too, is a function of the overall context.

The imperfective aspect is the precondition of that discourse that views temporal states from within rather than from without: descriptive discourse. A familiar sign of the imperfective aspect, the French imperfect tense, thus tends to mark descriptive passages in nineteenth-century French novels: "[G]râce à la stricte observance des règles classiques de la prose du XIXe siècle dotant de marques temporelles particulières les unités textuelles distinguées en 'descriptions,' 'récits,' et 'dialogues': on sait que les unités descriptives y sont caractérisées par l'usage de l'imparfait et délimitees par des passés simples qui les encadrent."[44] The imperfective aspect of the imperfect tense does more than characterize the descriptive. It makes it possible as that act by which discourse constructs an ongoing temporal ("remembered") state in which spatial relations are possible.

Whether a discourse claims to describe a static object, such as a house, or a dynamic process, such as a passing car or the workings of a machine, it presupposes the temporal deferral and forgetting of marks of beginning and ending that define the imperfective temporal aspect. Deferral and forgetting construct the fiction of a temporal duration of the same in which a described object – people, place, thing, process – and an observing subject – a point of view within this duration – can also be constructed. The imperfective temporal aspect is thus a necessary precondition for the production of a seemingly atemporal spatial "background," of simultaneously juxtaposed objects, and of a simultaneous atemporal observer of this background: in other words, a spatial relation between a described spatial object and a describing subject.[45]

What is deferred and forgotten by the descriptive's imperfective aspect is not time, but one aspect of time, its perfective aspect. Nevertheless, the perfective aspect has often been identified with time itself. The imperfective aspect's deferral of the perfective aspect has been misread as a negation of time, and the descriptive has been reduced to the atemporal representation of space.[46] A first step in overcoming this misreading has been taken by Philippe Hamon, who has displaced spatial contiguity from the described object to descriptive discourse itself. Hamon's descriptive does not necessarily represent a spatial world; rather it is an "unité textuelle régie par des opérations à dominante hiérarchisante, taxinomique."[47] It is a "paradigmatic" structure composed of spatially contiguous signs.[48] Hamon calls for a reading of the specific textual function of the spatialized paradigms that the descriptive brings into play and that Greimassian narrative semiotics has backgrounded: "[L]es études narratologiques contemporaines nous semblent avoir un peu trop systématiquement mis l'accent sur cette dimension syntagmatique du récit, et avoir négligé les importants problèmes que pose la notion de hiérarchie d'un système."[49]

Hamon's descriptive necessarily presupposes the imperfective temporal aspect of incomplete duration: "le signe emblématique du descriptif paraît être ... le 'etc.' qui clôture, sans la clôturer, toute énumération."[50] His descriptive is thus temporally reversible.[51] A descriptive paradigm can be unfolded in any order. If the descriptive could be extended to an entire novel, as Hamon tries to do in his reading of Zola, it would render all narrative transformations reversible. The novel would be structured as an alternation between passages that hide descriptive paradigms and "focal points" that reveal them: "un système à variations davantage concentriques, à éloignement réversible plus ou moins prononcé et variable d'un ou de plusieurs centres et 'foyers,' plutôt qu'un système à extension linéaire ou irréversible et à orientation constante."[52]

Once the imperfective aspect's temporal reversibility has been added to Hamon's spatialized paradigms, the descriptive turns out to be the discursive means by which Freud's text structures the mind as an unconscious alternation between remembering and forgetting memory traces. This descriptive reversibility, like Freud's description of the unconscious, is potentially subversive. It threatens to render all relations between signs, not only syntagmatic, but also paradigmatic, reversible, in other words, to "neutralise[r] les différences" between discursive remembering and discursive forgetting of meaning or structure.[53] The descriptive is thus not just a temporal means of constructing spatialized relations between signs, of constituting memory; it is, as in many modernist novels, a temporal means of effacing signifying relations, of forgetting them.[54] It is capable of transforming the most "realist" of passages into a mere symptom of remembering.

In the novels of Balzac, Flaubert, and Zola, statements about characters' lying and forgetting give rise to meditations, albeit indirect ones, on the realist narrator's reliability.[55] These meditations prefigure the contemporary debate over whether discourse can be constituted in purely temporal terms as an irreversible narrative act of transformation that is indifferent to truth, or as a reversible descriptive erasure that is indifferent to power as well. Rather than choose narrative time or descriptive time, these novels end up by putting both into question.

This indirect questioning of realist discourse is structured by two rhetorical modes: ironic reversal and allegorical irreversibility.[56] Irony, Paul de Man proposes, is directed against the "mimetic mode of representation in which fiction and reality could coincide."[57] It appears when the cognitive function of discourse, which grounds the mimetic mode of representation, is treated by writer and reader ironically as a lie and subordinated to the performative function of narrative.[58] Such is the case with Nietzsche's artistic lie and Greimas's narrative deep structure. The hidden rhetorical mode of Nietzsche's discourse on lying, de Man argues, and of Greimas's discourse on narrative, I will propose, is an irony of irony that puts into question the referentiality of Nietzschean and Greimassian narrative. Each discourse claims to be "less deceitful" simply "because it asserts its own deceitful properties."[59] Yet it cannot help but ironically characterize itself as a lie. It thus ironically undercuts its own power to reduce discourse to an ironical lie.[60] Irony of irony puts into question discourse's sequential narrative relationships and replaces them with the simultaneous ironical juxtapositions that also characterize the descriptive.

Allegory, as de Man defines it, is directed against the "symbolic mode of analogical correspondences."[61] It is the "reversed mirror-image" of irony. Allegory transforms an analogical relationship between "the substance and its representation" (a relationship "of simultaneity, which, in truth, is spatial in kind") into a sequential relationship, by spreading it "out along the axis of an imaginary time."[62] The analogical relationship that allegory "spreads out," the one between representation and substance, is made possible by the reversibility of the descriptive. Romantic analogy, for example, asserts both the priority of the representing subject over the represented natural substance and the reverse.[63] Allegory spreads romantic analogy out over time by deconstructing its descriptive reversibility and disclosing a hidden "temporal difference" between itself as representation and its origin as substance.[64] This deconstruction of the descriptive "makes all the past appear as a flight into the inauthenticity of a forgetting," while it makes the present appear as an irreversible movement from past forgetting to future remembering of this forgetting.[65] Whereas irony is the tendency of language towards the descriptive, allegory is the "tendency of the language toward narrative."[66]

The theme of lying in Balzac's novels, and the themes of lying and forgetting in Flaubert's novels, produce an irony of irony and, in the case of Flaubert, an allegorical deconstruction of this irony. Both put into question characterizations of the novel as a narrative genre, and of the nineteenth-century realist novel as a regression from, rather than a repetition of, the eighteenth-century ironic novel.[67] The theme of forgetting in Zola's *L'Oeuvre* gives rise to an allegory that deconstructs representations of the novel as a descriptive genre, and of nineteenth-century realism as a blind antecedent, rather than a significant precursor, of those twentieth-century discourses that deconstruct the descriptive as a narrative illusion. Together, irony and allegory enable these nineteenth-century realist novels to go beyond, even as they fall back into, the belief that discourse lies or forgets, beyond the illusion that the novel is a (narrative or descriptive) representation of time.

CHAPTER I

Balzac: the power of lying and the irony of power

In Balzac, writing and social history take on the verbal appearance of lying, as if life were made up of words and as if words constructed rather than represented reality.

[Q]ui dit art, dit mensonge (*Peau* 10: 153).[1]

Il y a deux Histoires: l'Histoire officielle, menteuse, qu'on enseigne, l'Histoire *ad usum delphini*; puis l'histoire secrète, où sont les véritables causes des événements, une Histoire honteuse. (*Illusions* 5: 695)

Of course it has traditionally been thought that words for Balzac were a mere realist means of representing literally the concrete world he observed. But it has become increasingly clear that the world he observed was a verbal one, and that he was more realistic than generally thought about what words could, and could not, say or do.[2]

According to Balzac, lying exercises different powers in different situations. In literature, it reveals knowledge about details of contemporary society. "[C]et auguste mensonge," the *Comédie humaine*, "ne serait rien si ... il n'était pas vrai dans les détails" (*Avant-propos* 1: 15).[3] Within society, however, where the disclosure of knowledge "ne sert à rien," lying is a means of obtaining wealth, position, and power (*Goriot* 3: 140; *Illusions* 5: 703).[4] Whereas literary lies describe society's historical present in all its complexity and detail, social lies constitute society as a narrative sequence of acts of power.

Balzac's distinction between literary and social lies exemplifies two different ways in which the *Comédie humaine* constitutes the narrator's discourse as a lie. In passages where the narrator describes contemporary character types, settings, or social hierarchies, he often characterizes his words as revealing, albeit indirectly, reliable knowledge about his era. But in passages where he narrates individual, social, or political actions, he frequently acts as if his words wielded power and as if he were one of the most powerful "maîtres" of his era (*Avant-propos* 1: 12). Balzac's narrator indirectly represents himself either descriptively as a teacher or narratively as a seducer.

The characters' lying in Balzac's fictional world brings to the fore the manner in which the narrator of the *Comédie humaine* tries to reconcile the different ways in which he characterizes his own words as a descriptive discourse of knowledge or as a narrative discourse of power. The characters' failure to reduce discourse to a lie marks the narrator's failure to reconcile these two modes of constituting social history verbally. This failure leads beyond lying to Balzacian irony.

DESCRIPTIVE IRONY AND KNOWLEDGE: HISTORICAL CHANGE AS SOCIAL DIFFERENCE

When I imagine a Balzacian description of physical setting or physiognomy, I see an all-knowing teacher with a benevolent twinkle in his eye. The teacher anticipates that I will misread his words and provide him with the dual pleasure of pointing out my error and disclosing the correct reading. Rather than the passive mirror of reality created by realist myth, he is an active creator and demystifier of realities. This narrator (or describer) actively enjoys both the duplicity of words and their power to unveil knowledge about the complex tissue of people, places, and things that constitutes society during and after the Restoration. The means by which Balzac constructs this fictional "teaching" narrator is descriptive discourse. An understanding of its structure and function in some early novels of the *Comédie humaine* will bring to the fore the deceptive way in which he structures the social space of his historical era. It will also foreground the ironical distance that, in the later novels, increasingly separates the narrator from his descriptive mask as teacher of society and history.

Balzac's narrator provides a lesson in the indirect structure of his descriptive discourse at the beginning of *Le Père Goriot*. Before detailing the Parisian quarter and house in which much of the action will take place, he predicts that provincial readers will misunderstand his story of this action: "Sera-t-elle comprise au-delà de Paris? le doute est permis" (*Goriot* 3: 49). Most Parisian readers will misread his story as well, because it takes place in a "quartier ... inconnu" of Paris (3: 51). Only knowledge of the real setting based on real observation, he suggests, can make this quarter and the drama it stages comprehensible: "Les particularités de cette scène pleine d'observations et de couleurs locales ne peuvent être appréciées qu'entre les buttes de Montmartre et les hauteurs de Montrouge, cette illustre vallée ... " (3: 49–50).

Balzac's narrator is not limiting his readership to the (un)happy few who have seen the real background to his story, nor is he encouraging readers to go see it before reading the story. Rather, he is telling them that, if they follow their natural inclination to skip over the descriptions, they will fail to give the story its correct meaning. This meaning, he argues, is to be found in the observable details of the real setting that his description provides, "[l]es particularités de cette scène pleine d'observations"; not in each detail, but in the overall urban landscape – "entre les buttes de Montmartre et les hauteurs de Montrouge" – that the totality of the details reconstructs.[5] If readers wish to understand, not only these details, but his story, they must first recompose the original spatial context, just as Christianity reconstructs the meaning of flock or family by reintegrating a lost sheep or a prodigal son.[6]

By teaching readers to interpret his novel in terms of the spatial context that his descriptions reconstruct, Balzac's narrator warns them that his words, if taken out of this context, are deceptive. He illustrates this deceptiveness by qualifying the quarter as "illustre," and characterizing it metaphorically as a "vallée." The adjective "illustre" says literally that the quarter is well known or well regarded. The word "vallée," derived from the contemporary romantic lexicon, suggests that the quarter provides a natural refuge from social artifice, pain, and human mortality. It creates the expectation that the narrator will interpret his descriptive details romantically as metaphors and synecdoches of the same natural, happy, and eternal whole. But this expectation is false. The narrator immediately pulls the rug out from under his romantic metaphor by listing observable details of the quarter that suggest contrary qualities: "cette illustre vallée de plâtras incessamment près de tomber..." The reference to plaster threatening to fall on the head of unsuspecting romantic observers comically reverses the connotations of nature, joy, and immortality that romantic readers might wish to read. It hits them over the head with the quarter's visible artifice, pain, and finitude. Balzac's narrator reinforces this comic interpretation of his romantic metaphors by repeating the comic reversal, "et de ruisseaux noirs de boue" (3: 49–50).[7]

As in Balzac's *Avant-propos* to the *Comédie humaine*, the narrator of *Le Père Goriot* invites his readers to take an ironical distance from preconceived interpretations of the quarter or of the action taking place in it, and to pay greater attention to the observable details he provides. He also sets up the expectation that this descriptive irony is stable.[8] Stable irony expresses a true meaning by means of a false, contrary meaning. The narrator's descriptive irony falsely misrepresents the setting of his novel as natural, joyous, and immortal (as valley or stream) in order to foreground ironically the visible details (falling plaster and black mud) that reveal it to be in truth "remplie de souffrances réelles, de joies souvent fausses ... " (3: 50).[9]

Much more knowledge is provided by this indirect, rather than direct, method of description. Not only does it claim to convey a partial knowledge of the "real" quarter, it warns contemporary readers ("vous qui vous enfoncez dans un mœlleux fauteuil en vous disant: 'Peut-être ceci va-t-il m'amuser'" (3: 50)) about the romantic discourses which they, like many of the characters, will try to impose on its parts. Balzac's ironical description thus encourages readers to question actively, rather than accept passively, conventional descriptive metaphors for setting and character, and to construct, with the details his narrator provides, the overall spatial context that will house and explain the story.[10] Each detail must be read as a true synecdochical metaphor of a depressed quarter as a whole, one that really resembles, the narrator tells us, Paris's underground cemetery, the Catacombes (3: 51).

The narrator's lesson in ironical reading presupposes a more general theory of language. As Martin Kanes has noted, Balzac's statements, both in and outside his novels, suggest that words prescribe, rather than describe, reality according to conventional paradigms. In other words, they lie: "[A]rt is a lie in the world of rationality..."[11] But art is also the means by which language goes beyond its prescriptiveness, its lying, and indirectly expresses, describes, reality's uniqueness: "Where 'dire' is the common coin of conventional language, reproducible from one situation to another... 'exprimer' is a mode of language that enshrines the aesthetic uniqueness of each situation, which is incapable of repetition..."[12] Through art, language overcomes its lies and becomes a discourse of knowledge. In Balzac's literary art, the form of this overcoming is the ironical demystification of metaphors for observed objects, and the construction, from juxtaposed details, of theoretically true descriptions of people, places, and things, of a multiplicity of unique types.

Lying and irony have similar structures.[13] Both deliberately produce misreadings. Both can mislead a listener or reader. However, irony presupposes a third person who does not passively accept a misreading as true; rather he or she acts as an active accomplice in the speaker's production and demystification of this misreading.[14] Whereas lying primarily conceals, irony conceals in order to reveal. Whether irony reveals knowledge about reality or about itself is a central question raised by the *Comédie humaine*.

Indeed, the repeated ironical negation of the positive attributes of conventional romantic metaphors, such as a valley, does not necessarily guarantee that a metaphor with the contrary attributes, such as a cemetery, is any more true. Balzac's narrator must create the impression that the metaphors he calls "true" are based on actual acts of perception, rather than on mere convention, like the romantic metaphors. He must make them appear to be pure products of inductive reasoning grounded in empirical evidence. He thus provides a multiplicity of details that could potentially be seen ("deux monuments... assombriss[ent] tout par les teints sévères"), heard ("[un] silence... règne dans ces rues"), or smelled ("les murailles y sentent la prison") (3: 50). By adapting an eighteenth-century realist device, he attributes these potentially perceivable details to the real acts of perception of his narrator or of an observing character.[15] He heightens the sense that they are objective by creating observing characters who have not yet been corrupted by Parisian society's lies, because they are young or because they have just arrived in Paris, like the central character of *Le Père Goriot*, Rastignac (3: 56). The narrator addresses his readers as if he, they, and sometimes his observing character were seeing, then inductively interpreting, the details together. Only after noting the falling plaster and muddy streams does he read them as signs of suffering. Only after listing the typical sights, sounds, and smells of the quarter does he compare it to the Catacombes. The narrator's emphasis on perceivable details, his use of a credible observing character, his inductive order of presentation, along with his repeated ironical negation of false metaphors; all reproduce the same fictional story of writing and reading an objective description. Writer or reader begin with a false preconception of the area; next they passively see or read real details; they then actively compare them and discover their common characteristics; finally they ironically demystify their error. Realist technique makes Balzacian irony appear to be more than mere contrariness, to reveal the real essence of an empirically observed place.

The narrator's descriptive irony constructs, and makes the reader an accomplice in constructing, both the perceivable setting or physiognomy it theoretically represents and the observing narrator, character, or reader who theoretically perceives it. The ways in which the descriptive constructs an object have been extensively studied by the semiotician Philippe Hamon.[16] The descriptive is constituted by a metonymic juxtaposition (on the page) of signs signifying potentially observable details, organized around the name of a person, place, or thing.[17] It (mis)identifies these spatially related signs as references to juxtaposed and co-existing parts or attributes of a real, perceivable object.[18] The narrator's description at the beginning of Balzac's *Le Père Goriot* thus lists objects and attributes: roofs, streets, walls, sights, sounds, smells. He constructs a fictional set of spatial relationships between these objects or attributes and other unnamed ones by giving the whole a conventional name, "quartier." The narrator's particular sensitivity to the spatial aspect of this descriptive construct is evidenced by his constant repetition of the traditional comparison between the acts of describing and of painting: "on ne saurait trop préparer l'intelligence par des couleurs brunes, par des idées graves; ainsi que, de marche en marche, le jour diminue et le chant du conducteur se creuse, alors que le voyageur descend aux Catacombes" (3: 51).[19]

The descriptive produces a spatial effect – the impression that real attributes exist simultaneously rather than sequentially – by defining signs paradigmatically or typologically within a system of identities and differences. This spatialized system of signs relates them to other simultaneously co-existing signs.[20] Descriptive paradigms, as Roland Barthes has noted, are conventional codes of representation that define what constitutes a general category or a particular type of person, place, or thing, and what does not.[21] Discourse can construct a representation of space only by awakening these differential codes in the reader's memory.[22] The narrator's sketchy and general details of houses, walls, roofs, and streets at the beginning of *Le Père Goriot* – "les maisons y sont mornes, les murailles y sentent la prison" (3: 50) – thus awaken the codes that distinguish a place from a non-place, an inhabited one from an uninhabited one, a town from a country house. His references to many houses and walls, and to Paris as a whole, recall the paradigms that distinguish a city from a town or from the country. The attributes that he gives these parts – dark, damp, silent, smelly – call up the codes that distinguish typically poor areas of a city from rich ones, codes with inter-textual and ideological implications.[23]

Like Walter Scott, Balzac's narrator takes advantage of the fact that specific details imply general codes in order to interpret his descriptions as synecdoches of an entire historical era: contemporary Paris and France. The spatial paradigms awakened by his descriptive passages are his means of constructing the *Comédie humaine* in spatial terms as an enormous museum comprised of multiple galleries in which word paintings of "tout le pêle-mêle" of the historical present simultaneously co-exist (*Preface*, *Goriot*, 2nd edn. 3: 47). These paradigms constitute him as a "peintre plus ou moins fidèle, plus ou moins heureux, patient ou courageux des types humains, le conteur des drames de la vie intime, l'archéologue du mobilier social, le nomenclateur des professions, l'enregistreur du bien et du mal." (*Avant-propos* 1: 11). Given that this museum is the product of simultaneously co-existing signs and codes, the *Comédie humaine* is less a museum than a memory or library space that contains and organizes the vast collection of codes of character, story, furniture, profession, and action with which contemporary French culture constructed what it called empirical reality. Reversing the ancient art of using real places to memorize words, Balzac's literary memory palace used the descriptive's architectural structure to construct a contemporary reality that was memorable.[24]

Although the modern awareness that discursive paradigms construct, rather than represent, geographical and social space questions the claim of Balzac's narrator to "paint" contemporary reality, it does not question the traditional characteristics of descriptive discourse itself: knowledge and spatiality. It simply displaces these characteristics from an observed spatial context, contemporary France, to a linguistic spatial context, the conventional linguistic paradigms with which the author constructs an observable space. This displacement is insufficient to account for one of the most important products of Balzac's descriptive practice: temporal duration. Returning to a tradition that can be traced back to at least Achilles' shield, Balzac's descriptions give a temporal and historical dimension to the social space they construct. But, rather than narrate specific, complete actions, they give an ongoing, incomplete duration to the space itself.[25] The knowledge that the narrator's descriptive irony hides and reveals is knowledge of the ongoing historical changes that are molding an entire era, and of the "moteur social" that is producing these changes (1: 11).

Balzac's narrator uses the descriptive's imperfective aspect to spatialize the time of historical narrative. He constructs the fiction of a dynamic historical present, the Restoration, in which society is repressing and ironically disclosing the paradigms that distinguish Paris's gradually decaying areas and groups from its increasingly prosperous ones. Balzac inherited an awareness of the descriptive's temporal aspect from late eighteenth- and early nineteenth-century German thought and poetry.[26] Herder, and later Goethe, constituted the temporal present as an ongoing process of change, as a becoming. They did so by foregrounding the descriptive's imperfective temporal aspect which attributes to static objects or to dynamic changes an ongoing duration in time. As discussed in the introduction to this study, the imperfective aspect makes possible the concept of a duration, in which objects and movements simultaneously coexist, by deferring temporal completion. It also constructs the fiction of a character's or narrator's observing consciousness that is watching objects and movements in a pure present of perceiving.[27]

The foregrounding of the imperfective aspect in nineteenth-century French novels is most evident in a few of Balzac's early novels. Much of his narrator's descriptive practice, as in the traditional epic *ekphrasis* or the conventional comparison of writing to painting, tends to dampen the imperfective temporal aspect.[28] Inasmuch as they lack even the narratives inscribed on Achilles' or Aeneas' shields, many descriptions of milieu and of characters immobilize their objects and freeze the observer of these objects, as if they, like the aesthetic objects portrayed in the Greek novel, were situated outside time and action.[29] Never the less, within the petrified spatial frame of his narrative pause, the narrator's descriptions sometimes ironically reconstruct the ongoing temporal processes that are shaping the present of an historically changing world as a whole. Not only does the descriptive cease to be the eighteenth century's enemy of the sublime and Lessing's enemy of time, it becomes their "sublimated" source. It adds to the space of the eighteenth-century sublime, the imperfective aspect of ongoing historical change.[30]

The description at the beginning of *Le Père Goriot* is a good example of how Balzac's narrator ironically constructs the processes transforming the historical present. The passage methodically awakens the descriptive's imperfective aspect by means of verbs, relative clauses, and adjectives, all signifying activity or change that is continuing, or being repeated, in time. The utterance – "[l]a maison où s'exploite la pension bourgeoise appartient à Mme Vauquer" (3: 50) – seems to establish a purely static relation between house and owner, as do previous utterances which have set up a similar relation between the house and the quarter in which it is located. But the active verb "s'exploiter" gives these static relations a temporal dimension, the duration of an iterated activity: running the *pension*. Similarly, the adjectival phrase "près de tomber" in "vallée de plâtras près de tomber" produces the impression that buildings in the quarter are more than static entities; they are caught up in a dynamic process. Likewise, the adjective "agitée" in "vallée... si terriblement agitée qu'il faut je ne sais quoi d'exorbitant pour y produire une sensation de quelque durée" suggests that people are more than just inhabitants and owners of buildings; they are in a continuous process of emotional upheaval (3: 50). By signifying iterated or continuous activities and changes that necessarily take place in time, grammatically subordinate parts of the sentence ("où s'exploite," "agitée," "près de tomber") add the imperfective temporal aspect to the historical present tense, just as the English progressive does to verbs: "the *pension* is being run", "plaster is losing parts," "people are being tormented." They construct a temporal duration of negative change: an area of continuously falling plaster and emotional upheaval, a place being molded by physically and emotionally destructive processes.

As translation into the English progressive shows, the iterative and durative aspects of particular words ("s'exploite," "près de," "agitée,"), like the French imperfect tense, awaken the imperfective aspect that lies hidden in the verb which all descriptive utterances presuppose: "to be." By imposing the imperfective aspect on signs of linear change ("tomber," "s'attrister"), the narrator's descriptions belie the very impression they create: the impression that they remove the narrator from time when they "paint" a spatial tableau on the canvas of the readers' minds. The narrator brackets out, not time, but chronological narrative time, so as to pan in on marks of descriptive time: the imprint of historical change on seemingly backgrounded static objects as on the period as a whole. The imperfective aspect of particular words and, in this passage, the historical present tense place readers in the middle of these changes, as if they were observing them alongside the characters. Lists of sensations produced by a room in the Maison Vauquer create the fiction that readers are there seeing, hearing, and smelling the effects of the process that is degrading the entire quarter:[31] "Cette première pièce exhale une odeur sans nom dans la langue... Elle sent le renfermé, le moisi, le rance; elle donne froid, elle est humide au nez, elle pénètre les vêtements... " (3: 53).

The narrator's descriptive utterances suggest that the sensations they describe are in the process of affecting perceptions in the present of reading: smells are now being exuded; cold, humidity, and wetness are now penetrating clothes. Attributing these perceptions to a universal observer ("l'homme," "on"), he invites readers to share his and his characters' acts of observing, as if we too could observe the historical processes changing the building, and feel the emotional effects produced by these changes: "L'homme le plus insouciant s'y attriste... ainsi que, de marche en marche, le jour diminue et le chant du conducteur se creuse, alors que le voyageur descend aux Catacombes" (3: 50–51). Balzac's narrator thus collapses the difference between the present of reading and the represented past. He constitutes a fictional reading subject who is experiencing effects similar to those that are being produced by his own real world: "ce drame... est si véritable, que chacun peut en reconnaître les éléments chez soi, dans son cœur peut-être" (3: 50).[32]

The traditional emphasis on the descriptive's spatial connotations, and the tendency to associate time with the narrative alone, tend to hide marks of the imperfective aspect. Readers presuppose that descriptions construct an empty stage, a "background," onto which time, in the form of the perfective aspect, will step, just as individual actions were painted on Achilles' shield. As a result, Balzac's narrator must explicitly teach readers to recognize signs of the descriptive's imperfective aspect that lie hidden behind the signs of its spatial aspect. In *Le Père Goriot*, he does so by parodying a common romantic interpretation of a "statue représentant l'Amour" in the yard of his Maison Vauquer. He first names the statue, and states its conventional, romantic meaning, as if he accepted that it were a spatial symbol of eternal feeling and a narrative prefiguration of time's, and cupid's, arrow. It would appear that the unique target of life's and Rastignac's actions is love. But the narrator then ironically contradicts this spatial and narrative reading by detailing its visual appearance: "A voir le vernis écaillé qui la couvre, les amateurs de symboles y découvriraient peut-être un mythe de l'amour parisien qu'on guérit à quelques pas de là" (3: 51).[33] The scaling of the statue's paint suggests that symbol and symbolized narrative are dying, that they are subject to temporal change. It ironically undercuts any literal reading of the romantic version of the myth, and foregrounds its conventional nature, which is based purely on consensus. The apparent permanence of objects, of spatial relations between them, and of the future state they might prefigure is mythical. The virtue of this quarter, in which "il faut je ne sais quoi d'exorbitant pour y produire une sensation de quelque durée" (3: 50), is that it cures the reader's misreading of spatial signs, just as the nearby hospital for venereal disease ("qu'on guérit à quelques pas de là") cures the belief that love conquers death.[34]

Behind their atemporal appearance, the spatial details of the scaling statue ironically reveal a continuous temporal process of disillusionment with atemporal signs of a unique narrative destiny. Rastignac will succeed only after he learns to read ironically Delphine's words of eternal love (for him and for her father, Père Goriot), when he learns that the relation between sign and meaning is contingent, mortal.

Although Balzac borrows from German literature his technique of describing objects in time, he parodies the romantic subordination of change to a duration of the same, Goethe's "dauer im wechsel."[35] On the contrary, Balzac's narrator finds within the appearance of permanence the reality of continuous change. To walk through this depressed area of Paris is to experience one's belief in natural identity being eroded by time. It is to realize that identity is a product of the differences wrought by social structure rather than an outgrowth of individual nature. Balzac's narrator throws the reader off the seemingly stable ground of the *ancien régime* and onto the moving sidewalk of history where individual identity is a product of middle-class labor.[36]

Balzac's critique of permanence and identity renders the notions of fixed character and background, central themes of the traditional description, highly deceptive.[37] Whereas perceivable details of character and place, such as those describing Père Goriot or the Maison Vauquer, seem to establish a presence of identity, contextual differences between details reveal the process of the disappearance of identity. Balzac attributes this interplay between hiding and revealing to the course of civilization. History leaves an imprint of its course on its victims, then hides its course by consuming them entirely:

> Cependant, il s'y rencontre ça et là des douleurs que l'agglomération des vices et des vertus rend grandes et solennelles : à leur aspect, les égoïsmes, les intérêts, s'arrêtent et s'apitoient; mais l'impression qu'ils en reçoivent est comme un fruit savoureux promptement dévoré. Le char de la civilisation, semblable à celui de l'idole de Jaggernaut, à peine retardé par un cœur moins facile à broyer que les autres et qui enraye sa roue, l'a brisé bientôt et continue sa marche glorieuse. (3: 50)[38]

The particular way in which Balzac's descriptive discourse hides and reveals historical difference and the questions that it raises are strikingly foregrounded in the early short story, "Le Colonel Chabert." Near the beginning, the narrator describes Chabert's physiognomy through the eyes of an observing character, the lawyer Derville. Derville ironically negates a purely literal reading of the similarities that he sees among all the parts of the colonel's appearance. He foregrounds differences among these details, which he interprets as marking the temporal process of differentiation that is producing Chabert's hidden, tragic emotions. The entire passage, which is exemplary, deserves quotation:

> Le jeune avoué demeura pendant un moment stupéfait en entrevoyant dans le clair-obscur le singulier client qui l'attendait... Le vieux soldat était sec et maigre. Son front, volontairement caché sous les cheveux de sa perruque lisse, lui donnait quelque chose de mystérieux. Ses yeux paraissaient couverts d'une taie transparente: vous eussiez dit de la nacre sale dont les reflets bleuâtres chatoyaient à la lueur des bougies. Le visage pâle, livide, et en lame de couteau, s'il est permis d'emprunter cette expression vulgaire, semblait mort. Le cou était serré par une mauvaise cravate de soie noire. L'ombre cachait si bien le corps à partir de la ligne brune que décrivait ce haillon, qu'un homme d'imagination aurait pu prendre cette vieille tête pour quelque silhouette due au hasard, ou pour un portrait de Rembrandt, sans cadre. Les bords du chapeau qui couvrait le front du vieillard projetaient un sillon noir sur le haut du visage. Cet effet bizarre, quoique naturel, faisait ressortir, par la brusquerie du contraste, les rides blanches, les sinuosités froides, le sentiment décoloré de cette physionomie cadavéreuse. Enfin l'absence de tout mouvement dans le corps, de toute chaleur dans le regard, s'accordait avec une certaine expression de démence triste, avec les dégradants symptômes par lesquels se caractérise l'idiotisme, pour faire de cette figure je ne sais quoi de funeste qu'aucune parole humaine ne pourrait exprimer. Mais un observateur, et surtout un avoué, aurait trouvé de plus en cet homme foudroyé les signes d'une douleur profonde, les indices d'une misère qui avait dégradé ce visage, comme les gouttes d'eau tombées du ciel sur un beau marbre l'ont à la longue défiguré. Un médecin, un auteur, un magistrat eussent pressenti tout un drame à l'aspect de cette sublime horreur dont le moindre mérite était de ressembler à ces fantaisies que les peintres s'amusent à dessiner au bas de leurs pierres lithographiques en causant avec leurs amis. ("Chabert" 3: 321–22)

Like the description of the quarter around the Maison Vauquer, this one constructs a realistic entity, here a character, by juxtaposing perceivable parts or attributes of a man's body with those of a Napoleonic officer's clothing. Once again, the significance of each detail does not lie in an inherent meaning.[39] It is not an example of Lavater's one-to-one typology which equates visible exterior signs of physiognomy with interior character traits.[40] Rather this significance lies in the contextual relationship, which constitutes the character's appearance as a whole. Chabert is sane. But the glassy eyes, the colorless face rendered cadaverous by the shadow of his hat, the absence of movement appear to be "les dégradants symptômes" of "l'idiotisme." Resemblances between signs of change thus construct a context that invites a false conclusion, precisely the one that Chabert's opportunistic and remarried wife hopes others will draw from the appearance of a husband who has so inopportunely come back to claim his money and spouse. Balzac's narrator renders this conclusion ironical by stating what an objective "observer," rather than this self-interested wife, would see, "indices d'une misère qui avait dégradé ce visage, comme les gouttes d'eau tombées du ciel sur un beau marbre l'ont à la longue défiguré" and signs of a future "drame." In this way, he tells readers that resemblances in his descriptions are misleading, that they lie. But they lie in order ironically to reveal a key to the character's identity as a type, the invisible emotions that are destroying his body and producing his future drama.

The narrator's intervention ("Mais un observateur ...") invites the readers' complicity in his repetition of this lie, as well as in its ironical demystification. He also invites readers to replace visible resemblances between signs with an invisible temporal difference. Chabert's overall appearance, he states, is a metaphor for a linear historical process that is differentiating past from present and present from future. The indices of differentiation are spatial differences between visible aspects of the colonel's appearance.[41] The narrator constructs these spatial differences by juxtaposing two series of similar, visible attributes with contrary connotations. One series includes attributes of Chabert's visible appearance. His face (glassy eyes), clothes (dirty black silk tie) and manner of wearing his wig (pulled down over his forehead) appear to most observers symptoms of madness, poverty, and weakness. The other series is composed of his visible choice of clothes. Wig, tie and hat identify, for qualified observers such as a lawyer, doctor, or author, the social and economic status of a colonel. This choice implies knowledge rather than ignorance of how clothes should be worn, sanity rather than madness, wealth rather than poverty, power rather than weakness. Taken alone, both series of similar signs are deceptive. Taken together, their difference can be interpreted as a spatial metaphor, not only for a particular Restoration character type – the Napoleonic officer – but for a temporal process of differentiation: the linear transformation of the sanity, wealth, power, and knowledge of the man who merited the clothes of a Napoleonic colonel into the apparent insanity, poverty, weakness, and ignorance of the one standing before Derville. Balzac's narrator reads this temporal transformation as evidence of the "douleur profonde" that distinguishes Chabert's identity and makes it representative of an historically identifiable character type. He constitutes identity as a spatial difference between perceivable signs.

Balzac's contextualization of perceivable signs renders all individual signs, all empirical evidence of the Colonel's individual type, deceptive products of social misreading. Neither his visible appearance, that of a bum, nor his visible choice of clothes, that of a colonel, can represent the process that is transforming him or the pain that is distinguishing him. He is neither a colonel nor a bum, and the typologies that give these signs fixed meanings are deceptive. Neither can create a realist "effet-personnage."[42] Balzac's narrator renders his description realistic only by making the colonel's most characteristic attribute, his pain, irreducible to a fixed paradigm. He does not abandon rational categorization in favor of intuition. Instead of categorizing individual signs, he categorizes differences between signs, by referring to a conventional code of difference that only a lawyer, a doctor, or an author would recognize. Differences between the colonel's choice of clothes and his overall state identify a precise temporal process of differentiation, a linear mental and physical deterioration over time. They also constitute the fiction of a superior observing type who can decode the spatial signs of this deterioration.

By unveiling, behind surface similarities, a hidden code of descriptive difference, Balzac's narrator constitutes not only

Chabert's identity, but French society in 1819, as an ongoing historical process of transformation with an imperfective aspect.[43] The specific change taking place in Chabert is the narrator's metaphor for the more complex, but just as irreversible, historical process transforming France during the Restoration. Chabert was a colonel in Napoleon's army. He was mistakenly declared dead at the battle of Eylau, just as the Empire would be declared dead by the Restoration. Years later, during the height of the Restoration, he made his way back to Paris. In the meantime his wife, like many other members of the middle class, had used her Napoleonic wealth to purchase social and political power from the increasingly poor Restoration nobility. She married Count Ferraud. When Chabert inopportunely reappears, not only does she refuse to renounce her newfound social and political power, she uses it to deny his identity just as Goriot's daughters, after they marry into wealth or nobility, try to deny the existence of their middle-class father. The countess deceitfully and opportunistically reads the signs of deterioration in her first husband's appearance as visible evidence that he is mad. Balzac's description of the symptoms that point to Chabert's madness is thus a concrete representation of the calculated misreading with which Restoration society tried to misinterpret signs of its Napoleonic past and aristocratic present: "Les bureaux voudraient pouvoir anéantir les gens de l'Empire" (3: 343).[44]

The description of Chabert's appearance is thus an indirect means of constructing the historical present of Restoration society in temporal terms, as a process of hiding signs of its Napoleonic past and foregrounding signs of its deceptively aristocratic and monarchical present. Like the signs of madness in Chabert's appearance, the Restoration's marks of its aristocratic and monarchical system are deceptive. These marks conceal a market strategy: the selling of inherited political and social influence in order to buy bourgeois wealth. Chabert's story constitutes the Restoration's historical present, therefore, as a temporal process of lying, of stating that the aristocratic sign system has an inherent use value rather than a contingent exchange value.[45] Such a system functions to buy economic power, to produce economic differentiation, rather than to reveal inherited hierarchical differences.[46]

Balzac's descriptive discourse constitutes the historical present as a continuous ironical process of disclosing history's course by concealing it. Society's powerful liars seek to gain complete control over the effects of their lies by hiding their market strategy.[47] But the victims of their repression have neither the wealth nor the power to conceal the marks that history's violence imprints on them. They rebel, as do Chabert and Goriot, by disclosing these marks of oppression to observing characters, like Derville and Rastignac, who might aid their rebellion. The latter read the physical imprints of Chabert's and Goriot's past identities as guarantees that their stories of repression are true, and they encourage their vain efforts to fight back (*Goriot* 3: 63).

Social coercion ironically unveils its own lie. Even when it forces its victims to be accomplices in denying their own identity, this denial reveals what it seems to conceal: "Pas Chabert! pas Chabert! je me nomme Hyacinthe...Je ne suis plus un homme, je suis le numéro 164, septième salle" ("Chabert" 3: 372).[48] Chabert's denial merely confirms what Derville has already read in his appearance: "Ce vieux-là, mon cher, est tout un poème, où, comme disent les romantiques, un drame. As-tu rencontré quelquefois la comtesse Ferraud?" (3: 371). The appearances of Chabert and of the poor quarter in *Le Père Goriot* are "poems" because they ironically reveal, not only the spatial multiplicity of character types and areas that history is destroying, but the process of lying that is hiding and producing this destruction. Balzac's ironical descriptive discourse constitutes society's historical present in its own image as an indirect disclosure of knowledge about that which it is hiding, about its own lying.

"Le Colonel Chabert" puts so much emphasis on this descriptive pattern that it seems to redefine the story's narrative in descriptive terms, as a process which has the incompleteness and reversibility of the imperfective aspect. The narrator situates the present in a temporal middle ground.[49] Derville encounters Chabert before the Restoration completely eliminates him, at a moment when its violence is still theoretically reversible. Hence the lawyer's attempt to defend the former colonel. But even when Chabert has been locked in an asylum, at the end of the story, the narrator embeds this complete narrative transformation within an incomplete repetition of similar transformations that he has repeatedly witnessed in the past and that his colleague will repeatedly witness in the future: "Je ne puis vous dire tout ce que j'ai vu, car j'ai vu des crimes contre lesquels la justice est impuissante ... Vous allez connaître ces jolies choses-là, vous ... " ("Chabert" 3: 373). By embedding the perfective aspect of Chabert's single destruction within the imperfective aspect of society's iterated acts of destruction, Balzac transforms his life into a mere part of society's ongoing repetition of repression and deceit that characterizes the era, indeed history, as a whole: "Quand les malheureux ont convaincu la Société de mensonge, ils se rejettent plus vivement dans le sein de Dieu" (3: 316). Balzac thus subordinates his narrative dramatization of the power of society's lies, its effacement of Chabert, to his descriptive and ironical revelation of the historical knowledge that it hides, which has the temporal reversibility of the imperfective aspect. Seemingly detachable descriptive passages in these two early works redefine the narrative as an historical allegory that unveils the spatial and temporal structure of the descriptive.

By presenting itself as a fundamentally descriptive discourse, "Le Colonel Chabert" gives the impression that the *Comédie humaine* as a whole is an ironical, yet indirectly realist, means of disclosing knowledge about history which is structured as a repetition of the same. The story constitutes the narrator as an objective point of view on society's lies, one who reveals, albeit ironically, what these lies conceal: the spatial differences that constitute his era's typical people, places, or things, and the historically repeated lies that are producing and destroying them. By ironically describing the truth of lying, and thus of his own lying, Balzac's narrator attempts to go beyond his own deceptiveness to irony. This stable ironical distance beyond lying is represented by Derville who, after observing Chabert's ultimate fate, recognizes that he must lie to survive. He can only take an ironical, spatial distance from his and Paris's lies: "[J]e vais vivre à la campagne avec ma femme, Paris me fait horreur" (3: 373).

Through Derville, Balzac's descriptive discourse constitutes social history as an ironical overcoming of society's repeated lying about its historical nature. It redefines historical time as a process of affirming and negating the sequence of lies with which his "auguste mensonge," the *Comédie humaine*, ironically constitutes the Restoration's multiple character types and its historical process of change. This representation of history has some similarities to Hegel's philosophy of history. Being for Hegel "falls into time," time being defined in Aristotelian terms as a sequence of countable NOWS that are passing away and coming into being.[50] This sequence, however, culminates in its own philosophical reversal, what Paul Ricoeur calls "*l'abolition de la narrativité dans la considération pensante de l'histoire.*"[51] In the philosophy of history, the sequence of NOWS takes the form of repeated ruses that reveal the nature of historical being by dissembling it, just as the sequence of lies performed by Balzac's powerful individuals indirectly reveals character type and historical change by concealing them.[52] In both Balzac's descriptive history and Hegel's philosophy of history, consciousness of lying ironically overcomes it and produces knowledge. The sequentiality of repeated lies constantly reproduces the simultaneity of unchanging self-knowledge.

As in some readings of Hegel, Balzac's ironical descriptive discourse does not ultimately bring an end to the category of time itself.[53] It simply replaces a narrative mode of constituting time (according to the perfective aspect of completion) with a descriptive mode of constituting time (according to the imperfective aspect of incompletion). In Hegel, however, time is the truth of space, and eventually negates it. But in Balzac's descriptive discourse, time's imperfective aspect (the process of differentiation that is destroying Chabert) and spatial contiguity (the difference between visible details of his appearance) co-exist. Rather than disclose a state of being that sublates historical time and space, Balzac's descriptive irony discloses a historical, but spatialized, being in time and space.

The descriptive, not just the narrative, enables Balzac to add a temporal dimension to his spatialized representation of the *Comédie humaine* as a museum. It treats the actions of the era's typical character types as if they could be contained, without being negated, within the juxtaposed spatial frames of his novel, not unlike animals in the cages of a zoo (*Avant-propos* 1: 18; *Préface*, *Goriot*, 2nd edn. 3: 47). By constructing his era's human zoo in terms of its multiple masks, Balzac melds the spatializing tendencies of the descriptive with those of irony to produce a revelation, rather than an elimination, of a fixed knowledge about time.[54]

The literary historical significance of Balzac's stable descriptive irony can be brought into focus by comparing it to Stendhal's unstable narrative irony. Stendhal subordinates descriptive time to narrative time, as did eighteenth-century French ironic novels. The initial description of Verrières in *Le Rouge et le noir* contains details of industry and social class that situate town and inhabitants historically near the end of the Restoration. It ironically subverts any conventional interpretation of its literal details, such as those that suggest the superiority of the mayor and husband of Julien's great love, Mme de Rênal: "A son aspect tous les chapeaux se lèvent rapidement." But, whereas Balzac's stable irony reveals, behind Chabert's apparent madness, signs of the historical forces that are destroying him, Stendhal's unstable irony discloses a knowledge only of the "atmosphère empestée des petits intérêts d'argent" motivating a typical provincial town: "On sent enfin que le talent de cet homme-là se borne à se faire payer bien exactement ce qu'on lui doit, et à payer lui-même le plus tard possible quand il doit."[55]

Stendhal's narrator interprets his spatial description of provincial character and place ironically, as a misreading of his narrative.[56] The details of M. de Rênal's garden, a traditional spatial and descriptive *topos* of love, as well as of the details of Fidelity Drive and of the mayor's appearance, disclose a provincial drive for gain that appears to explain Julien's rise in society. But this interpretation of Julien's actions proves to be a Parisian misreading of his life, one that fails to account for the unpredictability of his actions, which culminate in his abandonment of the brilliant Parisian Mathilde de la Môle and his shooting of the down-to-earth provincial Mme de Rênal.[57] Rather than ironically disclose typical historical change behind signs of typical historical space, Stendhal's descriptions disclose the failure of historical background, whether Parisian or provincial, to account for the singularity, ahistoricity, and unreadability of his narrative. Where Balzac's descriptive irony spatializes and historicizes the narrative, Stendhal's temporalizes and singularizes the descriptive. It thus keeps history in the background. Although Stendhal's ironical glorification of his characters' inexplicably individual acts is hardly characteristic of eighteenth-century narrative, his ironical subordination of descriptive to narrative time, of history to individual action, is. It side-steps the interplay between descriptive and narrative time that Balzac will introduce into the nineteenth-century novel.

Is Balzac's descriptive irony representative of his narrator's discourse as a whole? Does it reconcile time and space by reducing the former to its imperfective aspect? Some prefaces and early works, such as *La Peau de chagrin* and "Le Colonel Chabert", suggest that it does.[58] Certainly the descriptive plays a major role in the *Comédie humaine*. Nevertheless, the descriptive mode of constituting time raises serious questions. It cannot account for the complexity of Balzac's novels. The very imperfective aspect that enables the descriptive to give spatial differences a temporal duration, or to interpret them as marks of temporal differentiation, is not only temporally incomplete, it is logically, as well as temporally, reversible, as Derville is fully aware. Immediately after his first interview with the colonel, the lawyer realizes that he cannot decide whether he has seen a colonel transformed by history into a bum or "le plus habile comédien de notre époque" (3: 334), a bum who has masked himself as a colonel. The spatial differences in Chabert's appearance between signs of a colonel and signs of a bum may not have resulted from the tragic transformation of a past colonel into a present bum; they may have been produced by the deceitful masking of signs of a past bum as the present illusion of a colonel. If signs have a mere exchange value, then victimhood may only be a mask. Could it be that the mask of victimhood has been donned by those who would dispute the spoils of the Napoleonic past with those, like Chabert's wife, who have donned the mask of the Restoration? Did not Balzac hope to sell his fictional victim's story to readers who, like himself, preferred an absolute monarchy?

The fixity of the differential paradigms that constitute the descriptive is thus threatened by the potential, logical reversibility of the imperfective aspect. In itself, the descriptive cannot justify Derville's choice of one spatial paradigm over another. The identification of spatial and temporal differences is purely arbitrary. The signs of identity and historical temporality hidden behind Balzac's narrator's descriptive irony may themselves thus be masks hiding an absence of identity or of knowledge about historical change.[59]

The very means by which the descriptive ironically discloses a temporal duration, the imperfective aspect, thus ironically reverses this temporal duration. Irony of irony puts into question the descriptive's claim to disclose a knowledge about time, and reveals its blindness to whether it is hiding, or disclosing, temporal difference. The only knowledge revealed by Balzac's descriptive teacher is, ironically, a knowledge of his ignorance about whether society's lies hide a temporal and historical change or a continuity of the same.[60]

By disclosing descriptive discourse's ignorance about temporal change, Derville creates a desire for that to which the imperfective aspect is blind: the perfective aspect of complete individual transformations and complete historical change.[61] Irony of irony raises the possibility that descriptive reversibility is only an illusion produced by the narrative's irreversible acts of prescription. Behind the descriptive's deceptively detachable mask may hide irreversible semiotic transformations that have produced its illusion of reversibility and spatiality. If temporal change cannot be derived from the descriptive's reversible spatial paradigms, perhaps space can be derived from the narrative's irreversible temporal transformations. In that case, Balzac's descriptive rhetoric would merely displace, rather than transform, the priority of narrative in the eighteenth-century French novel.

NARRATIVE IRONY AND POWER: SOCIETY AS HISTORICAL DIFFERENTIATION

Although the *Comédie humaine* repeatedly characterizes itself descriptively as a discourse of knowledge, it increasingly discloses, particularly in the later novels, the ignorance that the descriptive hides. It then treats this ignorance strategically as a narrative means to discursive power. At first, the narrator seems to reject the descriptive as a source of knowledge and to replace it with the narrative. If the descriptive cannot make the narrative comprehensible, he argues, perhaps narrative can make the descriptive comprehensible: "[L]e récit des événements auxquels sont dus de si terribles bouleversements de physiognomie est la seule ressource qui reste au poète pour les faire comprendre."[62] But, rather than constitute an alternate source of realist knowledge, Balzac's narrative methodically deconstructs the descriptive assertion that words disclose knowledge at all (and thus the Restoration's presupposition that names describe a fixed social hierarchy).[63] By contradicting traditional statements of his belief in realist representation, Balzac's narrative of disillusionment redefines knowledge as a self-deception whose sole function is to confirm the writer's power to exchange words for desired readings.

Balzac's deconstruction of his descriptive discourse of knowledge comes to the fore in those early novels with uncomfortable transitions from long introductory descriptive passages to the narrative. *Le Père Goriot* provides a particularly striking example of this deconstruction. Immediately after describing the place in which Goriot lives and the cast of characters with whom he lives, the narrator focuses on Goriot himself and indirectly redefines his own discourse in narrative terms:

> Ce *patiras* était l'ancien vermicellier, le père Goriot, sur la tête duquel un peintre aurait, comme l'historien, fait tomber toute la lumière du tableau. Par quel hasard ce mépris à demi haineux, cette persécution

mélangée de pitié, ce non-respect du malheur avaient-ils frappé le plus ancien pensionnaire? Y avait-il donné lieu par quelques-uns de ces ridicules ou de ces bizarreries que l'on pardonne moins qu'on ne pardonnne des vices. Ces questions tiennent de près à bien des injustices sociales. (*Goriot* 3: 63)

The narrator's first comparison of himself to a painter echoes the traditional metaphor for a describer, but his second comparison to an historian suggests that he is a story-teller. A gradual modulation from describer to narrator ensues as he ponders the cause of Goriot's verbal persecution by the *pensionnaires*, causality being a function of narrative sequence rather than descriptive simultaneity. The question of Goriot's narrative function is then followed by a résumé of his life, from the moment he entered the Maison Vauquer to the present. This narrative provides a response to the question of causality.

Whereas the introduction to *Le Père Goriot* characterizes the subsequent narrative as a descriptive category, the transition to the beginning of the narrative redefines the descriptive as a narrative function. This transition dramatizes the triumph of a character who uses words as if they functioned narratively, Mme Vauquer, over a character who imagines that words function descriptively, Goriot:

Les yeux de la veuve s'allumèrent quand elle l'aida complaisamment à déballer et ranger les louches, les cuillers à ragoût ... "Ceci, dit-il à Mme Vauquer en serrant un plat et une petite écuelle dont le couvercle représentait deux tourterelles qui se becquetaient, est le premier présent que m'a fait ma femme, le jour de notre anniversaire ... Dieu merci! je pourrai prendre dans cette écuelle mon café, tous les matins durant le reste de mes jours. Je ne suis pas à plaindre, j'ai sur la planche du pain de cuit pour longtemps." (3: 64)

Goriot's words and belongings are signs that do not function in the way he thinks they do. He imagines that they simply disclose knowledge about his past life and his present well-being. Instead, they produce a powerful reaction in the mind of the widow who is seeing and hearing them. They give birth to the idea of her future fortune and well-being as his wife. Mme Vauquer is, in fact, incapable of interpreting his or anyone else's words descriptively, her only concern being what words can do for her, not what they might say. Words in her mind are speech acts of transformation. Goriot's words about his past thus become a present speech act that promises a future speech act, an "I do." When he does not keep his unwitting "promise," she reinterprets his speech acts as what Austin calls perlocutionary speech acts, that is, as acts of producing an effect on the listener, in this case, as deceitful acts of seduction.[64] She responds in kind by taking her revenge. She carries out her revenge by deceitfully choosing those words that support her allegation that he lies and that enlist the complicity of the other *pensionnaires* in this interpretation:

> L'opinion qui paraissait plus probable, et qui fut généralement adoptée, était celle de Mme Vauquer. A l'entendre, cet homme si bien conservé, sain comme son œil et avec lequel on pouvait avoir encore beaucoup d'agréments, était un libertin qui avait des goûts étranges. Voici sur quels faits la veuve Vauquer appuyait ses calomnies. (3: 70)

Mme Vauquer's lies serve to produce in her listeners the belief that her lies are truthful and that her victim's truths are lies.

As in so many of the *Comédie humaine*'s verbal battles, the conflict between a character who imagines that words convey meaning and a character who treats them as pure speech acts ends in the victory of the latter. This triumph of a discourse of speech acts redefines the descriptive in narrative terms of power. It answers the narrator's questions about the cause of Goriot's persecution and downfall. This persecution is brought about by his inability to recognize that society's words function narratively as acts of transformation.

In redefining the descriptive as a narrative transformation, this transitional passage deconstructs the notion that language, even in its narrative form, describes something real, that it is a discourse of knowledge. As a narrative function, Goriot's self-description becomes part of a transformation that takes place over time. This act, like Mme Vauquer's calumnies, may appear to communicate knowledge; it is as reversible and ambiguous as the description of Chabert. Is Goriot's choice to display his wealth and self-satisfaction to the most petty and egotistical of women a sincere act of confession, as he imagines? Or is it a masochistic rejection of her desire to marry in order to provoke her scorn and his own humiliation? The overall narrative context of his self-description raises the possibility that his words are as indifferent to what they describe as are Mme Vauquer's, that he chooses them in order to produce a desirable effect, not to represent something real. "J'ai vécu pour être humilié," he tells Rastignac after he is rejected, like Lear, by the very daughters to whom he gave his wealth (3: 275). Goriot's pretense that his words are descriptive allows him to blind himself to the fact that they function narratively, not descriptively, to bring about his martyrdom: "Je suis dupe!" (3: 277) "Je sais cela depuis dix ans. Je me le disais quelquefois, mais je n'osais pas y croire" (3: 273). "Oh! je souffre un cruel martyre!" (3: 274) The narrative of *Le Père Goriot* thus dramatizes a possibility that "Le Colonel Chabert" only suggests. When descriptive disclosure is embedded within narrative sequence, it becomes indistinguishable from its reverse, prescriptive hiding. Knowledge becomes a mask of ignorance. All that seems certain is the narrative in which the invitation to be persecuted is embedded.

"Le Colonel Chabert" gives the impression that language is descriptive by focusing on Derville's ironical observation of, and distancing from, Paris's acts of lying. But *Le Père Goriot* constructs a world in which language seems to be narrative by deconstructing Goriot's claim (and the introductory description's assertion) that words disclose knowledge. The title of *Le Père Goriot*, which names the novel's central character, may appear to identify a character; in fact it repeats the condescending and derogatory name prescribed by Mme Vauquer in order to carry out her social revenge.[65]

The title repeats the speech act of disparaging Goriot that Rastignac must ultimately adopt as his only road to success. At the end of the novel, he rejects familial sentiment for social performance when he abandons this doting father's grave and goes to dinner with the ungrateful daughter who speeded his death. As a speech act, the title thus repeats the narrative's act of transforming descriptive illusion into narrative power, the act that constitutes it as Rastignac's, rather than Goriot's, story. Does the novel not tell how a young man learns the social necessity of rejecting the descriptive illusions of an old fool who imagines that words express, how he adopts the narrative realism of society's knaves who use words to act? "[S]i vous avez un sentiment vrai, cachez-le comme un trésor" (3: 116).[66] Balzac's narrator's discourse on how words function in Parisian society discloses the error of imagining that words, including those in his titles or descriptions, inform, rather than seduce, a listener or reader. By negating the claim that language describes, and thus the discursive distinction between truth and falsity, *Le Père Goriot* redefines its "descriptive" utterances as covert speech acts of transformation within a purely narrative novel and *Comédie humaine*.

In commenting on his résumé of Goriot's life, the narrator explicitly replaces knowledge with power as the reality of language: "Peut-être est-il dans la nature humaine de tout faire supporter à qui souffre tout par humilité vraie, par faiblesse ou par indifférence. N'aimons-nous pas tous à prouver notre force aux dépens de quelqu'un ou de quelque chose?" (3: 63). Given that descriptive discourse is temporally reversible, the extremely long introductory description invites rejection. It implicitly asks its readers, as Goriot asks Mme Vauquer, to try out their word power by reversing its claim to be a discourse of knowledge. Have not generations of readers taken advantage of this power to discount, not only Balzac's introductory descriptions, but his entire novels, as irrelevant to (their) reality? Have they not accused him of what his narrator calls "poésie" (3: 50)? When the reversible imperfective aspect of the descriptive is interpreted as a purely narrative function, it provokes the reader into reversing its claim to convey knowledge, and into redefining it as an irreversible means of wielding discursive power with the narrative's perfective aspect.

Balzac's descriptive dialectics of hiding and disclosing do not produce a synthesis of contraries in an unfolding of knowledge about contemporary social space. They do deconstruct their own claim to conceal or reveal anything at all, and make the counter-claim that words perform acts of transformation.[67] This deconstruction of his descriptive discourse of knowledge remains implicit as long as Balzac's narrator ironically attributes it to the petty remarks made by the "veuve Vauquer" and her *pensionnaires*. It becomes explicit when *Le Père Goriot*, and later *Illusions perdues*, dramatize Rastignac's and Lucien de Rubempré's disillusionment after they are exposed to the theories and actions of the archcriminal Vautrin. Vautrin's theories and his attempts to act according to them redefine the *pensionnaire*'s petty attempts to feel powerful in terms of society and social history as a whole. When applied to Balzac's own words, they explode the literary historical myth that his narrator replaced a lucid eighteenth-century concern over the effects of words on a reader with a blind nineteenth-century concern over descriptive representation.[68] Rather they suggest a growing awareness of the exchange value of words as powerful tools in the increasingly market-oriented world of the first half of the nineteenth century. They reflect French society's increasing sense that the value of words, like that of property, is mobile, not fixed or moral, and that time may reflect the linear pattern of an amoral, profit-oriented market rather than the cyclical patterns of feudal or romantic organicist thought.[69]

Vautrin is the most powerful of a cast of characters that includes the politician De Marsay, the Archbishop Troubert, the master-criminal Ferragus, and the usurer Gobsek. Whereas petty characters like Mme Vauquer or Sophie Gamard wield word power for the sole purpose of taking revenge, and others like Grandet do so to accumulate wealth or, like Goriot's daughters, to attain social status, Balzac's powerful use words to demonstrate their power: "J'aime le pouvoir pour le pouvoir, moi!" (*Illusions* 5: 703) The means by which they produce a sublime feeling of power, says Vautrin, is a narrative poetry of action and feeling in time, as opposed to the descriptive poetry of hiding and revealing a sublime space, such as Chabert's appearance: "Je suis un grand poète. Mes poésies, je ne les écris pas: elles consistent en actions et en sentiments" (3: 141).[70] Just as Vautrin's actions are narrative poetry, so his words are actions. He substantiates his power by performing felicitous speech acts.

To act physically, mentally, or verbally is to perform an act of transformation with the irreversibility of the perfective aspect.[71] In Balzac, action is often linguistic and interpersonal (perlocutionary). Mme Vauquer transforms Goriot's self-description into a deceit in order to change his relationship to the other *pensionnaires* and satisfy her desire for revenge. Similarly, Vautrin manipulates society's words in order to produce the interpersonal changes that will confirm his power. Unlike Derville and Rastignac, who try legally and socially to make Chabert's and Goriot's names describe the past and present identity of a real man, Vautrin foresees the failure of names. He willingly changes names according to present circumstances and future goals. "Vautrin" is only one of his many pseudonyms, which include l'Abbé Herrera and Trompe-la-mort. All serve to increase the power of Jacques Collin.[72] Rather than names for reality, words, in Vautrin's mind, are arbitrary and substitutable means of performing the particular transformations he desires, just as names are the substitutable means by which Balzac's narrator identifies the powerful characters who mold his realms of politics, society, and finance. Vautrin's success in performing interpersonal transformations that demonstrate his social power thus appears to represent the power of Balzac's narrative to mold the minds and actions of his readers.[73]

Vautrin's theories explain the deconstruction of descriptive illusion that lies implicit in Goriot's encounter with Mme Vauquer. The criminal does so by means of an eighteenth-century skepticism that states the arbitrariness, and thus the reversibility, of the laws that distinguish one speech act from another: "Il n'y a pas de principes, il n'y a que des événements; il n'y a pas de lois, il n'y a que des circonstances: l'homme supérieur épouse les événements et les circonstances pour les conduire" (*Goriot* 3: 144). There are no immutable laws to decide whether actions, be they charitable or murderous, are good or bad, innocent or criminal. All laws are conventional acts of prescription.[74] This is Balzac's stated belief as well: "[L]'auteur n'est pas de propos délibéré moral ou immoral, pour employer les termes faux dont on se sert" (*Preface*, *Goriot*, 2nd edn. 3: 46–47). To prescribe general actions by laws as do law-makers, to prescribe specific actions by interpreting these laws as do judges, is to choose arbitrarily one law or interpretive paradigm over another: "L'on ne trouve pas dans les tribunaux trois juges qui aient le même avis sur un article de loi" (3: 144–45).

If the laws that make distinctions between actions possible are arbitrary and logically reversible, then the claim of Balzac's ironic descriptions to disclose knowledge is also arbitrary and reversible, like the historical connotations of Chabert's description. All that remains in Vautrin's model of history, as in Nietzsche's, is the temporal present of acting, the continuous advent of "circumstances," "events," and the repeated act of transforming them in a manner that confirms, rather than disconfirms, the actor's power to give them an irreversible direction.[75] The manipulation of historical circumstances by a few powerful men, not law, decides whether Mme Vauquer's petty misrepresentation of Goriot, or the Restoration's exploitative burying of Chabert, will be irreversible.

But Vautrin's denial of the laws that make knowledge possible necessarily presupposes that one law is true: the law that governs his, and later Nietzsche's, representation of discourse as a deceitful act of producing the illusion of knowledge.[76] His narrative theory constitutes discourse as a stable ironical lie, but one that is more subversive that the stable irony of the narrator's descriptive lie. Narrative deceives, not about discourse's object, but about what discourse does. According to Balzac's descriptive theory, discourse hides, in order to ironically disclose, knowledge about a contemporary social space of juxtaposed relationships and historical processes. According to Vautrin's (and Nietzsche's) narrative theory, discourse hides, in order to ironically reveal, the fact that knowledge is a discursive illusion.[77] Narrative discourse is a speech act that deceitfully creates and ironically demystifies the illusion that it refers. It is a lie in which the powerful, such as Vautrin, are willing accomplices.

Like Nietzsche, Vautrin sees his active complicity in discourse's lie as an aesthetic act of poetry that substantiates his power.[78] But, whereas Nietzsche concentrates on language as an ironical transformation, Vautrin focuses on language as an ironical transformation of others. For Balzac's chosen few, discourse serves interpersonal power.[79] The ironical speech act of lying is a perlocutionary speech act, a discursive means of producing a social effect. It is complete, felicitous, only when its listeners have been deceived.

By subordinating discursive to social acts of change, Vautrin gives historical time the deceptive appearance of a linear narrative plot: the rise of ambitious ironical liars to social, political, or economic power. He produces this rise by teaching his protégés to demystify society's hypocritical claim to possess knowledge about what is true or good, and by teaching them to lie as society lies to achieve its ends, "[s]e donner un but éclatant et cacher ses moyens d'arriver, tout en cachant sa marche" (*Illusions* 5: 701). However, the linearity of the successful apprentice's rise to power misrepresents the resulting pattern of social history as a whole. Once Rastignac succeeds in society, his life, like Vautrin's, becomes compressed into an historical present, into a repeated sequence of willed transformations whose sole purpose is to represent his power.

Through Vautrin, *Le Père Goriot* and *Illusions perdues* replace the descriptive notion of history presented by *Goriot*'s descriptive introduction, the repeated hiding and revealing of a real social space, with a narrative notion of history: a sequential repetition of acts of transformation that repress the weak, confirm the power of the strong, and produce, when useful, the realist illusion of knowledge. These novels replace, in other words, a description of spatial differences with narrative acts of temporal differentiation. Each change, like a Greimassian narrative transformation, has a perfective aspect. It is irreversible and complete. But it is not logical as is a Greimassian (or Hegelian) transformation. Nor is it historically necessary as is a Hegelian or Marxist transition.[80] Only the repetition of deliberate changes, history's narrative, is necessary. This repetition in itself does not change.

Whereas Balzac's descriptive discourse interprets historical acts of change as products of a hidden, but fixed, social structure in space, his narrative discourse structures spatial differences as products of unforeseeable, but individual, historical transformations in time:

Les ennemis de l'ordre social...jappe[nt] après la justice et se courrouce[nt] au nom du peuple de ce qu'on envoie aux galères un voleur de nuit et de poules dans une enceinte habitée, tandis qu'on met en prison à peine pour quelques mois un homme qui ruine des familles en faisant une faillite frauduleuse, mais ces hypocrites savent bien qu'en condamnant le voleur les juges maintiennent la barrière entre les pauvres et les riches, qui, renversée, amènerait la fin de l'ordre social. (*Illusions* 5: 701)

The powerful erect social space – the difference between the weak and the powerful, the poor and the rich – purely in order to maintain their ability to repeat the acts they will in time, to maintain society's temporal order. The enemies of this order are those who try to subordinate social time to an illusory knowledge of social space: "l'honnête homme est... l'ennemi commun" (*Goriot* 3: 140). Goriot, for example, attempts to impose on his daughters a fixed filial relationship that hinders their rise in aristocratic society. In order to overcome society's descriptive enemies, the agents of individual differentiation must hide their power and create an "Histoire officielle, menteuse" (*Illusions* 5: 695). They deceive society's honest dupes by masking their arbitrary acts of creating social space in time as products of a pre-existing and necessary hierarchy, as a spatial order. One of Goriot's daughters thus has herself adopted by an aristocrat, and then she conceals this useful transformation of social space.

For Balzac, the particular configuration of differences that composes the social space of an era is a function of the chance appearances of powerful men.[81] Hence his disappointment with the leaders of Restoration society who were too weak to ensure (what he felt to be) the monarchical and aristocratic heritage of power. This heritage belonged, he thought, to its most powerful, if not always aristocratic, actors.[82] Hence, too, his tendency, like the trend that was beginning to develop in nineteenth-century France, to blur class distinctions within the individual's search for market power. This is a search shared by aristocrats, parvenus, empire careerists, administrative officials of the constitutional monarchies, and (later) industrialists.[83]

What complicates Vautrin's practice of speech acts, however, is that he not only uses words to wield power, he uses them to enunciate a theory about word power. In other words, his is not only a discourse *of* power, it is a discourse *on* power. Vautrin systematically demystifies the illusion of his protégés (the law student Rastignac and the poet Lucien de Rubempré) that language is descriptive. If he teaches them about discursive reality, it is not to make them more knowledgeable, but to teach them as his apprentices the skill of using words to act.[84] This apprenticeship, notes Richard Terdiman, gives Balzac's works the form of a novel of initiation into liberal capitalist discourse.[85] It purports to train readers to "penetrate the dominant sign system ... and manipulate it freely from a secure position at its heart."[86] By means of characters like Vautrin, society's dominant discourse *on* power may mask itself as a Christian or Hegelian discourse of knowledge; it does so purely in order to achieve the non-Christian end *of* increasing individual power. Vautrin thus makes explicit an implicit goal of language in capitalist society: the achievement of individual power by interpreting words as having only an exchange value, as being mere means of manipulation. Such a will to exchange power surreptitiously took over the anti-bourgeois rhetoric of the Restoration, and began to surface in the rhetoric of the July Monarchy.[87]

What are the implications of Vautrin's discourse on/of power for the *Comédie humaine*? What does it imply for the relationship between realist author and reader? Theoretically, Vautrin's initiation transforms his apprentice into an ironical accomplice in his lies, and into a surrogate actor who performs the powerful acts his master wills, just as Vautrin the character performs the powerful historical acts that the novelist, Balzac, wills: "La première pensée de l'homme ... est d'avoir un complice de sa destinée ... J'aime à me dévouer ... Je veux aimer ma créature, la façonner, la pétrir à mon usage, afin de l'aimer comme un père aime son enfant ... [J]e me réjouirai de tes succès ... " (*Illusions* 5: 707–08). Were Lucien to succeed in using words as a discourse of power, he would confirm the power of his master's discourse on power to empower its listeners. He would demonstrate that the master's discourse on power is a discourse of power as well.

Vautrin's transformation of his discourse on power into a discourse of power is deeply ironical. It cannot help but question its own claim to be saying what it is doing. On the one hand, it discloses knowledge about the power of words in contemporary society. On the other, it produces an effect on listeners regardless of whether or not its meaning is true: "Les dernières phrases du prêtre espagnol [Vautrin] avaient remué beaucoup de cordes dans son cœur [Lucien's]" (5: 705); "Mon père, je suis à vous, dit Lucien ébloui de ce flot d'or" (5: 709). The very words that "benevolently" initiate Vautrin's listener into knowledge about society's dominant discourse of power ironically reveal their indifference to the act of disclosing knowledge and their performative goal of seducing Lucien. If Vautrin's words are truly a discourse of power, they resemble Austin's explicit performative. They are indifferent to whether they communicate knowledge about this act. They do not perform a cognitive act of description. But Vautrin's cynical rejection of rules also presupposes that a description of the rules governing speech acts may mislead a listener about what words are really doing.[88] A grammar of speech acts like Austin's becomes potentially deceptive.[89]

This realist character's assertion of word power indirectly invites an ironical reading of the narrator's discourse, just as some eighteenth-century narrators, like Stendhal's, invited an ironical reading of their narrative. If the narrator's ironical lie discloses knowledge about contemporary society's narrative deceits, if this lie liberates readers from belief in society's conventional laws, if it empowers them, it does so the better to dominate them.[90] Were not contemporary readers thirsting for knowledge about how to act in a world where aristocratic notions of eternal law or meaning were giving way to bourgeois market forces of exchange?[91] As Balzac's novels become increasingly narrative in nature, do they not, like Vautrin, give increasing evidence of his narrator's will to seduce his readers into a search for domination, into imitating a mastery that they will gratefully attribute to (the past and future purchase of) the author's novels?[92] Is the narrator not attempting to demonstrate his authority over a superior few among his apprentice readers by teaching them the discursive rules of Parisian life? It is hard not to react with suspicion when a narrator flexes his verbal muscles in a list of rhetorical questions: "N'aimons-nous pas tous à prouver notre force au dépens de quelqu'un ... ?" (*Goriot* 3: 63). Is this narrator affirming his own pleasure at being able to manipulate the reader's answers to his false questions?[93] This is certainly Lucien's reaction to Vautrin's revelations: "'Pourquoi me donnez-vous tout? Quel est votre part?'" (*Illusions* 5: 707)[94] Or is the narrator, like Goriot, asking his pupil to reject his model and to decide for himself?

The narrator's discourse on a few superior characters indirectly constitutes realist writing in the *Comédie humaine* as an ironical act of social injustice and political necessity. When his narrator says of his rhetorical questions, "[c]es questions tiennent de près à bien des injustices sociales" (*Goriot* 3: 63), then tells a story that justifies injustice as his hero's sole means to social power, he ironically affirms that these questions are political and performative. Rather than encourage readers to seek knowledge about society's victims as he did in his descriptive introduction, the narrator ironically reveals and performs the socially unjust act of justifying and recommending indifference, as well as the politically expedient act of fostering the word power of those who maintain society's temporal order. Balzac's narrator may pretend that his goal is to represent reality, just as his monarch pretends to be fair and his church to be religious. Realism is no more the primary goal of his writing than social welfare was the goal of the Restoration's powerful subjects or monarch.[95] The narrator's social realism, his descriptions of victimized groups and areas, do not, therefore, prefigure the descriptions of Zola's narrator, which cry out for a government that will rectify social injustice, nor do they foresee the social rhetoric of Napoleon III. The political role of Balzac's "auguste mensonge" is to lure a select few readers into maintaining the social order, while it deceives common readers into thinking that it is communicating knowledge about social reality: "Lucien revoyait Paris, il ressaisissait les rênes de la domination que ses mains inhabiles avaient lâchées..." (5: 705).

If we interpret the narrator's discourse according to Vautrin's discourse on power, the *Comédie humaine* is a narrative sequence of ironically deceitful acts of individual transformation (including Vautrin's empowerment of his apprentices) and of social transformation (Balzac's empowerment of his readers) that reinforce the temporal order of society. Its ironical descriptions of the social and topographical relationships linking Restoration and post-Restoration France's rich and poor, its Aristotelian narratives of action with distinct beginnings and ends, even its representations of word power, are ironical means of wielding power over readers. They transform readers into confirmations of the author's ability to compete against the professional writers in the rapidly growing, nineteenth-century market for words.[96] Realist discourse becomes an "histoire officielle, menteuse" that may or may not unveil reality, but that definitely demonstrates the power of its author (*Illusions*, 5: 695). Narrative irony is a transformation with a perfective aspect that serves to differentiate the author in society and in time.

Le Père Goriot's transition from a descriptive to a narrative notion of words thus prefigures Balzac's apparent evolution towards a more narrative conception of the *Comédie humaine*, as evidenced by *Splendeurs et misères des courtisanes*.[97] However, the power of the narrator's ironical discourse to perform the act of domination about which it speaks depends upon its ability to repeat itself in a plurality of historical circumstances. It must transform some readers' passive reception of knowledge about discursive power into an active practice of wielding it, and into indifference as to whether or not words communicate knowledge. Descriptive difference must become indifference to the descriptive within an act of narrative differentiation. It is precisely the *Comédie humaine*'s meditation on the contradictions that lie hidden in this attempt to transform a discourse *on* narrative dominance into a narrative discourse *of* dominance –

whether dominance be attributed to an individual agent, an historical force, or language itself – that produces an irony of narrative irony, an irony of power.[98]

IRONY OF NARRATIVE IRONY: POWER, RENUNCIATION, AND REPETITION

The *Comédie humaine* periodically foregrounds the irony of narrative irony that lies hidden in its discourse on power. It does so by recounting how seemingly powerless characters, like Lucien, occasion the failure of seemingly powerful characters like Vautrin. Whereas Balzac's powerful generally hold (legal or illegal) positions of social, political, or economic power and live in Paris, his subversive characters frequently exercise socially marginal vocations or no vocation at all. They come from, or end up in, marginal areas of Paris or the provinces. Some, like Lucien, are motivated by resentment of those who wield power. Others have renounced power and are indifferent to it.[99] By contributing to the failure of those seeking to confirm their power, Balzac's marginal characters ironically undercut the ironical lies and narratives with which a few exercise power. Irony of narrative irony decenters the very category of power, including the market power to exchange, within Balzac's novelistic discourse as a whole. It reintroduces the question, but only the question, of the descriptive and of knowledge.[100]

Balzac's narrator's ironical indifference to narrative power can be documented in some of his early, as well as his late, works. It is strikingly illustrated in the early short story, "L'Illustre Gaudissart," written during the same period as Balzac's ode to the few men who are "assez heureux pour avoir presque toujours réussi dans leurs desseins," *L'Histoire des treize* (*Histoire* 5: 787). Like Balzac's apostles of power for the sake of power, Gaudissart uses words to act. But his domain of speech action is neither society nor politics. It is commerce. Words perform the act of selling words: newspaper subscriptions and insurance policies. He is the most successful travelling salesman of words in his time. His attempt to exchange words for money establishes a close link in the *Comédie humaine* between discourse, monetary exchange, and power.[101] The story of how he incurs a loss, rather than makes a profit, in a small provincial town dramatizes the failure of Parisian capitalism to sell its discourse on word and exchange power in France as a whole.[102]

Commercial lies for Gaudissart, like social and political lies for Vautrin, are, in the words of Shoshana Felman, a "field of forces in which his will to power is affirmed."[103] "[J]e serai bientôt au pouvoir, moi!" he brags to his mistress, Jenny (4: 571). Gaudissart is absolutely indifferent to whether the words in his sales pitch or in the newspapers and policies he sells disclose knowledge: "Il est voyageur, il ne sait rien à fond; il connaît des noms d'hommes et de lieux et non les hommes et les lieux" (4: 1348).[104] Rather than communicate knowledge, words are a deceitful currency that can be exchanged for money, as money can be exchanged for power: "[L]a femme libre, le Saint-Simonisme, l'Antagonisme, le Fouriérisme, le Criticisme, et l'exploitation passionnée, hé bien, c'est... enfin, c'est dix francs par abonnement." (4: 572).

The pure exchange value of words for Gaudissart derives from their potential to produce a marketable descriptive illusion. They mask a narrative discourse of economic power as a descriptive discourse of knowledge about real future changes in the life of the buyer. A subscription to *The Globe*, he tells his clients, will alter their lives by providing them with knowledge about changes taking place in society as a whole: "[L]e journal *Le Globe*, bon nom qui en exprime nettement la mission, *Le Globe* est le *cicerone* qui vous expliquera tous les matins les conditions nouvelles dans lesquelles s'accomplira, dans peu de temps, le changement politique et moral du monde" (4: 591). An insurance policy on "intellectual capital" will insure positive change in the signer's future career. It will "solidifier les espérances, coaguler, financièrement parlant, les désirs de fortune de chacun, lui en assurer la réalisation!" (4: 589). Both statements are lies about their own narrative status. They sell the illusion that they are objective descriptions of the real changes that a subscription or a policy will cause in the buyer's life, of their use value. In exchange for this illusion, buyers blindly treat these words according to their exchange value by giving Gaudissart money. The salesman thus masks an irreversible narrative transformation, the exchange of words for money, as a descriptive representation, the exchange of words for knowledge. Moreover, he too performs his commercial lies ironically, by making his mistress, to whom he vaunts his success, an accomplice in his deceit.

Gaudissart's primary client, however, is himself. Before he can give descriptive illusion (to his clients) in exchange for narrative and economic power, he must sell his employers, as Vautrin sells Lucien, on the narrative power of his words. And before he can sell his employers on his word power, he must sell himself on the necessity that his words will deceive – "foi de Gaudissart! on les roulera! Ils seront roulés! roulés!" (4: 575) – and that he will never be deceived by the words of others: "'[E]nfoncer Gaudissart, jamais, jamais.' Et l'illustre Voyageur se posa devant Jenny, la regarda fièrement, la main passée dans son gilet, la tête de trois quarts, dans une attitude napoléonienne. 'Oh! es-tu drôle? Qu'as-tu donc mangé ce soir?'" (4: 571–72). Gaudissart can wield economic power only if he and his employers buy the belief that he is accurately describing the narrative power of his words.

It is precisely the reality of Gaudissart's narrative commodity that the man of power buys from himself, the power of his words to perform a narrative transformation. This is the commodity that "L'Illustre Gaudissart," unlike *Le Père Goriot* and *Illusions perdues*, puts into question. This questioning begins when Jenny refuses to play Gaudissart's ironical accomplice, and bets him that he will soon see evidence of the absence, not the presence, of his word power: "Je parie que tu ne seras pas seulement allé jusqu'à Poitiers que tu te seras laissé pincer?" (4: 571). Whereas Lucien quickly accepts Vautrin's description of his word power, Jenny teasingly questions Gaudissart's. She casts doubt on whether he can sell her, and even himself, on the belief that he is accurately describing his real word power. The story of his failure to sell himself on this description discloses an unbridgeable gap between what words say about power, and what they may or may not do. This gap ironically reverses any attempt to interpret discourses *on* power as discourses *of* power.

Gaudissart's failure takes the form of an allegory recounting the inability of a Parisian market discourse to dominate a provincial ironical discourse. As he distances himself from Paris, his ability to exchange words for money decreases: "[A] mesure que j'avance vers le centre da la France, les têtes deviennent singulièrement plus dures" (4: 573). The obstacle to economic exchange is not resentment of Parisian dominance, but indifference to it. The center of this indifference and the site of the story is the Touraine, Balzac's native province. When its inhabitants leave the Touraine, the narrator declares, they become some of France's greatest men. However, when they remain or when others enter, their collective mentality – "rusé, goguenard, épigrammatique," and "artiste" – destroys their will to act and thus to dominate, "les dispositions premières s'abolissent promptement": "Transplantez le Tourangeau, ses qualités se développent et produisent de grandes choses ... Allez dans cette Turquie de la France ... Fussiez-vous ambitieux comme l'était Napoléon, ou poète comme l'était Byron, une force inouīe, invincible vous obligerait à garder vos poésies pour vous, et à convertir en rêves vos projects ambitieux" (4: 575–76). Behind Paris's deceptive centrality, behind the Nietzschean construction of reality as a field of rival forces, the *Comédie humaine* ironically discloses rival centers, a force of indifference to social, political, economic, or literary speech action, a paradoxical power to destroy power.[105] Like a black hole hidden in the margins of its discursive universe, provincial indifference both generates and neutralizes the will to power of the Parisian Gaudissarts, Nucingens, Vautrins, De Marsays, and Balzacs. It ironically undercuts their claim to place their ironical lies at the center of French discourse.

Balzac undercuts his Parisian discourse on power by recounting a story in which Gaudissart blindly exchanges a subscription for two non-existent kegs of wine belonging to a madman, Margaritis. This exchange is set up by an ironical provincial, Vernier, who, along with several other Tourangeaux, watches it from the next room without Gaudissart's knowledge. Given the non-existence of the wine and the legal contradiction of an exchange with a madman, all that appears to change hands is a subscription and Gaudissart's illusory confirmation of his power. But even this exchange is ironically reversed and undone when he finds out that he has been tricked.

By pitting a sane salesman against a mad one, Vernier constructs a situation that ironically foregrounds the madness of all discourses of power. Like Gaudissart, Margaritis does not use words to disclose a meaning. He cannot. He is also incapable of manipulating discourse according to his desires or calculating its effects on a listener. He can no more use words as a discourse of power than as a discourse of knowledge, although he madly repeats a sales pitch which suggests that he can. The madman can deceive the salesman because the latter presupposes, in a paranoid manner, that anyone who does not use words to disclose knowledge must, like himself, use them to seek mastery. He concludes, accordingly, that the absence of any intention by Margaritis to make sense signifies the presence of a will to use words to produce an effect on the listener. All discourses of word power, in fact, confuse their negation of the referentiality of words with an affirmation of their ability to act.[106]

Balzac dramatizes the madness of the Gaudissart's presupposition – if words are not saying something they must be doing something – when the salesman interprets Margaritis's *non-sequiturs* as signs that he is performing speech acts:

"Monsieur," dit Gaudissart, "a été dans les affaires ... "
"Publiques," répondit Margaritis en l'interrompant. "J'ai pacifié la Calabre sous le règne du roi Murat ... "
"Oh! alors," reprit Gaudissart, "nous nous entendrons parfaitement."
"Je vous écoute," répondit Margaritis en prenant le maintien d'un homme qui pose pour son portrait chez un peintre. (4: 583)

Gaudissart hears only those words which seem to verify that the madman, like himself, is trying to dominate: "'Oh! la belle usure!' s'écria Margaritis. 'Et! diable! il est fin, le bonhomme ...' pensa Gaudissart" (4: 586). "'Bon, je tiens mon homme,' se dit Gaudissart; 'tu veux me vendre du vin dont j'ai besoin, je vais te dominer'" (4: 591). He transforms the meaningless formulas repeated by the madman into paranoid mirrors of his ideal perlocutionary speech acts, into imaginary confirmations of his discourse on word power. In this way he creates a purely fictional market situation. This imaginary market situation blinds him to the fact that his words are having no more effect on Margaritis than the latter's are having on him, to the absence of the conditions necessary for a market exchange of perlocutionary effects:

"Hé bien, vous avez parfaitement compris l'entreprise des capitaux intellectuels?"
"Parfaitement."
"Vous avez mesuré toute la portée du *Globe*?"
"Deux fois... à pied."
Gaudissart n'entendit pas, parce qu'il restait dans le milieu de ses pensées et s'écoutait lui-même en homme sûr de triompher. (4: 591–92).[107]

By putting France's greatest salesman in a situation where he produces a pure illusion that his and his listener's words are acting, that they are exchanging effects, Balzac foregrounds the implicit self-deception and irony of all discourses on the inherent power of words. Discourses on word power, like Gaudissart's bet with Jenny, wager that words act. But, like his insurance policy, they also act as if they guaranteed the performance of this act. They not only describe words as speech acts, they claim to prescribe these acts.[108] But, for Jenny and Vernier, words do not have an inherent power to prescribe a particular action, since they are always capable of producing the opposite effect from the one they say they are producing: "au seul mot de *garantie*, Vernier avait cessé de faire attention à la rhétorique du voyageur, il pensait à lui jouer quelque bon tour... " (4: 578).[109] Rather than produce a guaranteed deception of a client and corroborate the deceiver's word power, the word "guarantee" misfires. It discloses to the listener a knowledge of its own deceptiveness, as well as of the salesman's capacity to be deceived by his presupposition that his own words deceive.

The guarantee made by discourses of power – that words act – is ironically reversible because it presupposes what it denies: the reality of fixed descriptive paradigms. The power of words to act, we noted above, is guaranteed by the convention or law that prescribes it.[110] Civil law guarantees that Gaudissart's employers will honor their written guarantee to pay a certain sum of money if the policy-holder's career does not achieve the stipulated monetary goal. Gaudissart can sell this insurance policy only if his clients believe in the relative permanence of these civil laws. They will then treat the policy as an explicit performative.[111] Although Gaudissart and Vautrin do not believe in legal guarantees, they do presuppose that the weaker liar will be irreversibly guided by the more powerful liar's reference to laws. The weaker liar will eventually believe that the stronger liar's words both describe and prescribe a speech act that is advantageous to the former. He will fall prey to descriptive illusion. Every dialogue becomes a market exchange that results in an irreversible economic transformation: a net increase in the performative capital of the more successful liar, a net decrease in that of the liar who falls into descriptive illusion. The basis for believing in a law that dictates the economic superiority of the most successful liar is based, however, on a descriptive criterion. This belief presupposes that the liar who most successfully denies any value to the meanings of words will best see and describe the paradigms that govern what his words are doing in the weaker liar's mind. By assuming that he can describe the act of deceiving, the seducer ironically falls into the very descriptive illusion he claims to transcend, an illusion that renders him vulnerable to being deceived. This irony lies hidden, not only in Austin's description of certain formulas as pure speech acts or of an explicit performative that prescribes, rather than describes, the act it states, but also in the narrative semiotician's description of non-descriptive narrative acts of transformation, and in the historicist's description of an indescribable struggle between dominant and subordinate discourses.[112]

The salesman's failure to deceive the madman foregrounds the source of Balzac's irony of power.[113] As the provincial ironist demonstrates, the liar's description of what his words are doing in his listener's mind only deceives the liar himself if, as in this case, the listener is ironically or madly indifferent. By sending Gaudissart to a madman, who cannot possibly comprehend the rules governing marketable acts of exchange, Vernier puts the salesman in a situation where his words cannot possibly act according to his description of how they change his client's mind. Gaudissart thinks that Margaritis's words are an effect of the salesman's words. He imagines that they constitute a real offer to exchange wine (which Gaudissart needs) for subscriptions (which Margaritis does not need). He is certainly right to conclude that the madman's sales pitch is partially governed by a conventional logic, but he is wrong to assume that this logic is an effect of his sales pitch or that it promises an actual act of exchange. As a result, Gaudissart blindly exchanges a real subscription to a children's magazine for purely imaginary kegs of wine. He performs the opposite economic transformation from the one he thought he was performing: he loses rather than gains.

Balzac's provinces (and poor quarters) are much more than a source of powerful opportunists like Rastignac, powerful authors like Balzac, or weak victims like Eugénie Grandet, all apparent products of Paris's dominant discourse on power. A few marginal characters disrupt the smooth functioning of the seemingly irreversible triumph of the strong over the weak by ironically disclosing what this discourse hides, its reversibility. They also highlight the subversive role of repetition in *La Comédie humaine*. For the provincial ironist, as for the madman Magaritis, the repetition of words is governed neither by the logic of knowledge or the logic of power, but by the illogic of habit: "'Notre pays est un pays qui marche à la grosse *suo modo*, un pays où jamais une idée nouvelle ne prendra'" (4: 581). Vernier immediately recognizes Gaudissart's repetition of the word "guarantee" as a sign of Parisian habit, not of Parisian power: the habit of using words to constitute social history as an irreversible production, by a few powerful individuals, of new opportunities for gain. The provincial's irony, like Jenny's teasing, reveals the conventionality and vanity of this habitual rhetoric, as well as its susceptibility to the very poor, the female, and the provincial that it marginalizes.[114] Vernier's irony typifies Balzac's provincial irony which questions and decenters his Parisian discourse on power within the universe of the *Comédie humaine* as a whole, just as the "small nonlinearities" of chaos theory question and decenter the linearity of traditional science.[115] It paves the way for Flaubert's and Proust's critiques of power and lying, as well as their meditations on marginality and habit.

Whereas Balzac's narrator's descriptive and narrative ironies are stable, his provincial irony is not. Descriptive irony negates a false knowledge of reality, and replaces it with a contrary awareness of spatial and temporal difference. Narrative irony negates the illusion that words describe a prior knowledge, and replaces it with the act of producing knowledge in time. But the narrator's provincial irony interprets both the descriptive and the narrative as habitual repetitions, as "rhetorics," in which no knowledge is disclosed and no act of transformation performed. An irony of irony, it discloses the narrator's knowledge that he is ignorant about what language is or does. It thus reintroduces the question of knowledge.

Were Balzac's irony of power limited to provincial skeptics like Vernier, or disaffected Parisian observers like Derville, it might be considered a momentary insight within the *Comédie humaine*'s tendency to subordinate the narrator's descriptive to his narrative illusions. Is not Gaudissart a mere caricature of Vautrin and De Marsay, rather than an ironical commentary on their illusion of power? No ironical spectator seems to laugh at their defeats. Nevertheless, in "La Dernière incarnation de Vautrin," the last chapter of *Splendeurs et misères des courtisanes*, written late in Balzac's career, the narrator incorporates irony of power into the heart of his Parisian struggle for power and thus into his overall vision of (blindness to?) society and history. Vautrin comes to the paradoxical conclusion that he can increase his power only by renouncing the search for power, just as Vernier's and Margaritis's indifference overpowers Gaudissart. This paradoxical renunciation of power for the sake of power is, I believe, the "moteur" that constructs and deconstructs historical time and social space in the *Comédie humaine*.

Vautrin is not as unlike Gaudissart as he might appear. He, too, resembles Napoleon ("Illustre" 4: 572; *Splendeurs* 6: 789).[116] Like Gaudissart, he sells himself on his own power.[117] But his efforts to prove his power by transforming Lucien into its mirror image, like a stifling parent's attempt to live through a child, produce a mere caricature of power that is only a disembodied and impotent marionette. Like Gaudissart's blind attempt to transform a madman into a calculator like himself, Vautrin produces only an ironical mirror-image of his impotence to perform the transformation he wills: "Vous avez voulu me faire puissant et glorieux, vous m'avez précipité dans les abîmes du suicide, voilà tout" (6: 789).[118]

Soon after Lucien takes his own life, Vautrin interprets this reversal of his will to power as a law of historical reaction. Because the attempt to confirm one's power necessarily takes advantage of others, it eventually produces an act of revenge that disconfirms it:

> [J]'ai vu, depuis vingt ans, le monde par son envers, dans ses caves, et j'ai reconnu qu'il y a dans la marche des choses une force que vous nommez la *Providence*, que j'appelais le *hasard*, que mes compagnons appellent la *chance*. Toute mauvaise action est rattrapée par une vengeance quelconque, avec quelque rapidité qu'elle s'y dérobe. (*Splendeurs* 6: 922).

According to Vautrin's law of eventual retribution, the history of society cannot take the form, as he previously argued, of repeated and irreversible narrative acts of transformation. Rather, it is structured by an alternation between acts of transformation and acts of counter-transformation, acts of power and acts of revenge, that add up to no transformation, no change, at all. The will of Parisian individuals to show that they are powerful eventually produces only a reversal of this will, not so much by the marginal, as by society's powerful institutions or by powerful rival individuals. Vautrin's attempt to substantiate his power by changing a powerless poet, Lucien, into a powerful minister ultimately steps on the toes of another powerful individual, the Baron de Nucingen, and of a powerful representative of the state, Corentin. They take their revenge by bringing about Lucien's humiliation in court, and his ultimate suicide. A marginal subversive character, Mlle Michonneau, triggers this vindictive struggle between powerful individuals, and the state exploits the struggle, not to affirm, but to negate, the power of society's dominant discourse on individual power. The search for power thus contributes to the construction of a state whose function is to render this search self-destructive.

Rather than signs of power and pride, acts of transformation turn out to be signs of a self-destructive will to produce their own eventual reversal, a will to produce signs of impotence and humiliation. This necessary reversal does not mean that individuals are powerless in the face of history: "[J]e saurai réussir dans toutes les affaires qui me seront confiées." (*Splendeurs* 6: 928). Nor does it mean that attempts to show one's power *deserve* to be frustrated. It is not a moral law like the talion: "[L]'auteur n'est pas de propos délibéré moral ou immoral, pour employer les termes faux dont on se sert" (*Préface*, *Goriot*, 2nd edn. 3: 46). Vautrin's renunciation is neither an expression of charity towards others, nor a nostalgic return to a pre-revolutionary order.[119] Rather, it is produced by a purely structural, if paradoxical, law: any attempt to produce a sign of power will eventually produce a sign of impotence and error. The only irreversible power is the power to reverse the search for power. Freedom exists only within determinism.

Although Vautrin attributes this reversibility of power's signs to history, it is a function of the rhetorical nature of linguistic logic. Discourse can "describe" itself as a pure speech act, one that deceitfully masks itself as a description, only by means of another deceitful speech act that also masks itself as a description.[120] It can say that it lies only by saying, rhetorically and ironically, that it is lying in saying that it lies.[121] It can logically affirm the power of language only by ironically deconstructing signs of this power and stating its impotence to show that language has power at all.

Vautrin has already begun to put his theory into practice by subordinating his desire for power to the good of the criminals whose money he protects. But he now fully embraces his theory by joining, as did his apparent historical model Vidocq, one of history's instruments of reversal. He becomes a leader of society's formal justice system, which Balzac considers, along with Catholicism, "un système complet de répression des tendances dépravées de l'homme" (*Avant-propos* 1: 12).[122] By re-entering society, by ceasing to try to prove his dominance, Vautrin ceases to produce unwilling signs of impotence. But the power he wields on behalf of the state is totally ambiguous, since it is only the power to reverse and deconstruct erroneous discourses on power, the power to neutralize power that is the province of the ironical provincial, Vernier.

Vautrin's law of historical reversal alters the mode of representing society in the *Comédie humaine*. Society ceases to be a boundary between rich and poor, Paris and provinces, that is constructed and maintained for the sake of individually powerful acts in time. Instead, it becomes a dynamic alternation between constructing and deconstructing illusory discourses on individual power. If power hungry criminals want to avoid inevitable punishment by history's instrument of retribution, the state system of justice, they must become "le serviteur de cette puissance qui pèse sur nous" (6: 924). They must act as agents of the state's power to deconstruct and repress the criminal's depraved illusion of individual power: "Je n'ai d'autre ambition que d'être un élément d'ordre et de répression, au lieu d'être la corruption même" (6: 925).

Conversely, if the state is to maintain order, it must cease to use criminals as scapegoats for those who, like Rastignac, feign obedience to its laws. By treating the source of society's disorder as exterior to the state, social justice blindly encourages the search for power by those who act as if they obey its laws. This act of injustice condemns criminals to obsessively seek power outside the law:

> Vous vous arrangez pour que le forçat soit clairement désigné, reconnu, parqué, puis vous croyez que les citoyens auront confiance en lui, quand la société, la justice, le monde qui l'entoure n'en ont aucune. Vous le condamnez à la faim ou au crime. Il ne trouve pas d'ouvrage, il est poussé fatalement à recommencer son ancien métier qui l'envoie à l'échafaud. (6: 923–24)

Rather than encourage disorder by scapegoating its criminals, the state can discourage disorder by enlisting them in the repression of those who seek power inside, as well as outside, its laws. Vautrin proposes that he, a former master-criminal, replace the corrupt Chief of Criminal Investigation: "Si vous me donnez la place de ce gredin, vous aurez rendu le plus grand service à la société" (6: 925).[123] By turning the powerful against themselves, Balzac's "*monde meilleur*" purges them of their illusion of power (*Avant-propos* 1: 15). His state perfects them: "[L]a Société, loin de le dépraver [l'homme]... le perfectionne" (1: 12). Society thus constructs its power by deconstructing the illusion of individual power.

The actions of the powerful on behalf of the state's repression of power cannot be reduced to a narrative function or a descriptive structure.[124] Attempts to interpret them as signs of seeking or abandoning power, of establishing or destroying order, only produce evidence that they are saying or doing the opposite. Vautrin's confession of his own corruption ("nous serons toujours... d'atroces canailles" [6: 921]) is also, according to his argument, an ironical means of defending the state against unscrupulous servants like himself. Thus when he supplants the corrupt Chief of Criminal Investigations in *Splendeurs et misères des courtisanes* or insures the death of the corrupt Valérie Marneffe in *La Cousine Bette*, he uses criminal methods to defend society's victims against a powerful individual. Conversely, his statements of devotion to the state and its order ("Je n'ai d'autre ambition que d'être un élément d'ordre" [6: 925]) ironically express the will to power of a multiplicity of rivals within a state of apparent disorder: "Nous en serons plus forts chacun de notre côté," he tells Corentin, the policeman who engineered Lucien's final downfall (6: 921).

Once all signs confirming or disconfirming Vautrin's will to power ironically point to their contrary, the polarities power/impotence, dominance/subordination cease to be of use in describing the individual's relation to the state. Rather than a capitalist glorification of the individual as free agent, Balzac's state ironically undercuts, not only the economic basis of individual power, but also the notion that the market of words exchanges any value at all. Vautrin's final model thus does not displace power from the individual or the market to the state, history, a dominant discourse, or language.[125] Rather, it ironically deconstructs from within the very categories of power and market exchange by rendering all acts of transformation or exchange implicitly reversible, by making them indistinguishable from non-acts. Together, the early "Gaudissart" and the late *Splendeurs* express Balzac's ironical awareness, over his entire career, not only of the pervasiveness of bourgeois market structures, but also of the failure of bourgeois individualism or of liberalism to explain the complex discursive world that the *Comédie humaine* creates.[126]

Although the *Comédie humaine* periodically represents discourse as if it were a pure function of power, a Nietzschean ironical lie, it does so in order to purge itself of this illusion, to go beyond the illusion of power, of lying ironically. Language can lie only if it conceals knowledge about an object, whether this object be society, history or its own act of transformation. But it is precisely the power of words to represent what society, history, or words do that Vernier's and Vautrin's irony of power deconstructs. By showing that any description of language as a lie can only highlight its own error, Balzacian irony of irony leads beyond, not the act of lying, but the belief that language in itself is a lie. It undercuts any attempt to reduce the *Comédie humaine*, and thus the realist novel, to a narrative form, a mere repetition of an eighteenth-century ironical narrative. By dramatizing the novel's failure to become narrative, a failure that is anything but sublime, it introduces once again the nineteenth-century concern with the relationship between the novel, the descriptive, and knowledge.

For Balzac, the realist novel, like Auerbach's mimetic discourse, can be reduced neither to a descriptive nor to a narrative genre.[127] The imperfective aspect of his descriptions of social structure produces only that which it logically excludes: the perfective aspect of historical transformations. But the perfective aspect of the narrative which recounts these transformations produces only an ironical awareness of that which it tries to exclude: the eventual reversibility of historical transformations.[128]

Descriptive as well as narrative representations of social history are always misrepresentations of the *Comédie humaine*, which takes the form of a repeated alternation between the two. The allegory of its repeated alternation neither discloses a spatial structure of society, nor performs an historical transformation in time. It is neither descriptive nor narrative. Rather it locates the novel in the interval that this alternation repeatedly opens and closes.

If Balzac's allegory alternates between incompatible descriptive and narrative representations of reality, why in his prefaces did he represent novels as paintings, and the *Comédie humaine* as a museum with galleries of paintings? Was he simply falling back into descriptive illusion? This tendency to return to the descriptive, I would argue, is a mark of the fundamental mode of Balzacian discourse: irony of irony. By replacing a seemingly irreversible sequence with simultaneous and reversible readings, irony undercuts the narrator's increasing preference of narrative and makes it tend towards, without becoming, descriptive. Like Vautrin's ironical adaptation to the space of social institutions, Balzac's irony of narrative repeatedly appears to embed the actions it produces within the fixed spatial frame of a descriptive paradigm. But, because society's order, like Vautrin's renunciation, is unreadable, the narrator's irony of allegory can only open up a space between the incompatible structures it brings together. The *Comédie humaine* is a grammatical non sequitur, an anacoluthon, that juxtaposes the perfective grammar of narrative transformation (which creates the deceptive unity of Parisian action in time) with the imperfective grammar of the descriptive (which creates the deceptive plurality of France's spatial margins).[129]

CHAPTER 2

Descriptive and narrative self-deception: Flaubert's allegory of parody

In Flaubert's novels, nineteenth-century French fiction is beginning to parody the textual aspects with which the realist novel constructs the concept of reality.[1] Balzac's narrator makes the descriptive and the narrative appear to be discrete discourses that can be isolated in distinct passages, and that can represent, albeit ironically, the distinctive types of character, place, or action that compose contemporary social reality. In contrast, Flaubert's narrator treats the descriptive and the narrative as discursive illusions with which his characters deceive themselves into believing that they are conscious of their lives or of society's history. Although his "impersonal" narrator tends to avoid judgment statements, his characters methodically demystify and parody discourse's claim to describe reality or perform real acts of narration. Through the characters, Flaubert's narrator redefines realist discourse and the novel as parodies of the discourses they repeat when they create the illusion that they remember reality. He transforms realist fiction into a parodic precursor of modernist fiction.[2]

Demystification and parody in Flaubert are not ends in themselves. Rather, his fiction traces the process by which characters purge themselves and the text of the illusion, created by early nineteenth-century Balzacian and romantic representation, that discourse can remember what it is or does.[3] By making his characters accomplices in discourse's forgetting of itself, Flaubert's texts open themselves up to a repetition that goes beyond, yet reinscribes, the opposition between forgetting and remembering, parody and self-deception.

TEMPORALIZING, INTERIORIZING, AND TEXTUALIZING BALZACIAN SPACE

Flaubert's most explicit and striking redefinition of realist discourse as a parody of realist self-deception takes place in *L'Education sentimentale*.[4] Whereas Balzac's fiction frequently begins with seemingly detachable, descriptive passages which constitute place, character, or historical processes in primarily spatial terms, *L'Education sentimentale* begins with a passage that deconstructs both descriptive and narrative discourses. This introduction paradoxically situates the narrator's discourse beyond the realist fictions of place, character, and action it is about to create.

The first sentence of *L'Education sentimentale*, in the manner of a Balzacian novel, initially appears to anchor the novel within historical time and social space: "Le 15 septembre 1840, vers six heures du matin, *la Ville-de-Montereau*, près de partir, fumait à gros tourbillons devant le quai Saint-Bernard" (2: 33). Precise date and time, boat, Parisian quai, imperfect tense – all appear to announce a traditional Balzacian description of a relatively fixed, spatial background against which action will soon take place.

But, whereas Balzac's initial passages construct a spatial relationship between the inside and outside of a character, building, area, city, or social group, this sentence redefines spatial relationships – the contiguity of boat and quay – within a temporal and aspectual relationship: the relationship between the present imperfective aspect of the boat's pouring smoke and the perfective aspect of its imminent departure from the quay.[5] The sentence subordinates the spatial aspect of the descriptive to its temporal imperfective aspect, its deferral of change, as if the spatial relationship between boat and quay were merely a passing moment within a temporal transition from one point of view on time to another. Where Balzacian discourse adds temporalized signs of historical change to traditional descriptive space, Flaubertian discourse temporalizes and aspectualizes Balzacian space. It sets classical space afloat on the sea of time and history.

Although the first sentence establishes a chronological relationship between present pouring of smoke and future departure, the following sentence and paragraph bracket out this temporal chronology and focus on the simultaneous actions taking place in the present of boat and quay. These actions seem to have an imperfective aspect:

> Des gens arrivaient hors d'haleine; des barriques, des câbles, des corbeilles de linges gênaient la circulation; les matelots ne répondaient à personne; on se heurtait; les colis montaient entre les deux tambours, et le tapage s'absorbait dans le bruissement de la vapeur, qui, s'échappant par des plaques de tôle, enveloppait tout d'une nuée blanchâtre, tandis que la cloche, à l'avant, tintait sans discontinuer. (2: 33)

Passengers, sailors, collisions, packages, barrels – all are represented, not as discrete spatial objects, people, or things, but as subjects of action verbs in the imperfect tense. These verbs appear to signify present ongoing actions: hurrying, refusing to respond, colliding, rising, absorbing, ringing.

Flaubert's narrator attributes this emphasis on the imperfective aspect of ongoing action to an identifiable, interior point of view. An initial series of verbs signifies exterior actions that can be seen (arriving passengers, objects obstructing circulation, rising packages), felt (passengers colliding), or heard (hurrying passengers trying to catch their breath and unresponsive sailors): actions that produce sensations. By contrast, the final series of verbs replaces these exterior actions with inner sensations: the drowning out of the noise of departure by the sound of the steam escaping from the boat and the enveloping of visible actions in the cloud of steam. Not only does the sentence define people and things by the actions they are performing, it replaces these actions with the sensations they are producing in the mind of an arriving passenger or passengers. It interiorizes Balzacian space.

Is Flaubert's narrator exchanging an exterior physical space for an interior perceptual one, juxtaposed characters and objects for juxtaposed perceptual images of objects and actions? Such an exchange, which is strongly reinforced by frequent use of free indirect discourse, would in itself constitute a major novelistic innovation. But Flaubert's narrator goes much further. He dramatizes an erasing of spatial differences themselves, exterior or interior, within a modernist dramatization of the temporality of perception. Passenger or passengers do not see a coherent visual space filled with distinct perceptions. Rather, they see a chaotic space filled with obstructing and colliding perceptions. Moreover, this chaotic visual space is in the process of disappearing within an impressionistic vision of the boat's steam, just as the sounds of individual actions are being drowned out by the sound of the steam. The passage dramatizes perception as a temporal process that is methodically erasing, rather than tracing, spatial differences between visual and auditory parts of a possible mental space, that is transforming perceptual space into an illusion.[6]

The narrator's destruction of perceptual space in this passage initiates, I will argue, the novel's deconstruction of the very basis of descriptive discourse. Rather than a description of simultaneous actions on a Parisian quay or of simultaneous perceptions of a quay, the paragraph dramatizes the erasing of the fixed differences between lexical items that make possible, not only the perception, but the naming of an object or sensation.[7] It does so by grammatical and thematic means. Its imperfect tenses only appear to be duratives. They do not, in fact, describe continuous sensations of passengers arriving out of breath, colliding, etc. Rather they describe iterated actions. The effacement of particular sights and sounds by the steam dramatizes the erasing of any particular lexical references (specific actions) by iterative generalizations. The iterative aspect of "des gens arrivaient hors d'haleine," effaces differences between individual acts of arrival or individual sensations of arrival to which the verb "arriver" might refer. It signifies only the general concept of arriving. The temporal present of sensation disappears within a mental generalization marking an absence of sensory presence, of lexical difference, an absence of the descriptive.[8]

The paragraph attributes this disappearing of descriptive difference to the inner anxieties of an arriving passenger. By listing actions that normally connote means of, or obstacles to, boarding, it suggests that its iteratives refer only to the general actions that passengers hope or fear to experience as they try to board. In this way it creates the fiction of a passenger who is paying attention only to sensations that might aid or obstruct this intended act. For such a passenger, the naming of sensations, "perception," is purely a narrative means of distinguishing those that help from those that hinder the performance of an anticipated narrative transformation.[9] Flaubert's second paragraph thus erases particular descriptive differences by redefining them within an apparently narrative, chronological difference, just as Stendhal interprets the initial description of Verrières in narrative terms.[10] As if to confirm that mental space and text are products of temporal change and narrative, the narrator immediately recounts the departure of the boat: "Enfin le navire partit"(2: 33).

At the very moment that Flaubert's text appears to transform descriptive differences into narrative functions, however, it dramatizes an effacing, rather than a tracing, of narrative differences. Just as the cliched narrative transformations with which society constructs Julien's rise to success are subject to Stendhal's ironical reversal, so the mental transformations with which the mind constructs the general concept of change are subject to Flaubert's ironical reversal:[11] "Enfin le navire partit; et les deux berges, peuplées de magasins, de chantiers et d'usines, filèrent comme deux larges rubans que l'on déroule" (2: 33). Banks do not unroll; they only appear to unroll in the eyes of a passenger who is unaware that the boat on which he is standing is moving. As sensations pass through a passenger's mind, his thought can interpret the resulting sequence of perceptions either as an exact repetition of an exterior chronological sequence in time, the movement of the perceived point of departure away from the perceiver, or as a metaleptic reversal of the real movement, the movement of the perceiver away from the point of departure. In the case of Flaubert's narrator, the passenger's thought reverses the chronology. It exchanges the movement of the perceiver for the repose of the perceived. This thought actively performs a mental transformation in time and masks it as a perceived transformation, as moving banks being perceived by a passive, immobile perceiver.

Flaubert's interiorization of narrative sequence, Proust noted, puts into question any empirical relationship between real action and thought: "[C]'est le raisonnement qui après [coup] assigne à tout phénomène visuel des causes extérieures, mais dans l'impression première que nous recevons cette cause n'est pas impliquée."[12] Sensation can provide no evidence that the sequence chosen by thought is correct, in other words, that it is the effect rather than the cause of what thought believes to be real temporal chronology. Sensation cannot even demonstrate the existence of a real sequence. This reversibility and arbitrariness of narrative difference within the thought of Flaubert's characters renders all narrative structurally indifferent, not only to the direction of change in time, but to the difference between change and non-change, transformation and non-transformation. Within the text of Flaubert's characters' minds, the very concepts of movement and time become purely relative.

Reversibility and arbitrariness in Flaubert break down any narrative distinction between character, as the agent of action, and place, as the background of action. When the minds of Flaubert's characters create fictional acts of transformation, they animate inanimate objects, transforming them into fictional agents of these fictional acts. "Les choses ont autant de vie que les hommes," Proust says.[13] In the third paragraph of *L'Education sentimentale*, the passenger's mind not only transforms place into action, it creates a moving crowd of buildings, a cast of characters: "... et les deux berges, peuplées de magasins, de chantiers et d'usines, filèrent comme deux larges rubans que l'on déroule." As it transforms place into action and character, the passenger's mind converts the latter, moving boat and gazing passengers, into a place: the seemingly static background against which the crowd of buildings move away. Thought in Flaubert cannot objectively distinguish the narrative from the descriptive. It cannot differentiate its own mental act of transformation (its "cognitive doing") from a mental non-act, thought from non-thought.[14]

Having redefined the apparent description of a quay as part of an irreversible, interiorized narrative transformation, the beginning of *L'Education sentimentale* proceeds to reveal this narrative transformation to be implicitly reversible. In doing so, it rhetoricizes a traditional narrative representation of the beginning of life and of prose fiction: the departure of a boat. Rather than the beginning of a linear temporal sequence, departure signifies a repeated mental act of writing and reading which creates the illusion that life is an irreversible chronology (the passenger's momentary vision of a departing crowd of buildings), then demystifies this illusion by demonstrating that mental narratives are reversible (the passenger's discovery that the boat has departed). This mental departure does not replace a narrative of exterior action with a narrative of inner mental action. Rather, it redefines all irreversible narrative syntax as part of the ongoing repetition of a rhetorical figure, a metalepsis of before and after, where cause and effect are as reversible as the spatial relations posited by the descriptive. It rhetoricizes and spatializes narrative time.[15]

By deconstructing both descriptive and narrative illusion, the beginning of *L'Education sentimentale* sends its characters on a voyage that has both already begun and already ended. Its destination can only be their learning what they already know but do not admit to themselves, that their descriptions of spatial relations and their stories of temporal change efface, rather than trace, distinctions between change and non-change, departure and non-departure, voyage and non-voyage. They are deceiving themselves into believing that their minds are descriptions or narratives which remember, rather than forget, the temporal and spatial distinctions with which they construct what they call "reality."[16]

Flaubert's narrator textualizes reality by dramatizing reality as an interiorized process of breaking down discursive distinctions between time and space. His characters' thought is a process of writing and reading a mental text. Thought repeatedly creates and demystifies the illusions that its signs describe real objects or perform real narrative changes. It indirectly constructs the writing and reading of Flaubert's text, including utterances by his narrator that do not appear to represent a character's thought ("le navire partit"), as repetitions of the writing and reading of a (character's or narrator's) fictional mental text.[17]

L'Education sentimentale dramatizes thought, and indirectly its own writing and reading, as a rhythmical alternation between moments when a character misreads his mental text (as if it were a description of reality) and those when he rejects this misreading (as if it performed a narrative act of transformation). He creates this rhythm by alternating between formal marks of the imperfective and perfective temporal aspects and by alternately demystifying one then the other:

> La rivière était bordée par des grèves de sable. On *rencontrait* des trains de bois qui *se mettaient à onduler* sous le remous des vagues, ou bien, dans un bateau sans voiles, un homme assis *pêchait*; *puis* les brumes errantes *se fondirent*, le soleil *parut*, la colline qui *suivait* à droite le cours de la Seine peu à peu *s'abaissa*, et il en *surgit* une autre, plus proche, sur la rive opposée.
>
> Des arbres la *couronnaient* parmi des maisons basses couvertes de toits à l'italienne. Elles *avaient* des jardins en pente que *divisaient* des murs neufs... Plus d'un, en apercevant ces coquettes résidences, si tranquilles, *enviait* d'en être le propriétaire. (2: 34, my emphasis)

In the first sentence, signs of the imperfective aspect – the verb "to be" and the imperfect tense – seem to constitute a description of exterior reality. The next sentence, however, redefines the apparent outer object as an inner perceptual one by making inanimate objects ("des trains de bois") the subject of an active verb ("se mettaient à onduler"). But the passage demystifies this impression of perceptual reality by using iteratives rather than duratives ("rencontrait" and "se mettaient"). Since iteratives cannot represent continuous perceptions, only reconstruct general thoughts about repeated perceptions, they suggest that even the reference to a lone fisherman ("ou bien, dans un bateau sans voiles, un homme assis pêchait") might be an iterative signifying a general thought about a repeated vision, rather than a present perception of a single person.

After creating and demystifying the impression that the

passengers' minds are descriptions of immediate perceptions, the passage modulates from the descriptive to the narrative by means of the adverb, "puis," followed by a series of utterances in which inanimate objects are once again the subjects of active verbs in the *passé simple* tense ("les brumes ... se fondirent, le soleil parut, la colline ... s'abaissa," etc.). But these signs of the perfective aspect, like "les berges ... filèrent," construct the passengers' thoughts as sequences of narrative acts of transformation that produce fictional images. And some of them ("la colline ... s'abaissa, et il en surgit une autre"), like the departure, put into question the polarities upon which narrative is based: change/non-change, irreversibility/reversibility. The passage then modulates from deceptive signs of narrative back to deceptive signs of the descriptive aspect.[18]

This rhythmical alternation between descriptive and narrative illusion constitutes the character's thought and Flaubert's narrator's discourse as neither descriptive nor narrative in nature. Since the characters' mental text cannot be described in its entirety, it cannot be represented consciously. Since its writing and reading cannot be performed in their entirety, they are not acts, conscious or unconscious.[19] Mental text, writing, and reading are unconscious traces that only appear to take the spatial form of a text or to follow the temporal itinerary of an act of writing or reading. But, if the rhythm of thought demystifies and effaces the descriptive and narrative aspects of textual discourse, it also necessarily reinscribes them. When the mind constitutes itself descriptively as a fixed spatialized paradigm, it must forget the narrative act of transformation by which it arbitrarily produces this paradigm. When it constitutes itself narratively as an irreversible act of transformation, it must forget that, like the descriptive, this transformation is potentially reversible and atemporal.

Flaubert's dramatization of the interiorized reality of his characters' thought has an apparent precursor in Rousseau. The "Cinquième promenade" stages self-consciousness as "un état où l'âme trouve une assiette assez solide pour s'y reposer tout entière et rassembler là tout son être, sans avoir besoin de rappeler le passé ni d'enjamber sur l'avenir; où le temps ne soit rien pour elle, où le présent dure toujours sans néanmoins marquer sa durée et sans aucune trace de succession."[20] Like Flaubert's thought, Rousseau's self-consciousness has a temporal duration. But, whereas Flaubert's thought alternates between descriptive and narrative illusion, Rousseau's self-consciousness acts as if it were entirely descriptive. Rousseau constructs his self-consciousness by bracketing out narrative's perfective aspect and foregrounding the descriptive's imperfective aspect: "Le flux et le reflux de cette eau, son bruit continu mais renflé par intervalles frappant sans relâche mon oreille et mes yeux, suppléaient aux mouvements internes que la rêverie éteignait en moi et suffisait pour me faire sentir avec plaisir mon existence, sans prendre la peine de penser."[21] Iteratives ("flux et reflux," "renflaient par intervalles") and duratives ("son bruit continu"), both of which have an imperfective aspect, are unproblematically combined to create the fiction of a continuous subject experiencing, through the mediation of sensation, its continuous existence as its own object.[22] Rousseau thus interprets the imperfective aspect's deferral of marks of temporal change referentially, as a real negation of time and death. In this way he constructs an extra-textual, self-sensing self that feels itself to be immortal, "se suffit à soi-même comme Dieu," and that produces "un bonheur suffisant, parfait et plein, qui ne laisse dans l'âme aucun vide qu'elle sente le besoin de remplir."[23]

Of course society, Rousseau's source of victimization, repeatedly decenters his descriptive self, exiling it from its island of self-consciousness, but this exile in narrative does not explicitly question its at least potential plenitude and autonomy.[24] By contrast, thought's seemingly self-conscious journey up the river of thought at the beginning of Flaubert's post-romantic *L'Education sentimentale* repeatedly demystifies Rousseau's descriptive illusion of a full, immortal self-conscious self. Rather than a sense of enduring fullness and immortality, thought produces an iterated, bored feeling of emptiness and mortality: "A chaque détour de la rivière, on retrouvait le même rideau de peupliers pâles. La campagne était toute vide. Il y avait dans le ciel de petits nuages blancs arrêtées, – et l'ennui, vaguement répandu, semblait alanguir la marche du bateau et rendre l'aspect des voyageurs plus insignifiant encore" (2: 35–36). By obliterating the continuity of any durative, *L'Education sentimentale*'s iterative renders mental signs of place meaningless, renders signs of movement and immobility indistinguishable, and reduces signs of character to insignificance. Life, time, produce only an empty feeling of death, not because they are dead, but because life and death, difference and indifference, feeling and reason, continuity and discontinuity, have been replaced by purely conventional, repeated, and equally meaningless signs.[25] It is this overwhelming sense of linguistic indifference that Flaubert's characters must confront and try to go beyond.

Flaubert's characters' unconscious mental text transforms signs of consciousness, signs that life is a continuity of being or a discontinuity of doing, into momentary dreams of being or doing anything at all:

> [Les maisons] avaient des jardins en pente que divisaient des murs neufs, des grilles de fer, des gazons, des serres chaudes, et des vases de géraniums, espacés régulièrement sur des terrasses où l'on pouvait s'accouder. Plus d'un, en apercevant ces coquettes résidences, si tranquilles, enviaient d'en être le propriétaire, pour vivre là jusqu'à la fin de ses jours, avec un bon billard, une chaloupe, une femme ou quelque autre rêve. (2: 34)

Rousseau's "Promenade" dramatizes and decenters a feeling narrator's "prise de conscience" of the descriptive self-consciousness that constitutes the reality of his individual being. Balzac's fiction dramatizes and decenters an observing character's ironical "prise de conscience" of society's narrative of individual and social doing. But Flaubert's fiction dramatizes a character's falling in and out of the illusion that his mind's descriptions or narratives can represent reality at all. Like many twentieth-century narrators, his characters mourn then mock the death of consciousness, which they ultimately replace with a repeated writing and reading of fictional signs. By textualizing reality, they dramatize the impossibility and the inescapability of realist writing and reading.

PARODYING ROMANTIC DISCOURSE'S DESCRIPTIVE ASPECT

The introduction to *L'Education sentimentale* is followed by what appears to be a story of actions in one passenger's life: Frédéric Moreau's. But this is not primarily a story of action. Rather it recounts how Frédéric's mind writes then reads, creates then demystifies, signs that he is conscious of who he is and what he is doing in life. Given that the introduction has already traced the course of this story for all passengers on life's boat, Frédéric's can only be a repetition, an allegory.[26] Its all-too-predictable outcome is less interesting than the particular manner in which it repeats the common story. *L'Education sentimentale*'s allegory of life not only discloses, it repeats parodically, the received discourses with which contemporary society created fictions of consciousness.[27] It is a parody of mid-nineteenth-century discourses of consciousness.

Flaubert's parodic allegory begins, necessarily, by dramatizing the way in which his characters deceive themselves into believing that their minds describe reality. He creates, by negative means, the illusion that his mind is a subject describing a real object, that it is a consciousness.[28] He methodically denies a bourgeois discourse that imagines life to be a commercial act of exchanging lies for pleasure. This repeated denial comes to the fore when he encounters the entrepreneur Jacques Arnoux, a dealer in paintings and the publisher of an art journal, who shares Gaudissart's vain pride in wielding commercial power:

> Il vit un monsieur qui contait des galanteries à une paysanne, tout en lui maniant la croix d'or qu'elle portait sur la poitrine...
>
> La présence de Frédéric ne le dérangea pas. Il se tourna vers lui plusieurs fois, en l'interpellant par des clins d'oeil...
>
> [I]l exposait des théories, narrait des anecdotes, se citait lui-même en exemple, débitant tout cela d'un ton paterne, avec une ingénuité de corruption divertissante.
>
> ...
>
> Frédéric éprouva un certain respect pour lui. (2: 34–35)

Arnoux's flirting, bragging, and corrupt narrative rhetoric verbalizes Frédéric's unformed wish to use words performatively and narratively to satisfy his desire to seduce women and impress other men. Hence his respect for this paternal entrepreneur who constantly shows off his power by mentally calculating the rate of exchange for his mechanical (or sexual) needs: "[I]l marmotta vite un long calcul, afin de savoir 'combien chaque coup de piston, à tant de fois par minute, devait, etc.' – Et, la somme trouvée, il admira beaucoup le paysage" (2: 35).

Frédéric, however, feels only "un certain respect" for Arnoux. To emulate the entrepreneur's narrative discourse would be to deny the non-narrative discourse to which he is strongly attached. Initially, therefore, he rejects Arnoux's narrative discourse on life because he wishes to affirm a descriptive one in which words refer, rather than act. Soon after speaking to Arnoux, he sees the entrepreneur's wife and convinces himself that his mind is describing, that it is conscious of, a real romantic woman. He mentally repeats a romantic discourse that he has read in popular novels and he misreads it as a literal description of reality: "Elle ressemblait aux femmes des livres romantiques" (2: 41). Imagining that his mental repetition of romantic discourses describes a visible romantic reality, Frédéric constructs a fictional consciousness of a romantic "Mme Arnoux." Flaubert's narrator mimes this mental act of construction by means of free indirect discourse:

> [Q]uand il se fut mis plus loin, du même côté, il la regarda.
>
> Elle avait un large chapeau de paille, avec des rubans roses qui palpitaient au vent derrière elle. Ses bandeaux noirs, contournant la pointe de ses grands sourcils, descendaient très bas et semblaient presser amoureusement l'ovale de sa figure. Sa robe de mousseline claire, tachetée de petits pois, se répandait à plis nombreux...
>
> Une négresse, coiffée d'un foulard, se présenta en tenant par la main une petite fille, déjà grande. L'enfant, dont les yeux roulaient des larmes, venait de s'éveiller. Elle la prit sur ses genoux. "Mademoiselle n'était pas sage, quoiqu'elle eût sept ans bientôt; sa mère ne l'aimerait plus; on lui pardonnait trop ses caprices" (2: 36–37).

Frédéric constitutes his mind as a conscious subject, one that is passively describing a real object, by creating a romantic object of consciousness. He confuses the conventional romantic rhetoric of innocence, maternal nurturing, and non-aggressiveness connoted by Mme Arnoux's appearance – her peasant-like clothes, hairstyle, black servant, and refusal to discipline her child whom she puts on her lap – with visible metaphors of a real innocent and nurturing nature. This confusion of outer rhetoric with inner character, the creation of a fictional metaphor that is typical of descriptive portraits, enables him to construct a romantic character and imagine that she is a real person who exists independently of him: "Il n'aurait voulu rien ajouter, rien retrancher à sa personne" (2: 41). Frédéric masks his mental act of constructing a fictional character as a passive act of describing a real romantic person. Like Balzac's narrator, he argues that he is passively describing a prior object of consciousness, rather than actively writing a fictional object. He is an observer of reality rather than an author of fiction.

Frédéric can convince himself that he is a passive consciousness of romantic reality only by denying that romantic signs – the romantic novels he has read, Mme Arnoux's clothes, servants, words, gestures – are narrative means of producing romantic effects. He must deny the possibility that she would use her romantic rhetoric to flirt.[29] She would certainly not, he imagines, profane her romantic rhetoric in the way that her husband profaned the peasant woman's cross. She could not possibly try to use a symbol of purity to satisfy actively her desires. Only by denying to himself that Mme Arnoux might turn her romantic discourse of knowledge into a narrative discourse of persuasion can Frédéric persuade himself that his mind is describing a real romantic woman.

By rejecting the possibility that romantic discourse actively produces, rather than describes, his consciousness of a romantic world, Frédéric constructs a describable universe, a set of fixed relations between a fictional subject, himself, a fictional object of consciousness, herself, and all other things: "Elle était le point lumineux où l'ensemble des choses convergeait." By creating a consciousness of a describable universe, he fills the boring void created by the unconscious rhythm of thought on the boat of life: "L'univers venait tout à coup de s'élargir" (2: 41).

Descriptive space in Flaubert thus does not precede the narrative as it seems to do in Balzac. Nor is it a reality described in a detachable passage. Rather the descriptive arises as an illusory product of the character's mental actions. Frédéric creates a fictionally prior romantic space by misreading romantic discourse as a fixed lexical space, as a dictionary whose entries name discrete parts of a fixed universe. At the same time, he denies the historical signs in 1840 that the romantic lexicon is already a passing fad. He ignores the mechanical and irreversible steaming of society's boat up history's syntax of etymological change which inevitably empties some lexical items of meaning as it appears to fill others. In this way, he persuades himself that he can stop the boat of life's irreversible transformations: "Cependant, un long châle... allait tomber dans l'eau; Frédéric fit un bond et le rattrapa. Elle lui dit: 'Je vous remercie, monsieur.' Leurs yeux se rencontrèrent" (2: 37). By preventing one romantic sign, Mme Arnoux's shawl, from being destroyed ("Elle avait dû, bien des fois, au milieu de la mer, durant les soirs humides, en envelopper sa taille, s'en couvrir les pieds, dormir dedans!" [2: 37]), Frédéric reassures himself that romantic signs in general do not change, that their meaning will not die, that history will not transform them into clichés.

But he does not want to have to prove that he is worthy of being included in his imaginary romantic space, for to do so would be to continue to transform reality, to defend it actively against the ravages of historical time. Rather, he imagines he can step outside change and become a passive consciousness of an eternally describable world. He constructs a counter-narrative that transforms the boat of life's horizontal change and sequentiality into the vertical non-change and simultaneity of a romantic paradise:

Une plaine s'étendait à droite; à gauche un herbage allait doucement rejoindre une colline, où l'on apercevait des vignobles, des noyers, un moulin dans la verdure, et des petits chemins au delà, formant des zigzags sur la roche blanche qui touchait au bord du ciel. Quel bonheur de monter côte à côte, le bras autour de sa taille, pendant que sa robe balayerait les feuilles jaunies, en écoutant sa voix, sous le rayonnement de ses yeux! Le bateau pouvait s'arrêter, ils n'avaient qu'à descendre! (2: 39)

Frédéric's romantic story attempts to produce a purely paradigmatic and lexical discourse in which names of things, places, people, and actions co-exist simultaneously, a descriptive discourse with an imperfective aspect of continuous non-change. He does so by purging romantic discourse of its syntactical and lexical signs of the perfective aspect. He replaces verbs signifying horizontal change in time ("allait ... rejoindre") with verbs signifying vertical movement within the same space ("monter") or with verbs and nouns signifying the ongoing consciousness of a bucolic paradise ("touchait," "écoutant," "le rayonnement de ses yeux"). He imagines that the verb "pouvoir" ("pouvait s'arrêter"), which here signifies only a possible end to horizontal movement in time, and the conditional tense of "balayerait," which here expresses only a possible sweeping away of dead leaves as they move up the hill in space, take on the imperfective aspect of his perceiving ("apercevait"). And, like much romantic discourse, he fantasizes that his replacement of the perfective aspect (beginning/ending) with the imperfective aspect (deferral) eliminates time itself. A momentary perception of the same space, a momentary deferral of a change in perceptions, thus become an unchangeable vertical space in which objects, people, and actions are eternal and nameable. The romantic story ignores its own perfective aspect, its act of negating change, in order to create the illusion of an eternal, maternally nurturing, lexical, and describable space: "Quels étaient son nom, sa demeure, sa vie, son passé? Il souhaitait connaître les meubles de sa chambre, toutes les robes qu'elle avait portées, les gens qu'elle fréquentait; et le désir de la possession physique même disparaissait sous une envie plus profonde, dans une curiosité douloureuse qui n'avait pas de limites" (2: 37).

Frédéric can construct a romantic consciousness of space only by ignoring painful signs that the paradise he seeks to describe, and the descriptive discourse with which he tries to describe it, are unattainable. His description/perception of a mountain paradise contains syntactical reminders, such as inanimate objects made animate ("un herbage allait doucement rejoindre une colline"), that it is only a fleeting product of perspective. In a constantly changing mental world, not only perceptions, but also romantic transformations of these perceptions, will disappear when the boats of life and history go around the next bend. Whereas Balzac's narrator claims to situate character and action within a spatially fixed milieu, Flaubert's central character can never entirely believe that he is in the spatial milieu his mind constructs, that his thought is describing a real, rather than prescribing an imaginary, milieu. Romantic discourse can never quite make him believe that he is conscious of a romantic world.

In Flaubert, discourse's very attempt to become descriptive foregrounds signs that it is narrative in nature. When Balzac's narrator claims to describe contemporary reality accurately, when he compares a character's appearance to a Rembrandt painting or declares that only doctors and authors interpret reality correctly, he vainly praises his own memory of contemporary discourses on reality, his ability to transform them into realistic and artistic works of art, and his superiority in interpreting their hidden meanings. He brags about his superior power to produce an artistic world, even as he claims to be a passive consciousness of a superior real world. This implicit and recurrent reference to the author's power to produce an "auguste mensonge" indirectly questions his claim to describe a real world, for it discloses its act of producing a fictional consciousness. Where Balzac's narrator hides this reference to his authorial act of producing a consciousness, Flaubert's narrator brings it to the fore in the form of parody.[30]

L'Education sentimentale parodies romantic discourse's construction of a descriptive illusion of consciousness. Flaubert's narrator dramatizes Frédéric's attempt to misread romantic discourse as the description of a space whose womb-like enclosure protects him from time. When he first dines at the Arnoux's Paris apartment, he listens avidly to the painter Pellerin's romantic theories of art, then uses them to deceive himself into believing that his mind is a romantic painting that objectively describes the real Mme Arnoux and subjectively expresses his true feelings of love. By comparing this romantic descriptive illusion to a painting, a comparison that conventionally identifies the descriptive (*ut pictura poesis*), the narrator extends his parody of romantic description to all descriptive misreadings of discourse.[31] Whereas Stendhal merely parodies contemporary discourses on reality, Flaubert parodies the very notions of the descriptive and the conscious.

Frédéric can transform his mind into a painting that describes a real romantic woman who expresses a real romantic self only by believing the part of Pellerin's discourse that is compatible with a more naive romantic discourse, like Lamartine's, that confuses the imagination with objective perception:[32]

> "Laissez-moi tranquille avec votre hideuse réalité! Qu'est-ce que cela veut dire, la réalité? Les uns voient noir, d'autres bleu, la multitude voit bête... Le souci de la vérité extérieure dénote la bassesse contemporaine... Vous n'arriverez pas à son but [de l'art], – oui, son but! – qui est de nous causer une exaltation impersonnelle... sans l'idée, rien de grand! sans grandeur, pas de beau!... Mieux vaut l'exubérance que le goût, le désert qu'un trottoir, et un sauvage qu'un coiffeur!"
>
> Frédéric, en écoutant ces choses, regardait Mme Arnoux. Elles tombaient dans son esprit comme des métaux dans une fournaise, s'ajoutaient à sa passion et faisaient de l'amour.
>
> Il était assis trois places au-dessous d'elle, sur le même côté. De temps à autre, elle se penchait un peu, en tournant la tête pour adresser quelques mots à sa petite fille; et, comme elle souriait alors, une fossette se creusait dans sa joue, ce qui donnait à son visage un air de bonté plus délicate. (2: 78–79)

Rather than reject reality, Frédéric fantasizes that his mind paints a privileged romantic reality: a nurturing mother who is leaning towards her daughter and reassuring her with a smile.

But, according to the narrator, Frédéric's passion can create his Lamartinian illusion only by blindly following Pellerin's other words. His imagination "makes" love. It fabricates a pictorial consciousness of a lovable woman. Just as the iteratives in the "description" of the quay dramatized the anxious passenger's repeated memory of those actions as filtered through his inner anxiety, so the iteratives in this "description" dramatize Frédéric's repeated selection, out of all Mme Arnoux's gestures over the course of the dinner, of the gesture that best conforms to his romantic discourse. His imagination and "exubérance" project his romantic "idée" of female beauty onto his memory of this repeated maternal gesture, and cause the "exaltation personnelle" he desires. The mere memory of a repetition becomes a fixed tableau of the continuous being of maternity. This transformation of iteratives into duratives creates Frédéric's illusion that he is remembering more than a remembered gesture, more than the production of a compassionate effect. He is seeing a real nurturing woman. By masking a generalized memory of iterated romantic signs as a present consciousness of a real romantic woman, Frédéric deludes himself into believing that he is remembering the woman his perception passively painted, rather than the one his imagination actively constructed. He erroneously reverses the priority of imagination over perception that makes his romantic illusion of duration possible.[33]

Rather than a prior consciousness of reality, descriptive signs in Flaubert remember only prior repetitions of conventional signs, just as Frédéric's memory of Mme Arnoux's maternal gesture only remembers her repetition of a conventional sign of maternal love. The descriptive is a remembered iterative masked as a durative. Discourse can make itself appear to be the description of a continuous consciousness only by misreading the fundamentally iterative nature of its signs, by creating the illusion that lexical items represent a real duration of meaning. This misreading of iteratives as duratives makes possible the realist illusion that the novel describes an observed world, and the romantic illusion that it describes an enduring, observed natural world or a world that expresses an enduring natural self. It makes possible the fiction of an observing and feeling present of consciousness.[34]

The more Frédéric misreads romantic discourse as a description and produces a fictional consciousness of a real romantic woman, the more he brings to the fore signs that he is deceiving himself, that he is performing a narrative act of transformation. His very attempt to paint Mme Arnoux as an asexual mother figure employs, as in his vision of her dimple, a rhetoric of sexual possession: "Au moment des liqueurs, elle disparut. La conversation devint très libre; M. Arnoux y brilla, et Frédéric fut étonné du cynisme de ces hommes. Cependant, leur préoccupation de la femme établissait entre eux et lui comme une égalité, qui le haussait dans sa propre estime" (2: 79). Frédéric can compare his romantic love for the wife to the husband's sexual preoccupation; he can feel a similar pride, because he experiences the act of projecting his romantic ideal as an act of inseminating Mme Arnoux with his romantic soul: "Il regardait attentivement les effilés de sa coiffure, caressant par le bout son épaule nue; et il n'en détachait pas ses yeux, il enfonçait son âme dans la blancheur de cette chair féminine ..." (2: 80).

Frédéric's active projection of romantic discourse onto a perceived space is a means by which he introjects a romantic soul into himself: "Mme Arnoux ... tendit [la main] ... à Frédéric, et il éprouva comme une pénétration à tous les atomes de sa peau" (2: 81). During the dinner he feared he might perceive signs disconfirming his romantic ideal of himself ("il n'osait lever ses paupières, pour la voir plus haut, face à face" [2: 80]). But at home he can imagine that reality mirrors an ideal self: "Son visage s'offrait à lui dans la glace. Il se trouva beau; et resta une minute à se regarder" (2: 82). In the mirror, Frédéric imagines he sees the self that this mother figure will see when she once again looks him in the eyes, as she did on the boat after he saved her shawl. He fantasizes that she will gaze at him and love him the way she gazes at, and loves, her daughter.

Flaubert's narrator does more than parody this narcissistic reversibility of the object and subject of Frédéric's gaze. His parody discloses an irreversible narrative, rather than a reversible descriptive, object of his desire. What Frédéric wants above all is to brag to himself, as Arnoux brags to the other male guests, about his power to make a woman see him as the ideal object of her desire. Like Pygmalion, he imagines he is a god powerful enough to create a universe that glorifies him as its spatial center and temporal destiny. But even this desire to be desired is deceptive. For, like Pellerin, he does not really care whether his fictional adoring universe and adorable self coincide with reality, as long as the act of creating them gives him the "exaltation personnelle," the sense of power, he desires. This is the power to deceive himself, like a little child, into believing that his idealized mother will give him the strength to do whatever he chooses: "Il se demanda, sérieusement, s'il serait un grand peintre ou un grand poète; – et il se décida pour la peinture, car les exigences de ce métier le rapprocheraient de Mme Arnoux. Il avait donc trouvé sa vocation! Le but de son existence était clair maintenant, et l'avenir infaillible" (2: 82).

Frédéric's pride in his power to deceive himself suggests that he is not entirely unconscious of his act of self-deception. Unlike Balzac's describing narrator, Flaubert's character averts his eyes from the reality he describes, because he knows he may be deceiving himself. If he is not entirely deceived by the romantic world he constructs, then he cannot be really "conscious" of this world. Rather he tries and fails to deceive himself into believing that he is conscious of it.

This failure to be conscious of a spatial and temporally enduring, romantic world is not unique to Frédéric's indecisive mentality; it is inherent in descriptive illusion. The spatial aspect and the imperfective temporal aspect exist only as differences from the perfective temporal aspect of complete change. As a result, the imperfective's negation of the perfective aspect cannot help but ironically affirm it. Discourse necessarily demystifies and parodies its descriptive illusion by taking on the appearance of narrative.

Because discourse implicitly marks its descriptive self-deception, romantic discourse, like Frédéric, cannot be entirely deceived by its descriptive illusion.[35] It invites a deconstruction of the very descriptive illusion it creates by the obsessiveness with which it repeatedly constructs a self, just as Frédéric asks to be rejected by trying to prove that he is lovable. Obsessive repetition marks only a will to mastery over discourse, a will to use it as a narrative tool of power. The attempt to make discourse descriptive of an atemporal natural world or expressive of an atemporal natural self, the will to construct a spatially fixed background or cast of characters, foregrounds only the effort to produce a narrative transformation, to construct a fictional world and self in time.[36]

Through Frédéric, Flaubert's narrator parodies the "positive" spatial and imperfective aspects of the descriptive, and thus the fiction of a space of consciousness. He redefines the descriptive as a purely negative difference from that which it denies, the perfective aspect of narrative. So-called descriptive passages are mere illusions created by a repeated negation of discourse's perfective aspect. This parody of descriptive self-deception demystifies two common misreadings by, and of, many nineteenth-century texts: the assertion that realist novels merely repeat nineteenth-century discourses of knowledge, and the claim that romantic poems only repeat nineteenth-century discourses on the self.[37] It also parodies the notion that the novel is a descriptive genre. Does this parody mean that discourse in Flaubert, in the novel, or in "descriptive" poetry, is constituted by narrative acts of transformation? Does the narrative act of producing meaning in the present of reading the text remember only the original nineteenth-century act of producing the text's lies about world and self, the historical conditions of its written production?[38]

PARODYING DISCOURSE'S NARRATIVE ASPECT: FROM LYING TO FORGETTING

L'Education sentimentale discloses its parody of the descriptive when Frédéric comes to realize that romantic discourse is a means of self-deception. As he gradually comprehends that romantic discourse can at most parody its descriptive illusion, he begins to interpret all discourse as a Balzacian narrative, as a perlocutionary act of producing the illusion of consciousness in others and in himself. He ceases to lower his eyes before the women he desires or to dream in front of the mirror and, like Rastignac, he begins to explore discourse's power to perform narrative transformations on itself and on others: to lie. But in Flaubert the attempt to constitute discourse (and the novel) narratively is as doomed to parody and disillusionment as the attempt to constitute them descriptively. Frédéric's eventual discovery that he can produce only a parody of narrative transforms *L'Education sentimentale* into an allegorical revelation that the novel parodies, whether wittingly or not, its descriptive and narrative discourses on consciousness and on genre.

Frédéric tries to make the transition from descriptive self-deception to narrative deception after he and Mme Arnoux begin to exchange romantic words. He gradually discovers that romantic discourse seems not only to describe, but also to perform, acts. Like the folds in Mme Arnoux's peasant dress or her dimple, it produces desire, seduces:

> Et [Frédéric and Mme Arnoux] s'imaginaient une vie exclusivement amoureuse, assez féconde pour remplir les plus vastes solitudes, excédant toutes joies, défiant toutes les misères, où les heures auraient disparu dans un continuel épanchement d'eux-mêmes, et qui aurait fait quelque chose de resplendissant et d'élevé comme la palpitation des étoiles.... Quelquefois, une sorte de pudeur sexuelle les faisait rougir l'un devant l'autre. Toutes les précautions pour cacher leur amour le dévoilaient; plus il devenait fort, plus leurs manières étaient contenues. Par l'exercice d'un tel mensonge, leur sensibilité s'exaspéra ... et, quand des doléances échappaient à Frédéric, elle s'accusait elle-même.
>
> "Oui! je fais mal! j'ai l'air d'une coquette! Ne venez donc plus!"
>
> Alors, il répétait les mêmes serments, – qu'elle écoutait chaque fois avec plaisir. (2: 303–04)

Mme Arnoux and Frédéric would like to imagine that their repetition of romantic words and gestures is a "continuel épanchement d'eux-mêmes," a purely descriptive representation and expression of their superior souls. He prefers "qu'elle se donnât" physically after she recognizes that he fits her romantic description of an ideal lover, rather than to "la prendre" (2: 304), rather than to induce her abandonment by means of flattery, seduction. But Frédéric's denial of romantic discourse's power to produce a flattering effect, its narrative aspect, only makes it function all the more narratively, coquettishly, to produce desire: "Par l'exercice d'un tel mensonge, leur sensibilité s'exaspéra." The more they deny that their words act, and the more they wait for each other to act, the more they frustrate themselves and make themselves aware of their desire for their words to act: "J'ai l'air d'une coquette!"

Frédéric's and Mme Arnoux's love consists of a repeated self-delusion. They produce narrative desire and effects by claiming only to describe each other's romantic superiority: "'Ne venez donc plus!' Alors, il répétait les mêmes serments, – qu'elle écoutait chaque fois avec plaisir." But their relationship ends when her need to deny the seductiveness of her words and actions leads her to sacrifice their first planned sexual encounter in a new romantic hideaway. She makes her sacrifice in the name of motherly devotion to her son, whom she incestuously fantasizes will some day die, like a gallant hero, to save her honor (2: 313). Mme Arnoux's continual displacement and repetition of her descriptive idealization and narrative coquettishness finally succeed in exasperating Frédéric to the point that he tries to renounce any belief in the descriptive aspect, which he reduces to a hypocritical illusion: "[S]on amour disparut" (2: 314). He attempts to replace the descriptive with that which it and Mme Arnoux deny – with action, aggression, and complete change: "Il en ressentit un soulagement, une joie stoïque, puis un besoin d'actions violentes" (2: 314).

Frédéric's disillusionment with romanticism's descriptive discourse on love, and his desire to replace it with a narrative discourse on action, coincide with the workers' and bourgeoisie's disillusionment with the July Monarchy's aristocratic discourse on society and its attempt to exchange this discourse for a republic in February of 1848: "Il y avait dans l'air quelque chose de gaillard et de belliqueux." Walking "au hasard," Frédéric just happens to pass by the apartment of Jacques Arnoux's mistress Rosanette (La Maréchale) at the moment when she has been abandoned by her most recent protector, M. Oudry, and become terrified by the imminent revolutionary violence: "[U]ne idée folle lui vint" (2: 314). Perhaps action, "la prendre" rather than "l'attendre," will bring satisfaction:

"Ah! merci, tu viens me sauver! c'est la seconde fois! tu n'en demandes jamais le prix, toi!"
"Mille pardons!" dit Frédéric, en lui saisissant la taille dans les deux mains.

"Comment? que fais-tu?" balbutia la Maréchale, à la fois surprise et égayée par ces manières.
Il répondit:
"Je suis la mode, je me réforme."

Elle se laissa renverser sur le divan, et continuait à rire sous ses baisers.

Ils passèrent l'après-midi à regarder, de leur fenêtre, le peuple dans la rue. Puis il l'emmena dîner... Ils s'en revinrent à pied, faute de voiture...

Dans la garde nationale... les officiers, rouges d'enthousiasme, brandissaient leur sabre en vociférant: "Vive la réforme!" et ce mot-là, chaque fois, faisait rire les deux amants... (2: 314–15)

Just as the revolution of 1848 continued the replacement of the aristocratic hierarchy with the bourgeois struggle for political, economic, and social power, the "reform" of Flaubert's bourgeois, Frédéric, simply continues his replacement of the romantic tyranny of a "superior" idol, Arnoux's wife, with a struggle for sexual power over Arnoux's mistress, Rosanette. Desire for a descriptive referent gives way to the struggle with a rival for narrative power: "[I]l la désirait, pour le plaisir surtout de la vaincre et de la dominer" (2: 180).

Frédéric's reform explicitly rereads romantic discourse ironically as an iterative, rather than the durative it claims to be. He seduces Rosanette by repeating the same romantic signs with which he expressed his love to Mme Arnoux. He takes her to the apartment that he prepared for Mme Arnoux and seduces her with the clothes, flowers, and words with which he planned to express his "sincere" romantic love:

[P]our mieux outrager en son âme Mme Arnoux, il l'emmena jusqu'à l'hôtel de la rue Tronchet, dans le logement préparé pour l'autre.

Les fleurs n'étaient pas flétries. La guipure s'étalait sur le lit. Il tira de l'armoire les petites pantoufles. Rosanette trouva ces prévenances fort délicates.

Vers une heure, elle fut réveillée par des roulements lointains; et elle le vit qui sanglotait, la tête enfoncée dans l'oreiller.

"Qu'as-tu donc, cher amour?"

"C'est excès de bonheur," dit Frédéric. "Il y avait trop longtemps que je te désirais." (2: 315)

Just as Arnoux "souvent, reprenait à l'une ce qu'il avait donné, pour l'offrir à l'autre" (2: 176), so Frédéric gives to the mistress,

Rosanette, the same fetishistic romantic discourse he prepared for the wife and mother, Mme Arnoux. This substitution deliberately profanes the content of a discourse in which he still partially believes, the concept of a uniquely lovable, superior subject and object of description, in the same way that Arnoux profaned the peasant woman's cross on the boat. Romantic discourse becomes a narrative speech act, a parodic lie, which performs the act of seduction that it literally denies, but which the seducer makes it rhetorically perform.[39] After their first night together, as Frédéric and Rosanette walk through the streets, they interpret the cheers for social and political reform as ironical references to their reform in his love life: "[C]e mot-là ["la réforme"], chaque fois, faisait rire les deux amants" (2: 315).[40]

Frédéric's parodic repetition of romantic discourse denies the existence of the descriptive subject and object it affirms: a significant self and other with an imperfective aspect of ongoing duration. The romantic lexical items that he repeats – gifts of apartment, slippers, flowers, words of happiness – may be used to refer to specific things, attributes, or people; the referential difference they posit makes no inherent difference to the act of seducing Rosanette, as her surprise upon receiving them shows: "Rosanette trouva ces prévenances fort délicates." In repeating romantic discourse, Frédéric realizes that he is only following "la mode," social convention, which differentiates between words that act seductively and those that do not at a particular moment in history. He profanes much more than his memory of Mme Arnoux; he violates the very concept of lexical difference that lies at the heart of the descriptive. He transforms descriptive discourse into a purely deceitful means of producing a descriptive illusion of difference, an illusion whose sole significance is determined by whether it aids or hinders a narrative act of differentiation.[41]

Frédéric's narrative reform is defined, not by male conquest and female submission as he believed when he first desired Rosanette, but by a bourgeois, economic model of exchange.[42] He learns, upon entering the cocotte's house, that her most recent protector has abandoned her. He seizes her waist and, for the first time, he "demande[] le prix" for the money and protection he has provided her in the past and promises to provide in the future. Clearly, she has value only as a commodity, a value that is high only because her services are in demand. Outside this economic exchange, he, the well-to-do bourgeois male who has just received an inheritance, and she, the popular mistress, are nothing. The exchange alone differentiates them from others by creating the impression that he is a man of action with real buying power, and she an attractive female commodity with real selling power.

Rosanette and Frédéric think that their exchange gives them economic power because they presuppose that it is governed by a binding narrative contract which guarantees its future repetition. By accepting her sexual services, Frédéric promises to support her financially in the future, or so the mistress believes. By accepting his payment she binds herself to providing these services to him alone in the future, or so the protector presumes. Thus, when he helps her furnish a new apartment, he imagines that he is buying her fidelity: "[I]l éprouvait la joie d'un nouveau marié qui possède enfin une maison à lui, une femme à lui" (2: 343). But, unlike the marriage contract which dictates (but hardly guarantees) Mme Arnoux's sexual fidelity to her husband, the contract between protector and mistress is more fragile. Its conventionality is more apparent because it is guaranteed by unwritten, rather than written, law. It can easily be broken if one of the parties decides not to fulfill its terms. When Frédéric does not give Rosanette enough money, therefore, she immediately sells her services to someone else.

Indeed, Rosanette's and Frédéric's attempt to eliminate the descriptive, and ironically employ the narrative aspect of discourse and economic power, is self-deceived. It shares the same "alliage de mercantilisme et d'ingénuité" that characterizes Arnoux (2: 425). By assuming that this contract promises, rather than merely posits, future fidelity, they presuppose that the act of exchange has fixed rules, a fixed narrative syntax that can be described by the social semiotician. Rather than eliminate descriptive illusion, they displace it from an unchanging romantic self to unchangeable rules of speech action. By rejecting the naive belief that discourse has the power to describe significant differences between people, places, or things, they fall prey to the equally naive belief that discourse has the power to describe significant differences between narrative acts of transformation.

Frédéric's and Rosanette's narrative model hides a descriptive presupposition. This presupposition explains why their commercial exchange coincides with the novel's movement outwards towards a more detailed account and satire of contemporary social mentality. The descriptive constitutes the fiction of a perceived object and a perceiving subject. Romantic discourse's descriptive aspect, for example, constitutes a private subject and object of loving consciousness. It gives Frédéric and Mme Arnoux the illusion that they alone matter and that they live only for each other. The narrative contract between mistress and protector, like Arnoux's business contracts, also has a hidden descriptive aspect, but one that constitutes a public, rather than a private, subject and object. It presupposes three, rather than two, people: the partners in the exchange, Frédéric and Rosanette; and a spectator of this exchange, the vanquished rival whose acquiescence represents society's recognition and respect of the contract governing the exchange.[43] As long as Frédéric hopes that his romantic fantasy with Mme Arnoux will come true, he avoids being seen publicly with Rosanette. He acts as if society's gaze would bind him to a narrative contract with a mistress, and betray his spiritual infidelity to Mme Arnoux's romantic twosome. But, once he gives up Mme Arnoux, he displays his relationship with Rosanette openly, as if it gave witness to his having become a powerful and manly part of consumer society, rather that a passive adolescent object of motherly love. Later, Rosanette begins one of the first "salons des filles (c'est de ce temps-là que date leur importance)" and Frédéric "se [pose] comme le maître" (2: 421). He tries to convince himself that French society is a mass consciousness that describes and guarantees their exchange according to an unbreachable narrative contract.[44]

A discursive "reform" in a character's psychological maturation – a young man's coming to believe that he is performing a socially guaranteed speech act – thus motivates the novel's "realistic" inclusion and satire of historical changes in French society around the revolution of 1848.[45] It constitutes *L'Education sentimentale* as a parodic allegory of contemporary French society's predominant discourses on historic changes in the individual and the state: the rejection of the interiorized romantic discourse of a Lamartine for more socialist and active romantic discourses in defense of the workers, such as the idealist social discourses of bourgeois republicans or the socially pragmatic discourses of bourgeoisie and liberals. For Flaubert's narrator, this is not an historical movement from individual error to social truth. Rather it is a replacement of one error with another, a repetition. Before the revolution, Flaubert's Second Republic takes its socialist and idealist rhetoric of equality and freedom literally. But, once in power, it, like Frédéric and Rosanette, imagines that it is governed by a classical model of capitalism, a free market contract.[46] By repeating a common bourgeois metaphor of the time, it acts as if it were the product of a free act of exchange between a protector, the well-to-do influential bourgeoisie, and a mistress, the government: "[E]lle se fait entretenir, ta République" (2: 340)![47] In exchange for the bourgeoisie's economic and political support, the Second Republic's workers, represented by the character Dussardier, helped establish a government that they hoped would improve their lot, particularly by providing work for the employed in the abortive *ateliers*. Just as Rosanette, the daughter of a Lyon silk-factory worker (2: 360), aids Frédéric's attempts to overcome the tyranny of Mme Arnoux's romantic symbols of spiritual superiority, so the workers helped the bourgeoisie in their attempt to free themselves from the tyranny of the monarchy's symbols of hereditary political and social superiority. Instead of profaning a romantic hide-away, however, the workers profane the king's palace: "Une curiosité obscène fit fouiller tous les cabinets, tous les recoins, ouvrir tous les tiroirs. Des galériens enfoncèrent leurs bras dans la couche des princesses, et se roulaient dessus par consolation de ne pouvoir les violer... (2: 321).[48] Rather than achieve freedom, workers and republic, Flaubert's narrator suggests, simply prostitute themselves to the bourgeoisie in a grotesque parody of Delacroix's "Liberty Guiding the People": "Dans l'antichambre, debout sur un tas de vêtements, se tenait une fille publique, en statue de la liberté, – immobile, les yeux grands ouverts, effrayante" (2: 321).[49] Flaubert's workers thus do unwittingly what Rosanette does deliberately: they sell their bodies and ideals to the bourgeoisie according to a market contract, one that the bourgeoisie, like Frédéric, will eventually break. Accordingly, the sincere socialist Dussardier will be killed by the former socialist Sénécal when, after the June Days, the latter sells out to the new bourgeois government.

For Flaubert, the republic's profanation of the monarchy's symbols of class superiority is a powerful means of deceiving itself about its hidden economic motives: "Quel mythe!" dit Hussonnet. "Voilà le peuple souverain!" (2: 320) Its rhetorical negation of class differences deludes the republic into believing that it represents an absence of difference between classes, and a sameness of economic opportunity. Negation masks the real exchange value of its discourse on freedom as an illusory use value that will satisfy the worker's, the artisan's, and a growing industry's demands: "Le spectacle le plus fréquent était celui des députations de n'importe quoi, allant réclamer quelque chose à l'Hôtel de Ville, – car chaque métier, chaque industrie attendait du Gouvernement la fin radicale de sa misère" (2: 325). The workers' illusion of freedom and equal opportunity is increased by the rampant opportunism of the former ruling classes: "[Rosanette] se déclara pour la République, – comme avait déjà fait Monseigneur l'Archevêque de Paris, et comme devaient faire avec une prestesse de zèle merveilleuse: la Magistrature, le Conseil d'Etat, l'Institut, les Maréchaux de France, Changarnier, M. de Falloux, tous les bonapartistes, tous les légitimistes, et un nombre considérable d'orléanistes" (2: 324). Flaubert's Second Republic convinced itself that it was a well-oiled economic machine, one whose functioning could be seen and described by its citizens, just as Frédéric's and Rosanette's liaison can be seen by those who visit their salon: "Quelques-uns ... se rendaient près [du Gouvernement] pour le conseiller, ou le féliciter ou tout simplement pour lui faire une petite visite, et voir fonctionner la machine" (2: 325).

But, rather than produce "equal" market opportunity to perform narrative acts of exchange, rather than constitute equal partners in a binding contract, the well-oiled rhetoric of Flaubert's Second Republic acts out a struggle for power that benefits only those who repeat it ironically or parodically: "[T]ous se rangèrent sous [l'ombre du drapeau tricolore], chaque parti ne voyant des trois couleurs que la sienne – et se promettant bien, dès qu'il serait le plus fort, d'arracher les deux autres" (2: 325). The resulting struggle for economic power is as unequal and as hierarchical as the feudal system which it claims to reform, but which it in part repeats. The search for wealth and power will thus motivate bourgeois, like Frédéric, to replace daughters of workers like Rosanette with the wives of increasingly wealthy bankers like Mme Dambreuse, whose husband invests in monopolies that enchain a supposedly "free" market (2: 402).[50]

The attempt to ironically negate descriptive differences and to describe a narrative act of differentiation thus does not produce equal opportunity to perform these acts. It does not result in a free market of words. Rather it generates a struggle for the power to perform speech acts that treats all narrative contracts ironically. Frédéric's and the Second Republic's efforts to sell a free market and egalitarian rhetoric to Dambreuse and to the *haute bourgeoisie*, their attempts to buy seats in the National Assembly, are doomed to parody and failure:

Dès la seconde page, qui signalait comme une honte la prépondérance des intérêts pécuniaires, le banquier fit la grimace. Puis, abordant les réformes, Frédéric demandait la liberté du commerce.

"Comment?... mais permettez!"

L'autre n'entendait pas, et continua. Il réclamait l'impôt sur la rente, l'impôt progressif, une fédération européenne, et l'instruction du peuple, des encouragements aux beaux-arts les plus larges.

...

Le tout finissait par des conseils aux classes supérieures.

"N'épargnez rien, ô riches! donnez! donnez!" ... M. Dambreuse était tout pâle.

> ...
> Martinon tâcha de le rassurer. Le parti conservateur, d'ici peu, prendrait sa revanche, certainement... [I]l fallait que M. Dambreuse, lui-même, se présentât dans l'Aube... (2: 331)

The Second Republic's unwitting parody of free market rhetoric ironically performs the opposite speech act from the one it thinks it is performing. It encourages the *haute bourgeoisie*'s opposition to the market notions of equality and freedom, as well as its support for economic, political, and social inequality and for government restraint. Rosanette's attempts to persuade Frédéric to make their unwritten economic contract legal ("Il était maintenant sa chose, sa propriété" [2: 385]) will ironically and masochistically encourage him to leave her for Mme Dambreuse: "[T]outes les défectuosités de la Maréchale lui apparurent" (2: 391).[51]

The Second Republic's failure to perform the speech act, the "reform," its rhetoric claims to perform, its inevitable ironical reversal of this reform, suggest that all claims to describe, whether a non-verbal object or a verbal narrative syntax, are deceitful. If that is the case, then discourse is a Balzacian lie which, as for Vautrin, obeys no fixed contract, no syntax. It is an act of transformation whose deep structure, if it has any at all, is indescribable, and whose sole function is to perpetuate its power to act. The Second Republic's and Rosanette's attempts to reduce discourse to a describable narrative contract thus ironically disclose an economic will to power in French society and Frédéric: "[I]l fallait 'relever le principe d'autorité'; qu'elle s'exerçât au nom de n'importe qui, qu'elle vînt de n'importe où, pourvu que ce fût la Force, l'Autorité!" (2: 421). The rhetoric of freedom invites, paradoxically, a repetition of tyranny: Napoleon III.

Flaubert parodies the historical reduction of discourse to an indescribable narrative act of lying by recounting Frédéric's gradual replacement of Rosanette with Mme Dambreuse after the bourgeoisie's brutal repression of the workers during the June Days. Frédéric abandons his free market model, the entrepreneur Arnoux, in favor of a monopolistic model, Dambreuse, who is even more impervious than Balzac's Baron de Nucingen to dependence on an idea or a contract.[52] In the mind of this mid-nineteenth-century banker, all social contracts are deceitful means of increasing his individual power: "[I]l avait acclamé Napoléon, les Cosaques, Louis XVIII, 1830, les ouvriers, tous les régimes, chérissant le Pouvoir d'un tel amour, qu'il aurait payé pour se vendre" (2: 408). To take Mme Dambreuse from her husband, Frédéric imagines, is to confirm that he is even more powerful than the financier: "Avide, sans doute, de pouvoir et d'action, et mariée à un homme médiocre qu'elle avait prodigieusement servi, elle désirait quelqu'un de fort pour la conduire?" (2: 398). Perhaps Frédéric himself is the inscrutable figure of authority that French society desires, the one who will repair the chaos brought by the workers: "Le Progrès, peut-être, n'est réalisable que par une aristocratie ou par un homme? L'initiative vient toujours d'en haut. Le peuple est mineur, quoi qu'on prétende!" (2: 400).

Whereas Frédéric's and Rosanette's parody of romantic and revolutionary discourses sought confirmation for its narrative contract in an imaginary social consensus, Dambreuse takes an ironical distance from the speech acts he feigns to perform in public. His words in marriage, finance, and politics take the form of irony of irony. At the moment of his death, for example, he allows his wife and her lover, Frédéric, to believe that their lies are deceiving him. By deceiving his would-be deceivers, he shares and ironically undercuts their ironical complicity:

> "Ah! ça va mieux! Mais j'ai manqué faire le grand voyage!"
>
> "Pas sans moi!" s'écria Mme Dambreuse, notifiant par ce mot qu'elle n'aurait pu lui survivre.
>
> Au lieu de répondre, il étala sur elle et sur son amant un singulier sourire, où il y avait à la fois de la résignation, de l'indulgence, de l'ironie, et même comme une pointe, un sous-entendu presque gai. (2: 405)

Frédéric and Mme Dambreuse imagine they are ironical accomplices in her lie: her false statement that she will die if Dambreuse dies. Their complicity is based on the presupposition that their lies are performing specific speech acts of persuasion that will prevent her dying husband from disinheriting her. But Dambreuse knows full well what they think her words are doing. He covertly shares their ironical complicity and ironically undercuts their ironical bid for power. His smile discloses his knowledge that their words are powerless to possess an inheritance that he has already willed to someone else.

Although Mme Dambreuse loses the battle over her inheritance, she never abandons her husband's vision of discourse as a struggle for word power based on irony of irony: "[E]lle devait mentir à son confesseur" (2: 420). She is Frédéric's Vautrin. She teaches him, as he tries to teach Rastignac and Lucien, the notion of a couple that is based on a struggle for mutual domination. Rosanette simply repeats social clichés as if they performed, albeit ironically, stable, socially defined speech acts. But Mme Dambreuse uses social discourse, including irony, as an ironical means of wielding discursive power:[53] "[Mme Dambreuse], au moins... amusait [Frédéric]!... [S]'il lui échappait des lieux communs, c'était dans une formule tellement convenue, que sa phrase pouvait passer pour une déférence ou pour une ironie. Il fallait la voir au milieu de vingt personnes qui causaient, n'en oubliant aucune, amenant les réponses qu'elle voulait, évitant les périlleuses!" (2: 392) For Mme Dambreuse, as for her husband, speech acts of social lying ironically pretend to conform to a public contract. They are a private means of manipulating others that feigns ("passe pour") public complicity. But, unlike her husband, she tries to share her irony of irony with a lover, Frédéric.

The Dambreuse irony of irony may appear, like Vautrin's, to be a function only of circumstances, but it too presupposes a shared attitude towards language: a narrative contract based on the negation of all describable contracts. When Frédéric tries to seduce Mme Dambreuse with the same conventional speech acts of seduction that seduced Rosanette, she teaches him to take an ironical distance from the acts he imagines he is performing: "Il se servit du vieil amour. Il lui conta, comme inspiré par elle, tout ce que Mme Arnoux autrefois lui avait fait ressentir, ses langueurs, ses appréhensions, ses rêves. Elle recevait cela comme une personne accoutumée à ces choses, sans le repousser formellement ne cédait rien..." (2: 396). Bored rather than flattered by Frédéric's sophomoric assumption that she will jump into bed the moment he repeats the accepted romantic formulas, she continues to frustrate his wishes until he ceases to believe in his conventional description of their power:

Pourquoi ne pas obéir à l'impulsion qui nous pousse [Frédéric says]? L'amour, après tout, n'était pas en soi une chose si importante.
"Mais c'est immoral, ce que vous dites là!"
Elle s'était remise sur la causeuse. Il s'assit au bord, contre ses pieds. "Ne voyez-vous pas que je mens! Car, pour plaire aux femmes, il faut étaler une insouciance de bouffon ou des fureurs de tragédie! Elles se moquent de nous quand on leur dit qu'on les aime, simplement! Moi, je trouve ces hyperboles où elles s'amusent une profanation de l'amour vrai; si bien qu'on ne sait plus comment l'exprimer, surtout devant celles ... qui ont ... beaucoup d'esprit." (2: 397)

By calling his repetition of romantic discourse a profanation of true love, Frédéric rejects its conventional perlocutionary force: the tragic drama that charmed Mme Arnoux and the comic play-acting that seduced Rosanette. He treats it as a lie that misrepresents discourse's hidden perlocutionary force, its power over elite women with "beaucoup d'esprit." This power is theoretically indifferent not only to what words conventionally say, but also to what they conventionally do. It can be exercised by affirming or by denying love, by repeating or by rejecting the conventional formulas. Frédéric's successful seduction of Mme Dambreuse begins, therefore, with his cynical denial both of love and its conventional formulas of seduction, precisely because this denial convinces Mme Dambreuse that he is constrained by neither: "Pourquoi ne pas obéir à l'impulsion qui nous pousse?" Only when she hears his rejection of the conventions of love and seduction can he return to these formulas in a purely parodic mode and seduce (or rather be seduced by) Mme Dambreuse: "'Vous êtes si belle.' Mme Dambreuse ferma les yeux, et il fut surpris par la facilité de sa victoire" (2: 397).

For Frédéric, dialogue with Mme Dambreuse is an ironical (and, in its repetition of romantic discourse, parodic) lie that denies the very narrative contracts it affirms. This denial does not function to express love, but only to create a feeling of power: "Frédéric se considéra comme un homme très fort ... Sa vie, maintenant, avait des douceurs partout" (2: 403). In order to make himself feel powerful, he must repeatedly tell himself that he is not bound by the contracts he pretends to make with others. By obsessively breaking these contracts, he persuades himself that they are purely ironical means of increasing his power. Long after seducing Mme Dambreuse, therefore, he continues to make passes at Mme Arnoux, to send messages to Louise in the provinces, and to sleep with Rosanette: "[C]es mensonges le divertirent; il répétait à l'une le serment qu'il venait de faire à l'autre, leur envoyait deux bouquets semblables, leur écrivait en même temps, puis établissait entre elles des comparaisons..." (2: 418–19); "[I]l se dit: 'Quelle canaille je fais!' en s'applaudissant de sa perversité" (2: 401).

Frédéric's ironical lies appear to work, at least for a time, because he has learned from Mme Dambreuse to let the women he seduces know that his protestations of love are ironical. Like a mid-nineteenth-century Valmont with his Mme de Merteuil, he implicitly says "je mens" every time he says "je t'aime," thus making his lovers ironical accomplices in his speech acts of lying to them. More interestingly, he makes them feel that he is forgetting them.[54] It is their complicity in being forgotten, as well as deceived, by him that seduces them: "[P]lus il avait trompé n'importe laquelle des deux, plus elle l'aimait, comme si leurs amours se fussent échauffées réciproquement et que, dans une sorte d'émulation, chacune eût voulu lui faire oublier l'autre" (2: 419). Frédéric's mistresses want him to forget them because being forgotten makes them feel that he wields power over them. It also sparks their desire to exercise power over him, to make him forget the others and remember them. But the ensuing struggle for power over his forgetting culminates only in a bittersweet desire for him at least to repeat the same romantic lies. It seems to increase their awareness of his deceit and his power.

Rather than a source of memory, discourse in Flaubert's late Second Republic has become an ironical means of forgetting what words conventionally say or do, and of producing a feeling of power over others, over oneself, and over discourse.[55] The notion that discourse forgets and that forgetting produces a feeling of power will be advanced by Nietzsche a few years after the publication of *L'Education sentimentale*.[56] It is critical to an understanding of the difference between Balzac's and Flaubert's irony of irony. Balzac's Vautrin may irretrievably hide what he knows, and Restoration society may bury its Napoleonic past; this hiding is the product of a strategic choice between the memories they hide and those they display. Neither the "reformed" Vautrin nor Chabert's remarried wife seek to forget the past that they strategically deny. Balzac attributes Vautrin's power as a criminal, and his own as an author, to their prodigious memories which enable them to choose between necessary strategic alternatives.

But in Flaubert, as in Nietzsche, irony of irony produces a feeling of power by effacing memory of the past and constituting a self-deceived consciousness of the present. Dambreuse, the financier of monopoly capitalism, forgets past regimes in order to imagine that he truly believes in the superiority of the present one. Once the July Monarchy is in place he ceases to remember his past opposition to that regime and loyalty to the Restoration. He forgets in order to deceive himself into believing that the present regime, unlike the past one, exists to increase the power of finance and industry, and thus his own. He is quite surprised, therefore, when the July Monarchy gives way to the Second Republic: "L'état nouveau des choses menaçait sa fortune, mais surtout dupait son expérience. Un système si bon, un roi si sage! était-ce possible! La terre allait crouler!" (2: 327). But he soon forgets his "loyalty" to the July Monarchy, as he forgot his allegiance to the Restoration. He blindly convinces himself that he is "seeing" a present regime under which finance and industry will thrive. And this forgetting and self-deceived idolatry seem to contribute to his financial and political power to manipulate government and market.

Frédéric's amorous forgetting indirectly reveals that Dambreuse's forgetting is more extensive than it first appears. Not only does Frédéric forget an absent mistress, as the financier forgets a past regime; his thoughts about a present mistress, like those of Dambreuse about a present regime, are also a form of forgetting. Eventually, Frédéric can feel desire for Mme

Dambreuse and make himself feel potent only by forgetting her and reawakening an idealized memory of an absent mistress: "Il reconnut alors ce qu'il s'était caché, la désillusion de ses sens. Il n'en feignait pas moins de grandes ardeurs; mais pour les ressentir, il lui fallait évoquer l'image de Rosanette ou de Mme Arnoux" (2: 404). As he makes love to Mme Dambreuse, he imagines that he is possessing, not the memory of the real Mme Arnoux or the real Rosanette, but an idealized memory. He prefers to imagine that he is making love to Mme Arnoux, precisely because she always refused him: "[I]l y en avait une troisième toujours présente à sa pensée. L'impossibilité de l'avoir le justifiait de ses perfidies ..." (2: 419).

Frédéric's will to power over his mistresses is a pure parody of Dambreuse's and the late Second Republic's will to power. Given that the only woman who can make him feel the sexual desire to possess is one over whom he is powerless, his feeling of potency is produced by a profound sense of impotence. He takes out his resentment on those who will sleep with him by imagining that he is sleeping with someone else. In his eyes, therefore, his lovers gradually lose all value. They come to resemble Mme Arnoux's "coffret," which Mme Dambreuse buys at an auction in order to profane and erase his "souvenirs les plus chers" (2: 444–45): "Les cœurs des femmes sont comme ces petits meubles à secret, pleins de tiroirs emboîtés les uns dans les autres; on se donne du mal, on se casse les ongles, et on trouve au fond quelque fleur desséchée, des brins de poussière – ou le vide!" (2: 420). Frédéric's heart is clearly just as empty.[57] Possessing only a void, Flaubert's possessors, Frédéric and Mme Dambreuse, cease to possess anything at all. Subject and object of Nietzsche's will to power become pure self-deceptions.

The assertion that forgetting increases power presupposes that discourse can be freed of its descriptive and narrative constraints, its discursive "syntax," and that it can be transformed into an irreversible narrative reaction to present circumstances and an expression of the individual's will to power. But this presupposition of a syntax-free discourse contradicts itself. It presupposes in its turn a quite logical syntax. Flaubert's characters make themselves feel powerful only by methodically negating syntax: descriptive syntax, which treats words as representations, and narrative syntax, which treats words as a binding contract. They confuse this denial of syntax with an absence. Rather than liberate discourse from syntax, they enchain it to an anti-syntax.[58]

Frédéric's negation of his mistress's memory may temporarily give him a feeling of freedom and power; it ironically enslaves him to the necessity of its repetition. Memory of the absent mistress becomes anticipation of the future moment when he will see her and be disappointed with her. It imprisons him in a labyrinth where he must constantly flee the present and seek an ever receding future: "[Frédéric] mena dès lors une existence double, couchant religieusement chez la Maréchale et passant l'après-midi chez Mme Dambreuse, si bien qu'il lui restait à peine, au milieu de la journée, une heure de liberté" (2: 417). Flaubert's emergent monopoly capitalism, it would appear, also ironically enslaved itself to forgetting governmental allegiances in order to construct an impossible future government that would give it the power to satisfy freely its economic desires: "[I]l fallait que M. Dambreuse, lui-même, se présentât dans l'Aube" (2: 331).

However, Frédéric's irony of irony, or more precisely his parody of his parody, does not culminate, as does Vautrin's or the dying Dambreuse's, in ambiguous acts of power. Rather it transforms all ironical lies into acts of self-deception about the very concept of discursive power. The appearance that discourse irreversibly increases power is, in Flaubert, a reversible, self-deceived sign. The more Frédéric tries to feel powerful and the more monopoly capitalism tries to believe that it controls government, the more they feel powerless to escape their search for a power that the present always defers. They become addicted to producing a pure illusion of present power.[59]

For Flaubert, any attempt to show that discourse is an irreversible narrative act of transformation, an ironical lie, whether by asserting or negating a fixed syntax, produces its own parodic reversal. This parodic reversibility means that no act of transformation, no sentimental or revolutionary "réforme," takes place at all. The very attempt to describe the course of Frédéric's love life or of society's history (either as a description of romantic being or as a narrative of Balzacian power), the attempt to attribute it to chance, circumstances, individual power (as did Balzac), or historical processes (as will Zola), gives evidence only of error: "[Frédéric et Deslauriers] accusèrent le hasard, les circonstances, l'époque où ils étaient nés" (2: 455). When discourse acts as if it remembers what it is or does, when the novel acts as if it is descriptive or narrative in nature, it only parodies its attempt at self-remembering by giving evidence that it has forgotten itself. If the novel as a genre is distinguished by its narrative or descriptive nature, then *L'Education sentimentale* is a parody of the novel as genre.

The narrator of *L'Education sentimentale* thus parodies Balzac's irony of irony, his assertion of a discourse of power against power in service of the state.[60] Like the dying Dambreuse in front of his wife and her lover, like the final Vautrin, Flaubert's narrator sometimes appears to be defined by irony of irony. He seems to revel in his power to undercut ironically the ironical attempts of his characters to appear powerful. Consider only his description of Frédéric's efforts to prove to Mme Dambreuse and to himself that he is "quelqu'un de fort": "Afin de l'amuser, il s'offrit comme domestique, se prétendant capable de donner des assiettes, d'épousseter les meubles, d'annoncer le monde, d'être enfin un valet de chambre ou plutôt un chasseur, bien que la mode en fût passée. Il aurait voulu se tenir derrière sa voiture avec un chapeau de plumes de coq" (2: 396–97).

L'Education sentimentale seems exclusively ironical and parodic only as long as Frédéric persists in trying to show what he cannot show: that the individual's and society's words can remember what they are doing. But resignation ultimately undermines Dambreuse's Balzacian illusion of power against power, indeed the very notion that irony of irony is ironical. The necessity of forgetting and self-deception ultimately takes Flaubert's allegory beyond, or perhaps prevents it from ever becoming, irony or parody.

BEYOND PARODY: FROM FORGETTING TO REPETITION

Frédéric's allegory of parody takes a step beyond parody when he rejects all three of his loves: "il exécrait Mme Dambreuse... en oubliait la Maréchale, ne s'inquiétait même pas de Mme Arnoux..." (2: 446). His denigration, forgetting, and indifference are directed only temporarily at the three women. They indirectly express his resentment at having allowed himself to be deceived by the discursive aspects with which he constituted his loves for them: the descriptive aspect that enabled him to imagine he loved an unchangeable nurturing mother figure, and the narrative aspect that convinced him he possessed a commodifiable Rosanette or dominated a powerful rival, Mme Dambreuse. All he succeeded in doing when he tried to realize these loves was to make himself feel that he was doing the opposite: seducing a coquettish and changeable Mme Arnoux, being imprisoned by Rosanette's contract or being dominated by Mme Dambreuse. His initial disappointment with his three loves is only a first step towards understanding that the discursive aspects with which he constituted his and Paris's successive realities are self-deceived. This understanding implies that the narrator's discourse is other than a parody of realist illusion.

Flaubert dramatizes Frédéric's growing awareness of discursive self-deception as the character's gradual awareness of the fact that he cannot wield power over discourse. By repeatedly trying and failing to make words act narratively, he eventually gets his desire to act out of his system. He forgets it:

Il voyeagea.

Il connut la mélancolie des paquebots, les froids réveils sous la tente, l'étourdissement des paysages et des ruines, l'amertume des sympathies interrompues.

Il revint.

Il fréquenta le monde, et il eut d'autres amours encore. Mais le souvenir continuel du premier les lui rendait insipides; et puis la véhémence du désir, la fleur même de la sensation était perdue. Ses ambitions d'esprit avaient également diminué. Des années passèrent;

et il supportait le désœuvrement de son intelligence et l'inertie de son cœur. (2: 448–49)

This famous summary of 15 years of Frédéric's life, from 1852 (age 30) to 1867 (age 45), follows 400 pages that recount only 12, from 1840 (age 18) to 1852 (age 30). The extremely brief summary creates the sense of a sudden acceleration in time. It dramatizes Frédéric's iterated attempt to compensate, through action, his failure to perform the acts of love he wanted to perform, a failure that left him feeling "[h]onteux, vaincu, écrasé" (2: 448). This repetition only empties actions of meaning. The iterated definite articles – "*les* froids réveils sous *la* tente," "*l'*étourdissement *des* paysages et *des* ruines," "*l'*amertume *des* sympathies interrompues" (my emphasis) – transform the actions signified by the action verbs – "voyeagea," "connut," "revint," "fréquenta," – into trite iterations that defer, rather than complete, any satisfaction of Frédéric's desire to act. Like his candidacy to the National Assembly or his seduction of Mme Dambreuse, repeated travel, knowledge, society, and love, all change, do nothing. Flaubert's summary narrates, not a compressed series of actions, but rather a methodical erasing of any connotation of change, speech action, narrative, from conventional signs of action.

Flaubert's narrator dramatizes time's emptying of change from signs of action as the process of Frédéric's disillusionment. Each action is represented as Frédéric's mind would idealize it before he performs it: "Il connut la mélancolie des paquebots," etc. The definite articles and verbs in the *passé simple* combine to constitute action as a mere iteration of signs that is now complete and past, a mere memory. The "pastness" of these repeated signs is reinforced by the paratactic structure of the first three sentences, each of which comprises a paragraph: "Il voyagea"/"Il connut"/"Il revint."[61] The blanks between the short paragraphs evoke the passage of time between vain attempts to effect change, an absence that constitutes Frédéric's life as a series of meaningless transitions from one clichéd sign to another. The final action, "Il fréquenta," culminates the paratactic structure with a "mais" which marks, along with the imperfect tenses ("rendaient insipides," "était perdue," "avaient... diminué"), a final state of remembering ("le souvenir continuel du premier") that destroys all illusion that signs of action make a real change. Rather than narrate a series of actions, this summary narrates the series of conventional representations with which Frédéric's mind remembers his attempts to act at that moment when he no longer tries to act nor believes that he can. It creates a mature point of view from which his attempts to change, to do, anything at all in life seem purely parodic.

Frédéric's middle-age parody of his youthful belief in action arises out of disillusionment and resignation. He experiences time neither descriptively (as an expression of desire, emotion, sensation, or thought) nor narratively (as a performance of acts of seduction or thought). He accepts what the boat made him feel at the beginning of the novel: that time empties life of meaning. He redefines life as an iteration of meaningless loves and a parade of indistinguishable lovers. Life becomes devoid of signs of difference, of loving someone different, of being anyone different, of doing anything different: "... et il supportait le désœuvrement de son intelligence et l'inertie de son cœur." Frédéric's disillusionment with life gives time the form of a forgetting of differences between past actions, a blurring of distinctions in the memories of mere words. This forgetting of narrative differences makes him forget his will to act, or rather his will to wield power over the discourses with which he created the illusion that he could act. He thus takes an ironical distance from his desire to construct life descriptively as a sincere search for love or narratively as a deceitful act of power or appropriation.

The blank space that precedes this passage, of which Proust wrote so eloquently, dramatizes a transition in Frédéric's mental world from life to words.[62] Until now, the novel dramatized his mental experience as a repeated construction and deconstruction of self-deceived consciousnesses of life. But this passage clearly constructs his mental experience as an iterated remembering and forgetting, not of real past loves or real past actions, but of the conventional discourses with which his mind has repeatedly and retrospectively reconstructed past life, discourses from which past time is absent. The paratactic structure of the first three sentences re-enacts not only Frédéric's deconstruction of the conventional discourses with which his mind has constructed the temporality of his life, but also his construction of a memory space in which discourses, not life, are repeatedly forgotten and repeated.[63] It marks his acceptance and remembering that the discursive space of his memory is riddled by forgetting.

Frédéric's transition, between the ages of 30 and 45, from a self-deceived consciousness of life to a memory of forgetful words, constitutes an allegory of his apprenticeship in the discursive nature of mental life. It marks his acknowledgment that the mind can constitute the objects of consciousness only descriptively, as an enduring self, or narratively, as acts and agents of transformation. Consciousness is never more than a construct of iterated past discourses, a self-deceived and forgetful form of discursive memory.

The transition also marks Frédéric's acceptance that discourse does not constitute his mind as an identity to, or a difference from, real life, but as a difference within discourse itself. He has experienced this discursive difference as a necessary interplay between the forgetting of one discursive aspect and the remembering of the other. He could persuade Mme Arnoux and himself that his words of love described her realistically only by forgetting his desire that they act narratively to seduce her. He could convince Mme Dambreuse and himself that his romantic words were powerful narrative tools of seduction only by forgetting his desire that they literally describe Mme Arnoux. As purely discursive differences, however, the descriptive and narrative aspects can only pretend to forget each other and define the text. Every attempt to forget one recalls the other. It becomes a parody that repeats the other.[64] In the passage summarizing Frédéric's "adventures," therefore, Frédéric implicitly realizes that his efforts to forget the descriptive aspect and remember the narrative aspect, to constitute his life as action, simply remind him of the former and make him forget the latter: "[L]e souvenir continuel du premier les lui rendait insipides."[65]

The differential nature of discourse determines Frédéric's mind as a repetition of the alternation between the descriptive and narrative aspects that he experienced unawares on the boat. Nevertheless, his repetition of this alternation is strongly colored by his personal preference for romantic discourse, his tendency to foreground its descriptive aspect and background its narrative aspect. Thus even at the age of forty-five, long after he has experienced their falsity, he echoes the same romantic formulas of love to the now elderly Mme Arnoux when she pays him a final visit. He chooses to forget what he knows all too well, that romantic descriptions of unchangeable being forget the past and reawaken only the narrative aspect of its flight into death:

> Mme Arnoux ôta son chapeau. La lampe, posée sur une console, éclaira ses cheveux blancs. Ce fut comme un heurt en pleine poitrine.
>
> Pour lui cacher cette déception, il se posa par terre à ses genoux, et, prenant ses mains, se mit à lui dire des tendresses.
>
> "Votre personne, vos moindres mouvements me semblaient avoir dans le monde une importance extra-humaine. Mon cœur, comme de la poussière, se soulevait derrière vos pas. Vous me faisiez l'effet d'un clair de lune..."
>
> Elle acceptait avec ravissement ces adorations pour la femme qu'elle n'était plus. Frédéric, se grisant par ses paroles, arrivait à croire ce qu'il disait. (2: 451)

Frédéric's half-hearted attempts to delude himself into believing that his romantic words describe an unchangingly romantic, rather than a graying and changing, woman make him paradoxically forget the very desire they create, the descriptive desire for a nurturing mother. They reawaken his narrative desire to seduce the woman who always said "no": "Frédéric soupçonna Mme Arnoux d'être venue pour s'offrir; et il était repris par une convoitise plus forte que jamais, furieuse, enragée" (2: 452). But his admission that he wants to seduce Mme Arnoux only makes him forget this desire as well, and recall once again his romantic desire for a nurturing mother figure, but now under the sign of a prohibition: "Cependant, il sentait quelque chose d'inexprimable, une répulsion, et comme l'effroi d'un inceste" (2: 452). Alternating between the desires artificially awakened and erased by discourse's descriptive and narrative aspects, Frédéric momentarily remembers what he prefers to forget, that neither aspect can appropriate the real: "Une autre crainte l'arrêta, celle d'en avoir dégoût plus tard. D'ailleurs quel embarras ce serait!" (2: 452)

By rejecting Mme Arnoux's advances, Frédéric resigns himself to being repeated by, as well as repeating, discourse.[66] In conversations with his friend, Deslauriers, he renounces his will to power over words, and accepts the power they have over his mental life, along with the feeble sense of power they give him. He sometimes gives in to his desire to repeat discourse's descriptive aspect as he did during Mme Arnoux's last visit. But he no longer interprets this repetition as the representation of a real being, only as a means of putting off, deferring, forgetting the narrative aspect by creating the momentary illusion of describing a remembered romantic being. Indeed, "celui qui avait rêvé l'amour" reconciles himself to the inevitability of discourse's narrative aspect as well, for he renews his friendship with "celui qui avait rêvé le pouvoir," the one who always tried and failed to be a first-class Balzacian seducer, Deslauriers (2: 455). Deslauriers's burlesque stories of his vain efforts to seduce, like Frédéric's burlesque descriptions of his romantic memories, do not represent past reality: "Ils ... avaient manquée tous les deux [la vie]" (2: 455). Rather, both characters define themselves by their lack of the discursive aspect preferred by the other. Deslauriers faults his "excès de rectitude" and Frédéric his own "défaut de ligne droite" (2: 455). "Réconciliés encore une fois, par la fatalité de leur nature qui les faisait toujours se rejoindre et s'aimer", the friendship between Frédéric and Deslauriers stages discourse as a Derridean difference between narrative differentiation and descriptive deferral (2: 453).[67]

Frédéric's acceptance of his forgetful romantic formulas, and of Deslaurier's forgetful Balzacian stories, constitutes his implicit acknowledgment that discourse condemns him to create repeatedly descriptive and narrative illusion, to act as if he were repeatedly self-deceived by his desires. His awareness of having to feign self-deception, an awareness expressed by his acts more than his words, takes him beyond self-deception into a realm that appears, at first glance, to be entirely parodic. *L'Education sentimentale* seems to recount a linear allegory, to be a *Bildungsroman*, of how a naive adolescent learned to demystify and repeat, in the present of parody, his past sentimental illusions. But this parodic present is only an iteration of past parody, a parody of parody that cannot be said to be entirely parodic:[68]

Frédéric ... pria l'ex-délégué du Gouvernement provisoire [Deslauriers] de lui apprendre le mystère de la tête de veau.

"C'est une importation anglaise. Pour parodier la cérémonie que les royalistes célébraient le 30 janvier, des Indépendants fondèrent un banquet annuel où l'on mangeait des têtes de veau, et où on buvait du vin rouge dans des crânes de veau en portant des toasts à l'extermination des Stuarts. Après Thermidor, des terroristes organisèrent une confrérie toute pareille, ce qui prouve que la bêtise est féconde." (2: 454–55)

In order to mock the monarchy of Louis Philippe, the revolutionaries of 1848 repeated a parody of the monarchy by the revolutionaries of 1789, who themselves repeated an English parodic repetition of a royalist celebration. This parody spatialized a self-deceived past, the English monarchy's ceremonies, by making them coincide with an enlightened present, their parodic iteration by English independents. But revolutionary parody or satire, Deslauriers suggests, is a "bêtise ... féconde." Its parodic demystification of the monarchical illusion of enduring tyranny generated, in two French revolutions, only inverted repetitions of the error it mocked: the tyrannies of the Terror and of Napoleon III. In *L'Education sentimentale*, France's repeated revolutions become a parody of their pretense to parody and change monarchy, a parody of parody that is all too evident in the tyranny and inequality of the late Second Empire when Frédéric and Deslauriers converse. Parody of parody (parody of satire) breaks down the logical and spatial distinction between tyranny and freedom, permanence and change, error and truth, an empty calve's skull and a human head, upon which the possibility of parody depends.[69]

Frédéric dramatizes the breaking down of the parody/non-parody distinction in the last lesson of his sentimental education. Together, the two friends tell a comic yet nostalgic story of their first visit to, and flight from, a brothel in early adolescence. Upon arriving at the brothel, they presented the prostitutes with flowers picked from Frédéric's mother's garden. They thus transformed the buying of love into a profanation and parody of filial love. Like the English parody of the royalists, this parody is a "bêtise... féconde" that seems to engender multiple repetitions: Deslauriers's endless attempts to seduce women; Frédéric's failed attempts to seduce Mme Arnoux, his meaningless seductions of Rosanette, Mme Dambreuse, and others. But these repetitions are parodies of parody. Frédéric's seduction of Mme Dambreuse was a parody of the mistress/protector relationship that he had entertained with Rosanette. But his seduction of Rosanette was a parody of the romantic formulas culled from Mme Arnoux's discursive garden. However, his attempts to seduce Mme Arnoux are themselves repetitions of the original parody of his filial love for a nurturing mother: his first visit to the brothel. But is not his love for a purely imaginary, nurturing Mme Arnoux, a repetition of the adolescent's love for a purely idealized mother, itself a parody of a very real, non-nurturing woman? Is not his love for Mme Arnoux a parody of parody too?

Rather than reveal a "vérité romanesque" at the end of its parodic negations, rather than undercut its repetition of romantic error by disclosing a present truth, *L'Education sentimentale*'s final words reduce its parody of realist discourse and of the novel to a degraded repetition of a superior moment that took place before both parody and novel even began, the visit to the brothel:[70]

> "C'est là ce que nous avons eu de meilleur!" dit Frédéric.
> "Oui, peut-être bien? C'est là ce que nous avons eu de meilleur!" dit Deslauriers. (2: 457)

The friends' preference for this pre-narrative, unwitting parody over its narrated, and increasingly aware, repetitions denies that their sentimental and political education or their era's "revolution" has taught them, their contemporaries, or the reader anything at all. The chronological series of the novel's parodic negations thus culminates in a highly ambiguous negation of negation which is both a present repetition of past parody, and a non-parodic nostalgia for a superior past.[71] Hence the mixed tone of the passage which is both comic and sad.[72] Are the friends expressing literally a serious preference for their youth? Or is their idealization of the past simply one more parody? Parodic irony, which tends towards the simultaneity of pure present negation, gives way to allegory in which the sign can only "refer to another sign that precedes it."[73] Allegory reintroduces the question, but only the question, of linear time and history in the form of a seemingly conservative idealization of a pre-adolescent, pre-revolutionary past, as if, but only as if, it were sacred, and as if history (and revolution) were an irreversible decline.[74]

Flaubert's allegorization of parody also differentiates his novel from Balzac's ironization of allegory. On the surface, Flaubert's novels, like Balzac's, appear to spatialize time by reducing linear change to an ironic, spatial juxtaposition, although not of powerful actors in geographical space, but of irreconcilable discourses in mental space.[75] Like the space of Frédéric's memory or the discursive space of Paris in which Flaubert's Second Republic is born and dies, the "form" of Flaubert's novel seems to be composed of an unchanging difference between descriptive and narrative illusions: "[J]e cherche non pas la *vibration* mais le *dessin*."[76] The final "désœuvrement" and "inertie" of Frédéric's mind and heart suggest, in fact, that this spatialization is even greater than in Balzac. Whereas Balzac's ironic gallery of contemporary types juxtaposes characters struggling for power in time, Flaubert's parodic mental space seems to efface time. At the beginning of the novel, for example, not only the adverb of time, "puis," but the conjunction, "et," appear to narrate Frédéric's awareness of temporal changes in his perceptions: "puis les brumes... se fondirent... la colline... s'abaissa, et il en surgit une autre" (2: 34). At the end not only "et," but also "puis" seem to describe memories and qualities that co-exist simultaneously in his memory: "... et il eut d'autres amours encore. Mais le souvenir continuel du premier les lui rendait insipides; et puis la véhémence du désir, la fleur même de la sensation était perdue" (2: 448). The temporal connotations of "puis" in the early passage are replaced by the spatial connotations of "et" in the later one, which express the mere addition of one more description of the space of Frédéric's disillusioned mind.

Flaubert's allegory of Frédéric's apprenticeship in parody discloses a spatialization of discursive time that reoccurs throughout the narrator's discourse. In the passage recounting Frédéric's first dinner with Mme Arnoux, for example, the "et" brings together and spatializes the descriptive and narrative illusions of time that already co-exist, like friends, in the space of his mind: "Au moment des liqueurs, elle disparut. La conversation devint très libre; M. Arnoux y brilla, et Frederic fut étonné du cynisme de ces hommes. Cependant, leur préoccupation de la femme établissait entre eux et lui comme une égalité, qui le haussait dans sa propre estime" (2: 79). The "et" joining "eux et lui," like the "et" preceding it, juxtaposes Frédéric's descriptive illusion – that his love of Mme Arnoux has an imperfective aspect of temporal continuity – and the narrative illusion he shares with her husband – that his love-life is a narrative act of seduction. But, while Frédéric overtly imagines that this "et" functions metaphorically to conjoin similar entities, and while he covertly hopes that it functions performatively to make dissimilar entities act similarly, the narrator's spatial juxtaposition of the two undercuts and seems to parody both.[77]

Although Flaubert's apparent spatialization of time creates the impression that his novel's form is a describable and modernist juxtaposition of parodied temporal aspects, this appearance is deceptive: "[L]a forme me résiste."[78] His narrator's discourse may act as if writing and reading spatialize time; it can never succeed in becoming spatial. The narrator's discourse can never coincide with the mental discourse of its character, with its satire of the social discourses of the historical era, or with its parody of the novel.[79] In the very depths of parodic or satiric simultaneity, Flaubert's characters rediscover the sequence, repetition, and alternation of Frédéric's opening boat ride to his home town: in his final story of life as a continual regression through repetition; in Emma's search to express "la dissemblance des sentiments sous la parité des expressions" (1: 500); in Félicité's dying transformation of her stuffed parrot into the Holy Ghost; and in St. Antoine's discovery of life "au fond de la matière": "O bonheur! bonheur! j'ai vu naître la vie, j'ai vu le mouvement commencer" (1: 198).[80] Out of the fiction of spatial and parodic form, Flaubert's novels repeatedly resurrect the allegorical fiction of time as a search for difference through repetition and alternation: "Comme [la tête de Iaokanann] était très lourde, ils la portèrent alternativement" (2: 678).[81]

Flaubert's novels displace the centrality traditionally accorded to the space of memory by dramatizing a repeated forgetting in time of their parodic effect.[82] Parody in Flaubert, it has been noted, arises out of an erasure of the difference between past and present. It is a remembering that conventional signs of the past forget. The decentering of this parody by allegory is a forgetting of forgetting that necessarily reintroduces the categories of memory, representation, difference, and time, albeit in the form of repetition and error. Flaubert's interiorization and parodization of Balzacian space and irony thus culminate in a reversal of Balzac's spatialization of time, in the temporalization of discursive space, and in the production of an allegorical effect. This process of temporalization will become increasingly important in the latter half of the nineteenth century as the novel, philosophy, and psychology explore the theme of forgetting. Emile Zola in particular will unfold an allegory of history as an unconscious process that is effacing signs of descriptive deferral and narrative differentiation, an allegory that will "make[] all the past appear as a flight into the inauthenticity of a forgetting."[83]

CHAPTER 3

Forgetting and beyond: Zola and allegory

Since the Renaissance, the priority of past over present has increasingly come into question. *Inventio* has become a sign not only of discovering the old, but of creating the new.[1] Flaubert extends this questioning to the priority of memory over forgetting, one of the principal presuppositions of western thought, at least since Plato.[2] Forgetting becomes a positive means of demystifying memory, as if it were an unhealthy attachment to the past. It replaces memory with a modern acceptance of repetition. By learning to forget the discourses with which mid-nineteenth-century bourgeois society constructs its life and history, Frédéric Moreau redefines his memory as a middle-class mental habit that has no power to influence his habitual actions. He can repeat past romantic formulas to the presently graying Mme Arnoux precisely because he no longer believes that this repetition will deceive him into acting romantically or seductively. His forgetting replaces Balzac's memory system of contemporary bourgeois discourses with a collection of meaningless discourses on life that he can alternately repeat and forget, as he does the souvenirs decorating his apartment, without interfering in the meaningless habits of his life.

Zola's *L'Oeuvre* modifies the late nineteenth-century redefinition of the centrality of memory by dramatizing, not only forgetting's transformation of remembering into empty repetition, but also its historically determined overcoming of memory. Rather than a Rabelaisian, Balzacian, or Flaubertian accumulation of remembered discourses, Zola's historical unconscious structures the mind as a methodical effacement, not only of the real, but also of discourse itself.[3] Whereas Nietzsche, a decade earlier, posited that the powerful "forget most things so as to do one thing," Zola now suggests that history effaces even the individual's power to remember the one thing that would make individual power possible.[4] *L'Oeuvre* recounts an allegory of how late nineteenth-century France confronted, in order to question, the fear that history was ironically effacing, rather than inscribing, the past. It thus weds allegory to history as did St. Paul.[5] Zola's allegory of forgetting foreshadows the twentieth-century meditations on forgetting, as both negative repression and positive sublimation, that will engage Freud, Proust, Beckett, as well as late twentieth-century, postmodernist critics of a contemporary crisis of history.[6]

HISTORY, CONSCIOUSNESS, AND REVERSIBILITY

The power of forgetting in Zola's *L'Oeuvre* is closely linked to its particular mode of temporalizing consciousness. From the beginning, the novel constitutes consciousness as a dynamic alternation between Balzacian observation of the historical milieu and Flaubertian blindness to it, an alternation that will gradually efface consciousness of history. It is two in the morning and visibility is obscured by darkness and pouring rain. Only periodic lightning flashes enable the committed naturalist painter, Claude Lantier, to observe momentarily yet repeatedly the Parisian quarter in which he lives, and to know where his steps are guiding him:

> Claude passait devant l'Hôtel de Ville, et deux heures du matin sonnaient à l'horloge, quand l'orage éclata. Il s'était oublié à rôder dans les Halles, par cette nuit brûlante de juillet, en artiste flâneur, amoureux du Paris nocturne. Brusquement, les gouttes tombèrent si larges, si drues, qu'il prit sa course, galopa dégingandé, éperdu, le long du quai de la Grève. Mais, au pont Louis-Philippe, une colère de son essoufflement l'arrêta : il trouvait imbécile cette peur de l'eau ; et, dans les ténèbres épaisses, sous le cinglement de l'averse qui noyait les becs de gaz, il traversa lentement le pont, les mains ballantes.
>
> Du reste, Claude n'avait plus que quelques pas à faire. Comme il tournait sur le quai de Bourbon, dans l'île Saint-Louis, un vif éclair illumina la ligne droite et plate des vieux hôtels rangés devant la Seine,

au bord de l'étroite chaussée. La réverbération alluma les vitres des hautes fenêtres sans persiennes, on vit le grand air triste des antiques façades, avec des détails très nets, un balcon de pierre, une rampe de terrasse, la guirlande sculptée d'un fronton. C'était là que le peintre avait son atelier, dans les combles de l'ancien hôtel du Martoy, à l'angle de la rue de la Femme-sans-Tête. Le quai entrevu était aussitôt retombé aux ténèbres, et un formidable coup de tonnerre avait ébranlé le quartier endormi

Arrivé devant sa porte, une vieille porte ronde et basse, bardée de fer, Claude, aveuglé par la pluie... (4: 11)[7]

The novel's second paragraph constructs a seemingly Balzacian observing consciousness that is objectively perceiving the Parisian area where Claude lives. It does so by framing signs of the imperfective aspect ("c'était là" and spatial details), which suggest a continuity of being, within signs of the perfective or perfect aspects ("alluma," "était... retombé," adverbs, and nouns), which suggest action and change. It also attributes the described details to a universal act of observation ("on vit"). But this quite conventional, nineteenth-century mode of framing "objective" descriptive details is not as Balzacian as it might appear. In Balzac, the verbs in the *passé simple* tense that normally frame the description's imperfect tenses signify a momentary cessation and resumption of action. They bracket out signs of physical action in order to give the impression that the character's observation and the narrator's description of spatial milieu are uninterrupted and objective. But in Zola's description, signs of the perfective aspect not only frame, they infiltrate the descriptive details. They construct, rather than bracket out, action. Not only do they delineate observed details, they also mark the beginning and end of a mental act: an observing character's momentary vision of his milieu. Verbs in the *passé simple* tense thus signify the beginning of the act of seeing ("un vif éclair illumina"; "on vit") while a verb in a perfect tense and a past participle belatedly signify the end of this seeing ("le quai était aussitôt retombé aux ténèbres"; "Claude aveuglé"). Claude's limited act of vision clearly takes place within the unfolding of his life, for it reflects, rather than defers, his physical actions: he continues to walk home from the place he has observed to the workshop where he will paint it.

The perfective aspect of Claude's observations renders them as discontinuous as the lightning flashes to which Zola naturalistically attributes them. But the periodicity of the lightning flashes embeds the perfective aspect of these observations within the imperfective aspect of an ongoing repetition and alternation between light and darkness, vision and blindness. For the weather in *L'Oeuvre* metaphorizes involuntary historical forces, family and social history, which are temporalizing consciousness near the end of Zola's fictional nineteenth century, and transforming it from a continuous state into a discontinuous, repeated action. History, the central character of the *Rougon-Macquart*, is structuring society's consciousness as a repeated alternation between early nineteenth-century scientific empiricism and late nineteenth-century mysticism: "C'était fatal ... ce siècle, qui a fait déjà tant de clarté, devait s'achever sous la menace d'un nouveau flot de ténèbres ..." (4: 359–60). This historically determined periodicity of vision and blindness is aggravated, in Claude's case, by his family heredity. An inherited lesion in his eyes makes his power to observe and represent flash on and off like lightning:

Qu'avait-il donc dans le crâne, pour l'entendre ainsi craquer de son effort inutile? Etait-ce une lésion de ses yeux qui l'empêchait de voir juste? Ses mains cessaient-elles d'être à lui, puisqu'elles refusaient de lui obéir? Il s'affolait davantage, en s'irritant de cet inconnu héréditaire, qui parfois lui rendait la création si heureuse, et qui d'autres fois l'abêtissait de stérilité. (4: 53)

Claude's family history makes him an extreme example of the socially determined periodicity that repeatedly interrupts and renews the Second Empire's power to observe its historical milieu, the subject of Zola's *Rougon-Macquart*. Social and family nature determine a temporality of consciousness that prefigures the psychologically determined alternation of Proust's insomniac narrator's mind between awaking and falling asleep.[8] In Zola, however, it is history and historical representation that are neurotic. His novels recount an allegory of his analysis of history and his attempt to cure it.

Of course, Zola's temporalization of consciousness is not new. The beginning of *L'Education sentimentale* constitutes thought as an iterated, temporal alternation between signs of the imperfective aspect, of continuity, and signs of the perfective aspect, of change.[9] But Flaubert's novel does not describe this formal alternation as an epochal outcome of linear historical determination; rather the narrator attributes it to the ahistorical structure of discourse. Moreover, the poles between which thought alternates in Flaubert, the imperfective and perfective aspects, are both blind. By contrast, the imperfective aspect in Zola is the mark of consciousness, whether as moments of seemingly continuous lucidity, or moments of seemingly continuous blindness. The perfective aspect marks historically determined transitions between the two: the singular change from early nineteenth-century vision to late nineteenth-century blindness; the iterated ongoing transformation of vision into blindness and of blindness into vision near the end of Zola's nineteenth century.[10]

Problems arise in *L'Oeuvre*'s *fin-de-siècle* precisely because society's intermittent blindness to its historical milieu makes it blind to what it is doing in this milieu. During eras of historical blindness, society must continue to act, just as Claude continues to walk in the dark towards the doorstep of his workshop. The signs of the perfective aspect which signify for Zola transitions from light to darkness, vision to blindness, early nineteenth-century "clarté" to late nineteenth-century "ténèbres," thus also mark a transition from self-conscious action to self-blinded action. This transition creates difficulties that Balzac's observing characters can learn to avoid and possibilities that Flaubert's self-deceiving characters cannot encounter. Balzac's Derville can first observe objective signs of Colonel Chabert's future tragedy in his immobile physiognomy, then decide how this objective observation of historical change should guide his future actions. Although he chooses to ignore history's signs and defend Chabert, the colonel's downfall teaches him to base his future choice of actions on his objective observations. Objective observation of the milieu guarantees an objective consciousness of social history, and the calculation of future and individual actions. In *L'Education sentimentale*, by contrast, society's self-deceivers cannot base action on an historical knowledge they cannot achieve. They can only accept their blindness to history or invent a fictional one. Zola's painter, however, must alternate between moments when history illuminates life's path with the objectivity of a Balzacian observer, and moments when it makes him as blind to this past as a Flaubertian self-deceiver.

The historically determined, periodic blindness of Zola's characters to what they are doing enslaves them to history. It renders their vision too early or too late to guide the choice of those actions that take place outside the intermittent present of observation. It thus prevents individual will from becoming conscious or voluntary agency, and it subordinates will and action to family and social determination.[11] Claude likes to feel that he is in control of his actions, which is why he gets angry at himself when he begins running from the rain: "U]ne colère... l'arrêta: il trouvait imbécile cette peur de l'eau... il traversa lentement le pont, les mains ballantes." But the lightning illuminates the doorway to his workshop at too early a moment and from too great a distance for him to see where his steps are taking him. When he arrives, he must act according to a memory that is premature and incomplete: "Arrivé devant sa porte, une vieille porte ronde et basse, bardée de fer, Claude, aveuglé par la pluie, tâtonna pour tirer le bouton de la sonnette ..." (4: 11). Reaching blindly for the bell, he performs an act different from the one he intended, an act that his observation was simply too early for him to will or avoid:

> ... et sa surprise fut extrême, il eut un tressaillement en rencontrant dans l'encoignure, collé contre le bois, un corps vivant. Puis à la brusque lueur d'un second éclair, il aperçut une grande jeune fille, vêtue de noir, et déjà trempée, qui grelottait de peur. Lorsque le coup de tonnerre les eut secoués tous les deux, il s'écria: "Ah bien! si je m'attendais... Qui êtes-vous? que voulez-vous?" (4: 11)

As Claude's defensive reaction hints, an encounter with an attractive woman is deadly. The hereditary flaw that he shares with his brothers Jacques and Etienne, as with his sister Nana, transforms his sexual desire into a drive for death that overpowers his will to self-preservation.[12] Just as Jacques kills the women he desires, Etienne kills an amorous rival, and Nana vindictively provokes destructive sexual desire in Paris, so the hereditary lesion in Claude's eyes will make him "kill" his unique, naturalist talent at seeing and painting reality.[13] Until this involuntary encounter, he has maintained some power over his actions by fleeing women: "Il avait la méfiance de la femme ..." (4: 12). Had he seen the one in his doorstep, he would not have entered: "si je m'attendais..." But his desire to take precautions was too early, and now it is too late to withdraw. History has brought him face to face with the death-drive that sexuality awakens in him, although he avoids facing up to it by blaming the encounter on her: "Bon! une farceuse," pensa Claude, "quelque gueuse flanquée à la rue et qui cherche un homme" (4: 12).

The historically determined premature or belated nature of observation in Zola's Second Empire condemns any consciousness of history to discover only after the fact that it is paradoxically becoming unconscious of history.[14] Zola dramatizes this reversibility of historical consciousness by means of the third and fourth lightning flashes:

> Un éclair éblouissant lui coupa la parole; et ses yeux dilatés parcoururent avec effarement ce coin de ville inconnue, l'apparition violâtre d'une cité fantastique. La pluie avait cessé. De l'autre côté de la Seine, le quai des Ormes allignait ses petites maisons grises, bariolées en bas par les boiseries des boutiques, découpant en haut leurs toitures inégales; tandis que l'horizon élargi s'éclairait, à gauche, jusqu'aux ardoises bleues des combles de l'Hôtel de Ville, à droite jusqu'à la coupole plombée de Saint-Paul. Mais ce qui la suffoquait surtout, c'était l'encaissement de la rivière, la fosse profonde où la Seine coulait à cet endroit, noirâtre, des lourdes piles du pont Marie aux arches légères du nouveau pont Louis-Philippe. D'étranges masses peuplaient l'eau, une flottille dormante de canots et d'yoles, un bateau-lavoir et une dragueuse, amarrées au quai; puis, là-bas contre l'autre berge, des péniches pleines de charbon, des chalands chargés de meulière, dominés par le bras gigantesque d'une grue de fonte. Tout disparut...
>
> Mais elle jeta un cri, un nouvel éclair l'avait aveuglée; et, cette fois, elle venait de revoir la ville tragique dans un éclaboussement de sang. C'était une trouée immense, les deux bouts de la rivière s'enfonçant à perte de vue, au milieu des braises rouges d'un incendie. Les plus minces détails apparurent, on distingua les petites persiennes fermées

du quai des Ormes, les deux fentes des rues de la Masure et du Paon-Blanc, coupant la ligne des façades; près du pont Marie, on aurait compté les feuilles des grands platanes, qui mettent là un bouquet de superbe verdure; tandis que, de l'autre côté, sous le pont Louis-Philippe, au Mail, les toues alignées sur quatre rangs avaient flambé, avec les tas de pommes jaunes dont elles craquaient. Et l'on vit encore les remous de l'eau, la cheminée haute du bateau-lavoir, la chaîne immobile de la dragueuse, des tas de sable sur le port, en face, une complication extraordinaire de choses, tout un monde emplissant l'énorme coulée, la fosse creusée d'un horizon à l'autre. Le ciel s'éteignit, le flot ne roula plus que des ténèbres, dans le fracas de la foudre.

"Oh! mon Dieu! c'est fini... Oh! mon Dieu! que vais-je devenir?" (4: 12–13)

Through indirect and free indirect discourse, Zola's narrator constructs the consciousness of the woman Claude has met in his doorway, Christine, in terms of two nightmarish visions of the historical forces that are determining society's present. Impersonal pronouns ("on vit"), references to dilated eyes and to the cessation of the rain, and lists of "[l]es plus minces détails," suggest that, for the narrator, her consciousness, like Claude's, is objective.[15] Moreover, consistent references to parts of a working-class quarter (crane, work boats, chimney), well-known Parisian places, and the historical period (the "nouveau pont Louis-Philippe") identify the scene she objectively sees as a working-class area of industrial Paris, and the period in which they live as the late Second Empire.

Not only is Christine momentarily conscious of her place in space and her moment in time, she, like Balzac's observers, sees an historical process of change that is molding this space. Balzac's observers negate visible details ironically in order to disclose an invisible, historical relation between them. In contrast, Zola's literally see and feel historical tropes, each of which "naît avec la sensation, parce qu'il est dans les choses."[16] These tropes are both impressionist – they present the "spontaneous" effects of the perceived on the perceiver – and naturalist – the effects are constituted by (quite romantic) symbols of past and future death.[17] The Seine is transformed by the lightning into the "fosse profonde" of a cemetery in which "[d]'étranges masses peuplaient l'eau." Paris becomes a bloody and burning funeral pyre: "[E]lle venait de revoir la ville tragique dans un éclaboussement de sang. C'était une trouée immense, les deux bouts de la rivière s'enfonçant à perte de vue, au milieu des braises rouges d'un incendie." In Zola's *Rougon-Macquart*, the cemetery symbolizes the historical source of Second Empire life, the cemetery in the *Conquête de Plassans*, while the pyre symbolizes its destination, the fire and blood of the Franco-Prussian war in *La Débacle*: "soleil de sang," "Paris entier brulant," "[l]es incendies continuaient" (5: 911).[18]

Zola's historical consciousness is fundamentally self-referential. His observers, unlike Balzac's, are transformed by their very act of observing historical change. This self-referentiality explains why his narrator focuses his attention, less on the observed Parisian landscape, than on the drama of its suffocation of its observer: "Mais ce qui la suffoquait surtout, c'était ... la fosse profonde." The final description of a lightning-illuminated Paris culminates in Christine's belated realization that she, who has come to Paris to begin her life, has blindly walked into the doorway of her death: "Oh! mon Dieu! c'est fini ... Oh! mon Dieu! que vais-je devenir?"[19] She not only sees the Second Empire burying and burning itself, she indirectly destroys herself through the very act of seeing. Like Austin's explicit performative, her act of observation tragically performs the act of self-destruction it represents, which is why she cries out.[20] But even this cry for self-preservation performs the reverse action. It overcomes Claude's mistrust of women ("[u]ne pitié l'envahit" [4: 13]), seduces him into inviting her into his life, and allows his family heredity to destroy her as well as himself. Rather than enable Zola's observer to master her milieu, observation makes her "vieillie de dix ans et sans force ... Vous savez qu'elle en était venue à oublier jusqu'à son orthographe. Une déchéance, un écrasement, une demoiselle ravalée à une bassesse de servante!" (4: 355)

The self-referentiality of historical consciousness renders it reversible. This reversibility is foregrounded in *L'Oeuvre*'s dramatization of the effects of Zola's historically determined death-drive on naturalist observation. Claude observes a process that is destroying his eyes in the act of his seeing it. History transforms all action into a neurotic production of the opposite action. It creates a crisis of consciousness on the level of society not unlike the one that confronts Proust's insomniac narrator when the "pensée qu'il était temps de chercher le sommeil" awakens him.[21] The very attempt to will actions freely, including the act of observation, thus enslaves *L'Oeuvre*'s characters by increasing their will to do the opposite. Claude's impatience to get out of the blinding rain and into the light of his workshop, his decision not to wait for a flash of lightning to guide his way, makes him all the more susceptible to his will to perform the opposite action. His impatience to see helps history enslave him to his self-destructive will to be blind. Throughout the novel, the more he attempts to see his milieu accurately, the more heredity and society blind him to it. Only when it is too late will this naturalist painter be able to see at least his own blindness. "[C]omprenant bien que la réalité elle-même ne lui était plus possible," Claude belatedly sees that he cannot see the present of history (4: 347).

For Zola, Claude's ability to see only his blindness is exemplary of a crisis of historical consciousness at the end of the nineteenth century. According to his fictional, naturalist novelist, Sandoz, early nineteenth-century science's attempts to observe its milieu empirically were incomplete and premature. Impatience produced the opposite action, the late nineteenth century's fall into mysticism:

> On a trop promis, on a trop espéré, on a attendu la conquête et l'explication de tout; et l'impatience gronde. Comment! on ne marche pas plus vite? la science ne nous a pas encore donné, en cent ans, la certitude absolue, le bonheur parfait? Alors, à quoi bon continuer, puisqu'on ne saura jamais tout et que notre pain restera aussi amer? C'est une faillite du siècle, le pessimisme tord les entrailles, le mysticisme embrume les cervelles. (4: 360)

All that the writer Sandoz and the painter Bongrand can belatedly see after Claude's death is that they are too late to prevent him, society, or themselves from bringing about their own fall into illusion. The hereditary forces that enslave a few, and the social forces that imprison all, condemn society as a whole to perform the opposite action from the one it wills. *Fin-de-siècle* society is a Hegelian unhappy consciousness that is chained to decline: "Its deeds and its words belie each another continually."[22]

Zola constitutes the nineteenth-century's consciousness of history as a reversible speech act of irony. The attempt to achieve complete consciousness ironically produces only an unconscious fall into blindness that puts off completion: "[I]l faudra une génération, deux générations peut-être, avant qu'on peigne et qu'on écrive logiquement, dans la haute et pure simplicité du vrai..." (4: 358). The era's act of becoming conscious of change is thus an act of becoming unconscious to it. History is a terrifying force, which is both outside and inside the mind, and which is breaking down the very distinction between consciousness and unconsciousness.

It is this historically determined crisis of historical consciousness that *L'Oeuvre* sets out to describe and change. The theoretical task of the naturalist novel, as prescribed by Zola's *Roman expérimental*, is to describe the natural, social, economic, and political milieu during the Second Empire, dramatize its inevitable effects on a character, make society see and remember the "déterminisme des phénomènes," and induce it to eliminate this determinism.[23] The naturalist writer and painter are privileged perceivers who have "le sens du réel." Unlike Claude, they have no hereditary lesion, nor are they blinded by the "abstract" logic of seventeenth- and eighteenth-century artists or by the mysticism that Zola associates with religion and romanticism.[24] Rather, their eyes react mechanically and physiologically – in a manner that is "toute spontanée" – to concrete details and to the implicit determinist logic of the milieu that these details contain.[25] The tropes transforming Paris into a cemetery and funeral pyre – that Christine and Claude theoretically see, then lose the power to see – are the spontaneous physiological, and mechanical imprint of history.

Description, Zola suggests, not only remembers history's imprint, it spontaneously performs the act of producing an irreversible, complete, written narrative governed by history's natural logic: "Je définirai donc la description: Un état du milieu qui détermine et complète l'homme."[26] Zola's documentary descriptions of contemporary places – department stores, train stations, Les Halles, the Salons – *are* "states" of the Second Empire milieu that naturally produce narratives in the same way that Christine's eyes make her perform the tragic action of attracting Claude:

> Quand [nos grands romanciers contemporains] ont étudié avec un soin scrupuleux le terrain où ils doivent marcher, quand ils se sont renseignés à toutes les sources et qu'ils tiennent en main les documents multiples dont ils ont besoin, alors seulement ils se décident à écrire. Le plan de l'œuvre leur est apporté par ces documents eux-mêmes, car il arrive que les faits se classent logiquement, celui-ci avant celui-là; une symétrie s'établit, l'histoire se compose de toutes les observations recueillies, de toutes les notes prises, l'une amenant l'autre, par l'enchaînement même de la vie des personnages, et le dénouement n'est plus qu'une conséquence naturelle et forcée. On voit, dans ce travail, combien l'imagination a peu de part.[27]

According to Zola's theories, *L'Oeuvre*'s narrative – its tragic story of Christine's decline into servitude and Claude's fall into forgetting history – has been preordained by the Second Empire Parisian milieu that Zola has seen and described. His descriptions are thus historically determined, illocutionary speech acts. They are necessary and irreversible narrative acts of transformation. History, not the naturalist author, imprints the naturalist description and produces the naturalist narrative. History is, in great part, the author of the *Rougon-Macquart*.

However, this apparent servitude of the naturalist description to historical determinism is only a ploy. It is a covert means by which the socially committed, naturalist artist tricks history into revealing itself and giving up its power. By luring it into imprinting its logic in descriptive form, the naturalist artist, like the empirical scientist, provides experimental evidence of history's destructiveness. Once the *Rougon-Macquart*'s descriptions have mapped social space as a whole, once they have produced narratives that reveal history's temporal determinisms in time, they will become, through the mediation of society's scientists and reformers, irreversible perlocutionary speech acts. They will empower society to destroy history's determinist structures: "Notre vraie besogne est là, à nous romanciers expérimentateurs, aller du connu à l'inconnu, pour nous rendre maîtres de la nature..."[28] History's necessary repetition of its logic in a fictional description and narrative will thus cause society to destroy this logic and, with it, historical necessity. Society will gain the freedom to be "maître du phénomène":[29] "Comme le dit très bien Claude Bernard, du moment où nous pouvons agir, et où nous agissons sur le déterminisme des phénomènes, en modifiant les milieux par exemple, nous ne sommes pas des fatalistes."[30]

Were *L'Oeuvre* to act out Zola's theory of writing as he presents it in the *Roman experimental*, were the novel to be a truly "naturalist" novel, then its initial descriptions of a tragic Paris would be the spontaneous product of history's natural logic as it is imprinted in the observable milieu. The descriptions would produce a necessary story of the effects of this logic on a naturalist painter's consciousness: the story of how history made him unconscious of its imprint. Along with the rest of the *Rougon-Macquart*, these descriptions would map the entire network of history's "déterminismes." The stories would dramatize their danger and cause society to eliminate their power, including their power over consciousness. Society after the *Rougon-Macquart* would once again see the perils lurking in the milieu's dark doorsteps, and perform the irreversible act of exterminating them.

But the interest of *L'Oeuvre* is precisely that it does not blindly assume that the novel's descriptions will inevitably constitute a "maison de verre" or dominate history.[31] Rather, it asks the question that Fredric Jameson poses about "late capitalist" society at the end of the twentieth century. What are the implications of the crisis in Claude's historical consciousness for historical representation in general.[32] *L'Oeuvre* characterizes the painter's gradual blindness to his milieu as a forgetting and erasure, from the space of his paintings, of the means of representing his milieu. It interprets the implications of this erasure for naturalist discourse as a whole through the mediation of the naturalist novelist Sandoz, who strongly resembles Zola. *L'Oeuvre* thus interprets history in Zola's Second Empire as an allegory of the fall of all naturalist description from a remembering to a forgetting of the descriptive means of representing historical change, a fall that has serious implications for Zola's descriptive practice.

SPATIALIZING TIME: HISTORY, THE DESCRIPTIVE, AND FORGETTING

The plight of historical consciousness in Zola's late nineteenth century arises out of a crisis of discourse. History is transforming not only Claude's eyes and paintings, but all naturalist discourse, into a spatialization of time, an effacement of historical distinctions. If naturalist artists hope to produce genuine change, they must overcome this historically determined dehistoricization of the means by which they represent history. Their goal thus resembles Jameson's project to "historiciz[e]" the "resolutely ahistorical" space of what he calls "postmodernist" discourse in the late twentieth-century world market. Zola's reformers must historicize the forgetful and chaotic discursive space in a late nineteenth-century monopoly capitalism that has gone out of control.[33]

History, *L'Oeuvre* posits, is rendering discourse (and with it consciousness) forgetful by making descriptions of Second Empire France incomplete. Even artists who are not blinded by heredity, such as the successful painter Bongrand and the increasingly successful writer Sandoz, must sell their works before having painted or described historical space completely: "'Je me méprise de ... sentir [mes bouquins] incomplets et mensongers, malgré mon effort'" (4: 363). Spatial incompleteness reduces *fin-de-siècle* representational discourse to the spatial fragmentation that some will later attribute to modernist and postmodernist art: "des enfants infirmes, auxquels il manque toujours des morceaux, les jambes ou la tête, et qui ne vivent pas" (4: 363).[34] History has not condemned the descriptive to eternal incompleteness. It has simply put off completion to that future moment when experimental science might describe and overcome its deterministic structures. But by deferring the naturalist act of describing Second Empire

France, history is putting off the very means by which science can make that future possible.

History structures Claude's act of painting as an alternation between incomplete remembering and complete forgetting of the pictorial means of reproducing his milieu:

> Ses mains cessaient-elles d'être à lui, puisqu'elles refusaient de lui obéir? Il s'affolait davantage, en s'irritant de cet inconnu héréditaire, qui parfois lui rendait la création si heureuse et qui d'autres fois l'abêtissait de stérilité, au point qu'il oubliait les premiers éléments du dessin. Et sentir son être tourner dans une nausée de vertige, et rester là quand même avec la fureur de créer, lorsque tout fuit, tout coule autour de soi, l'orgueil du travail, la gloire rêvée, l'existence entière! (4: 53)

Claude's best painting, "Plein air," is incomplete precisely because his moments of remembering "les premiers éléments du dessin" are never sufficiently long to capture his Parisian milieu (4: 127). These moments are preceded and followed by others in which he forgets the basics of design and defers the act of describing. Periodic forgetting is thus fragmenting his naturalist paintings.

Claude's alternation between incomplete remembering and complete forgetting of pictorial technique makes him efface the spatial distinctions that structure Zola's reality. Zola, Philippe Hamon notes, tries to "penser le réel comme une *surface*, comme un *espace* rationalisé."[35] The novelist fantasizes the real as a readable space whose differential structure can be described by fixed relations between lexical signs, although he obviously constructs this readable space by means of a fixed, differentially structured lexicon.[36] Paris for him is thus a systematically organized space whose parts can be named and whose relations can be described by whoever sees accurately and knows the fundamentals of descriptive technique. But, because history is making the mind forget these fundamentals, naturalist descriptions are effacing, rather than tracing, the spatial differences that compose Second Empire Paris. Descriptions of Zola's tragic Parisian landscape, including its metaphors of history, are becoming unreadable.

History destroys descriptive readability by transforming the act of completing an artistic representation into an effacement of the real. Claude tries to capture the real by documenting women who are emblematic of real life and who express his artistic ideal. He thus displaces his desire for sexual appropriation onto the act of representation, although without complete success:

> [C]'était sa passion de chaste pour la chair de la femme, un amour fou des nudités désirées et jamais possédées, une impuissance à se satisfaire, a créer de cette chair autant qu'il rêvait d'en étreindre, de ses deux bras éperdus. Ces filles qu'il chassait de son atelier, il les adorait dans ses tableaux, il les caressait et les violentaient, désespéré jusqu'aux larmes de ne pouvoir les faire assez belles, assez vivantes. (4: 50–51)

In Christine, Claude finally finds his artistic ideal become "réalité" (4: 243): "[C]'était ça, tout à fait ça, la figure qu'il avait inutilement cherché pour son tableau ..." (4: 19). By representing her body, he can appropriate both the real and his ideal: "[I]l n'aimait plus en elle que son art, la nature, la vie" (4: 242). He thus tries to realize Zola's naturalist project of reconciling the rational spaces of reality with the descriptive space of art. But once he has found the real equivalent of his ideal, his attempts to trace it, like the era's efforts to be conscious of history, only efface it: "Tu as tort de t'acharner, mon vieux ... [T]u vas encore gâter ton affaire, comme l'autre jour" (4: 49). The act of representing the real only destroys and fragments it, just as Balzac's painter, Frenhoffer, captures a fragment of the real, a beautiful model's foot, only by effacing her body as a whole.[37] Zola extends Frenhoffer's self-destructive gesture to the representational art of an era and attributes it to historical determination. History renders historical description, like historical consciousness in the Second Empire, reversible.

History also renders Claude's desire to represent reality reversible. By making him forget the tools of his descriptive trade at the very moments when he tries to remember them, history eventually makes him want to forget the real. It creates a desire to forget by coquettishly putting off complete descriptive appropriation of the real, Christine: "[Q]uand il crut l'avoir conquise et qu'il voulut obtenir ses confidences, ainsi que d'un camarade qui n'a rien à cacher, elle s'échappa en phrases fuyantes, elle finit par bouder, muette, impénétrable... Elle était très femme, elle se réservait, en se donnant toute" (4: 149). Rather than increase his desire for descriptive appropriation, history's refusal to be appropriated makes Claude want to flee: "Christine était la réalité, le but que la main atteignait, et Claude en avait eu le dégoût en une saison, lui le soldat de l'increé..." (4: 243). He increasingly abandons his attempt to construct a rational description of his milieu's tragic, rational structure and chooses to paint artificial ("increé") metaphors of a non-tragic, non-realisable ideal "qui me fît oublier tout..." (4: 350). Whereas Frenhoffer's realistic obsession shatters the real into metonymic fragments, Claude's heredity fragments the real by replacing its rational metaphors of history's real tragedy with irrational metaphors of a desirable ideal.

Zola interprets Claude's increasing will to forget as an allegory of a process destroying the readability of scientific and naturalist discourse in general: "[O]n a attendu la conquête et l'explication de tout; et l'impatience gronde. Comment! on ne marche pas plus vite? la science ne nous a pas encore donné, en cent ans, la certitude absolue, le bonheur parfait? Alors, à quoi bon continuer, puisqu'on ne saura jamais tout et que notre pain restera aussi amer?" (4: 360) The impatient desire to complete a description and explanation of the real is producing a desire to do the opposite, to replace the real's metonymically juxtaposed details with metaphors of a non-existent ideal, fantoms: "C'est une faillite du siècle, le pessimisme tord les entrailles, le mysticisme embrume les cervelles; car nous avons eu beau chasser les fantômes sous les grands coups de lumière de l'analyse, le surnaturel a repris les hostilités, l'esprit des légendes se révolte et veut nous reconquérir, dans cette halte de fatigue et d'angoisse..." (4: 360).

Society's historically determined will to forget makes naturalist description fall into what all realist discourse will be two decades later for Proust: an act of self-deception.[38] This fall takes the form of a repetition of past, conventional discourses on the ideal, such as the medieval legends and mysticism that were revived by nineteenth-century romanticism.[39] Hereditary and social forces make Claude's mind and hands repeat these conventional discourses, instead of realist techniques, and make him want this repetition. He progressively deceives himself into believing that his eyes actually see a romantically idealized world: "J'ai ce sacré Delacroix dans l'œil" (4: 47). Similarly, society as a whole deceives itself into believing that it is seeing the world it wants to see: "[S]on mal n'était pas en lui seulement, il a été la victime d'une époque... Oui, notre génération a trempé jusqu'au ventre dans le romantisme, et nous en sommes restés impregnés quand même, et nous avons eu beau nous débarbouiller, prendre des bains de réalité violente, la tache s'entête, toutes les lessives du monde n'en ôteront pas l'odeur" (4: 357).

Society's self-deceived idealization of its milieu is especially seductive because it creates an erroneous consciousness of the self perceiving this milieu. When the public of the "Salon des Refusés" laughs at Claude's naturalist painting, "Plein air," a painting based on objective observations of Christine's ideal/real body, their mockery makes him want to flee representation. He imagines they are laughing because he has failed to achieve representational completeness: "Ils ont raison de rire, c'est incomplet..." (4: 127). Rather than seek to overcome this incompleteness, however, he seeks refuge in Christine's maternal love: "[E]lle s'oubliait maintenant, elle ne songeait qu'à lui, bouleversée par l'idée du chagrin qu'il devait avoir, grossissant l'amertume de cet échec de toute sa sensibilité de femme, débordant d'un besoin de charité immense"; "Tais-toi, tais-toi, je t'aime" (4: 140). In Christine, Claude finds a viewer who declares the superiority of his art purely because this declaration makes him feel better about himself: "O mon ami, ne vous faites pas de peine!... Je voulais vous voir et vous dire que ce sont des jaloux, que je le trouve très bien, ce tableau..." (4: 140). Representation becomes a means of producing a self-deceived sense of self-esteem based on the spectator's reaction, rather than complete representation.

Claude can deceive himself into feeling worthy only by forgetting naturalism's will to describe and change Parisian reality, the will that produced "Plein air." Is it not this will that produced his recent humiliation?[40] "[D]ans un de ces brusques désirs de solitude et d'oubli," Claude and Christine flee the vulgar crowds of Parisian reality for an idyllic romance in the country (4: 143). In its unpolluted air, he can forget Paris's tragic state, indeed forget his own forgetting, and deceive himself into believing that his future paintings will receive from the public what "Plein air" was refused, the same nurturing reaction offered by Christine: "Lui, saignant encore de son échec du Salon, ayant le besoin de se reprendre, aspirait à ce grand repos de la bonne nature; et il aurait là-bas le vrai plein air, il travaillerait dans l'herbe jusqu'au cou, il rapporterait des chefs-d'œuvre" (4: 145).

Claude's flight from representation into a self-deceived search for self-esteem is, for Zola, the product, not only of family heredity, but of a society for which art is a mirror of collective narcissism. "[E]tranglés par l'idéal," the public demands, not a representation of its historical reality, but a repetition of the received discourses that produce the sexual and narcissistic gratification it desires (4: 360). In a later salon, the same public that condemned Claude's "Plein air," not because it was incomplete, but because it was too representational, praises a plagiarized version of that painting by the opportunist, Fagerolles. The "force menteuse" of Fagerolles's pastiche derives only from the effect it produces. It is "adoucie, truquée, gâtée, d'une élégance d'épiderme, arrangée avec une adresse infinie pour les satisfactions basses du public." Fagerolles's deceitful pastiche satisfies the public's sexual desires and provides a narcissistic mirror of its "rêve du distingué" (4: 286). In exchange, society proclaims that his plagiarized work, rather than Claude's naturalist original, is an objective and new description of Parisian reality. It also buys his paintings: "Ce n'était pas lui qui se lâchait incongrûment en morceaux passionnés, d'une création débordante; non, quand il avait pris trois notes sur nature, il donnait les trois notes, pas une de plus. Un chroniqueur qui arrivait, s'extasia, trouva le mot: une peinture bien parisienne. On le répéta, on ne passa plus sans déclarer ça bien parisien" (4: 287).

Like Fagerolles's plagiarism, society forgets history by mixing representational and non-representational discourses which, for

Zola, are irreconcilable. This blending of discourses destroys the possibility of a complete, representational, naturalist description. Claude's last unfinished work is an enormous painting of "le port Saint-Nicolas à gauche, l'école de natation, à droite, la Seine et la Cité au fond" (4: 235). As he obsessively paints and repaints the contemporary Parisian scene, he increasingly forgets and paints over the metonymic and lexical differences that give each part its proper place, Zola believes, within the totality of historical space and time. These differences would produce empirically verifiable metaphors of history in the minds of their objective observers, just as the lightning-illuminated Paris made Christine see symbols of its historical tragedy. But Claude replaces them with totally borrowed clichés. He juxtaposes realist details, such as a "barque conduite par un marinier," with fantasized ones: "une autre barque, très grande, tenant tout le milieu de la composition, et que trois femmes occupaient," one with her "corsage à demi arraché montrant l'épaule," another "toute nue à la proue, d'une nudité si éclatante, qu'elle rayonnait comme un soleil" (4: 235). Whereas the mariner is in his proper place in the metonymic logic of the Parisian scene, the nude women are not: "Tiens! quelle idée!" murmura Sandoz. "Que font-elles là, ces femmes? – Mais elles se baignent," répondit tranquillement Claude. "Tu vois bien qu'elles sont sorties du bain froid, ça me donne un motif de nu, une trouvaille, hein?..." (4: 235) By replacing a working boat, which Parisians were likely see, with a pleasure boat carrying women in various stages of undress, which they were not so likely to see, Claude's pictorial discourse forgets the differential structure that dictates what a woman would or would not "naturally" wear or do in a Parisian working scene, the totalizing structure of Zola's historical reality. It fragments the real. But this mixing of real and ideal allows him to deceive himself into believing that he is painting a real world that will satisfy his desire to be loved by the woman (and the public) of his dreams.

Not only does Claude's mixing of discourses fragment, it dehistoricizes the space of the real by juxtaposing irreconcilable metaphors of history. The details of the port, like those that

Claude and Christine saw during the lightning flash, figure metonymically and synecdochically the complete reality he hopes some day to render, Paris's historical tragedy. But the sexually gratifying bodies figure an imaginary, romantically passionate city, an ahistorical comedy: "le tourment d'un symbolisme secret, ce vieux regain de romantisme... lui faisait incarner dans cette nudité la chair même de Paris, la ville nue et passionnée, resplendissante d'une beauté de femme" (4: 236). By forgetting the real metaphors of Paris's imminent fate in the Franco-Prussian war, Claude's fragmented, rhetorical space effaces the historicity of the present. It spatializes time.[41]

Claude's mixing of historical and ahistorical metaphors renders the acts of representing and remembering history reversible. He imagines that he is giving birth to a new and original work of naturalist art, one that will remember reality and be remembered by society: "[O]n aurait dit... un être qui naissait en lui, cette exaltation et cette nausée que les femmes connaissent" (4: 214). But he really aborts his painting by forgetting historical Paris: "La vie avorte" (3: 359).[42] Claude represents this reversibility of representational memory in his last submission to a salon. The painting depicts the corpse of his son who died out of obedience to his father's will to forget him: "Lui qu'elle trouvait si désobéissant, il venait de trop obéir. Elle lui avait tant de fois répété, quand il jouait: 'Tiens-toi tranquille, laisse travailler ton père!' qu'à la fin il était sage, pour longtemps" (4: 266). Claude's painting of his dead son memorializes *fin-de-siècle* descriptive art as a still birth of memory, a metaphor that foreshadows Beckett's stories of time – "A cheval sur une tombe et une naissance difficile" – and Jameson's postmodern: "The premise, in any case, is that memory has been weakened in our time, and that the great rememberers are a virtually extinct species: for us, memory, when it is a strong experience and still able to testify to the reality of the past, only serves to annihilate time and that past along with it."[43] Realist descriptive memory becomes a postmodern description of forgetting.

Zola's reversal of the lexical differences that make descriptive memory possible not only fragments representational discourse and makes it unreadable; it renders discourse homogeneous. According to Zola, only a complete description of outer reality, not a search for public esteem, can differentiate one painter's works from another's.[44] But Claude replaces this authentic differentiation with a formal search to appear different: "[S]on originalité de notation, si claire, si vibrante de soleil, tournait à la gageure, à un renversement de toutes les habitudes de l'œil, des chairs violâtres sous des cieux tricolores. La folie semblait au bout" (4: 248). Claude's paintings replace signs of his originality with a mad reversal of convention that creates only an illusion of originality. His original attempt to describe the milieu's differences and to create a different representation thus culminates in a homogeneous repetition of clichés and conventional techniques.

The wasting away of Claude's originality is a product of history's destruction and decentering of the individual within Zola's Second Empire society. The novelist dramatizes this decentering as Claude's gradual absorption into, and destruction by, the social clichés he repeats: "[I]nquiète de le voir si absorbé, saisie d'une sorte de peur religieuse... [Christine] l'entraîna, comme si elle l'avait senti en grand péril" (4: 214).[45] He progressively "s'oubli[e]," first in front of Fagerolles's successful plagiarism of "Plein air" (4: 287), then before his painted nude, which he hopes will make society love him as they love Fagerolles. But his dream of being drawn into the womb of society's love turns out to be an act of individual self-effacement. He eventually commits suicide in front of his unfinished nude: "[I]l crut avoir entendu une voix haute l'appeler du fond de l'atelier... 'Oui, oui, j'y vais!'... Claude s'était pendu à la grande échelle..." (4: 351–52).[46]

History's decentering of the individual within contemporary society's fragmented and homogeneous discourse, along with its destruction of historical signs, produce emotional indifference. The more Claude fanatasizes a passionate Paris that will love him through his paintings, the more he becomes indifferent to the difference between the real and the ideal, birth and death, past and present, originality and conventionality. Claude's fall into indifference is reinforced by society as a whole. The

Parisian community funds only a mass art, like Fagerolles's, whose repetition of clichés gives it a false collective memory of past and present. At the same time, through censure and the refusal to purchase, it condemns to forgetting those naturalist art works that make it remember its present historical situation. By methodically forgetting its own reality and forgetting its own forgetting, Zola's *fin-de-siècle* society replaces naturalist representation of history with the mass production of ahistorical, disposable commodities that are forgotten as soon as they are consumed, since their illusion of realism and originality quickly wears off:

> [Q]uelle publicité! un charivari d'un bout de la France à l'autre, de soudaines renommées qui poussent du soir au matin, et qui éclatent en coups de foudre, au milieu des populations béantes. Sans parler des œuvres, ces pauvres œuvres annoncées par des salves d'artillerie, attendues dans un délire d'impatience, enrageant Paris pendant huit jours, puis tombant à l'éternel oubli! (4: 184)

Historical representation becomes indistinguishable from, and defined by, the production and consumption of words. The journalist, Jory, only seems to criticize Fagerolles when he calls him a "simple gueuse"; he fully profits from the knowledge that subscribers buy his paper because it publishes reviews, like his rave one of Fagerolles's painting, that praise the attributes they prefer, just as the opportunist painter provides the clichés they want to see: "Le fait est, ricana Jory, que Fagerolles ne s'est pas laissé piller comme un niais" (4: 333). Words, like paintings, have the power to flatter the public's tastes and give them an illusory value: "C'est la fin," Sandoz moans, "c'est fatalement le journaliste qui traite les autres de ratés, le bâcleur d'articles tombé dans l'exploitation de la bêtise publique!..." (4: 336) Whether or not written or pictorial discourse represents, whether or not it is naturalist or fictional, becomes only a business decision. In itself, this question is a matter of indifference.

Those who control the means of producing and selling paintings or words, therefore, are pure speculators in representational currency. The cynical art dealer, Naudet, is "un spéculateur, un boursier, qui se moquait radicalement de la bonne peinture." He caters to the "amateur riche" who "ne se connaît pas en art" and "achète un tableau comme une valeur de Bourse..." (4: 186). For the few successful producers, merchants, and speculators in this market economy, representations of the historical present are disposable commodities without an inherent use value. All they have is an exchange value governed by the fleeting whims of the public.

By contrast, those who only buy, the public, confuse the mere exchange value of representational discourse with a fixed use value. They believe that Fagerolles's paintings, not Claude's, faithfully represent the era. They thus become the dupes of Zola's roguish speculators. What they really consume, however, is representations of the system of consumption itself.[47] By buying then forgetting empty naturalist pastiches, like Fagerolles's plagiarism or Jory's reviews, the public consumes metaphors of society's forgetting of its historical situation, metaphors of society's commodification and consumption of reality.

The distinction between an elite that is aware of the commodification of discourse and a mass audience that is not aware is most often associated with modernism.[48] But from the point of view of *L'Oeuvre*'s narrator and of its best artists, discourse in Zola's Second Empire resembles Jameson's postmodern. Not only does it mix discourses in a fragmented, decentered, and ahistorical space; it is out of the control of producers as well as consumers in this monopoly capitalist world. Although producers and speculators fantasize that their deliberate forgetting of historical reality gives them power over the market system as a whole, their will to power is self-destructive and thus self-deceived. Zola's monopoly capitalism is destroying itself in a process which he represents in *La Bête humaine* as a speeding train without an engineer and in *Germinal* as a mine become a voracious monster blindly consuming itself.[49] The will to power of Zola's Second Empire will achieve only a humiliating defeat in the Franco-Prussian war. Monopoly capitalism is thus decentered in a national market space that it cannot comprehend, just as power is decentered in Jameson's incomprehensible world market network.

As *fin-de-siècle* society decenters Zola's privileged means of totalizing its real space – the centrality of naturalist eye and art – it increasingly produces and consumes, not just images of its shattered, decentered, and commodified discursive space, but this space itself. France narcissistically consumes its own resources as Claude's narcissistic last painting consumes his naturalist talents. Without experiencing a modernist sublime, it becomes the "relentless saturation of any remaining voids and empty places" with purely commodified historical signs that Jameson attributes to the ahistorical, postmodern space of the late twentieth century.[50] But, for Zola, this late nineteenth-century consumer society is an enormous tragedy that brings an end to the Second Empire, not the relatively benign pastiche described by Jameson. It is structured by a reversal of all attempts to give it a direction, a transformation of construction into destruction.

If naturalist discourse is caught up in this historically determined act of self-consumption, if it cannot distinguish a description from the prescription of history, then how can it lead to genuine change?[51] Naturalist representation in *L'Oeuvre* is locked into an apparent no-win situation that it in fact creates. It attributes to historical forces consequences that its own mode of constructing history actually produces. The discursive structure of Zola's naturalist discourse is constituted by the repeated replacement of narrative's perfective aspect of irreversibility with the descriptive's imperfective aspect of reversibility.[52] The presupposition in Zola's theories that descriptive documents spontaneously generate narratives implicitly subordinates narrative irreversibility to the temporal reversibility of the descriptive. The construction of history in the *Rougon-Macquart* extends this reversibility from temporal duration to narrative logic. It generates a rhetorically reversible narrative and a rhetorically reversible notion of history.[53] If we call the set of rules that govern fixed narrative or descriptive differences a "grammar," then Zola creates his version of *fin-de-siècle* history by means of a methodical rhetorization of grammar, as well as a spatialization of time.[54]

The imperfective aspect of descriptive discourse is the means by which Zola not only constructs, but deconstructs, the naturalist illusion of a readable historical space. The deconstruction of the seemingly irreversible descriptive and narrative differences with which Zola wishes to construct his Second Empire Paris or Jameson's monopoly capitalism would prefer to construct the market, produces the fiction of a fragmented, reversible, homogeneous, decentered, and collective space. For both authors, the imperfective aspect is not only the future cure, the means by which Zola's descriptions and Jameson's "map" will gain mastery over historical determinism and rehistoricize the ahistorical; it is also the poison, the means by which historical determinism destroys the discursive means of achieving this historicist mastery.[55] It is the source of the *pharmakos* structure which plays such an important role in relating the crowd to the individual in Zola's fictional Second Empire and the mass producer to the consumer in Jameson's fictional world market.[56] The realization that these *fin-de-siècle* and postmodernist historical and collective spaces are products, rather than sources, of descriptive discourse, ironically reveals that their real tragedy or irony is their blind faith in the descriptive.[57]

Irony is indeed Zola's greatest enemy, hence the ironical structure of historical consciousness and naturalist description in *L'Oeuvre*. Irony quickly reverses the assertion it appears to make or the speech act it pretends to perform. In its most extreme form, it reverses all discourse on the real, including that of the speaker.[58] Zola's observers can maintain their belief in the existence of an original, prelapsarian world of objective observation only as long as they resist any extension of history's irony to their own descriptive presuppositions. Irony must thus be projected outwards, away from the author's own words. It becomes an objective reaction to society's, not the observer's, false sense of individual freedom from the collective forces that are determining its self-destruction.[59] Irony is the point of view of historical determinism itself in Zola. Fagerolles's ironical praise of Claude's last painting is one means by which history ironically increases not only Claude's and society's enslavement to the ideal, but the speculator's and journalist's enslavement to their search for market power: "[C]omme si cette ironie d'un habile homme lui fût porté malheur, [Claude] ne fit ensuite que gâter son ébauche" (4: 234).

The critical moment in *L'Oeuvre*, therefore, is the moment when it confronts the possibility that its paranoid condemnation of historical forces ironically states its own descriptive error. By deconstructing its own descriptive presuppositions, it goes beyond the *fin-de-siècle* and postmodernist fictions of an historically determined, ironical space of forgetting, and it reintroduces, albeit negatively, the categories of memory and historicity.

FORGETTING FORGETTING: BEYOND HISTORICISM AND BEYOND THE DESCRIPTIVE

By constructing the course of history as a necessary fall of discourse from early nineteenth-century remembering to Second Empire forgetting of history, *L'Oeuvre* indirectly constitutes the *Rougon-Macquart* and naturalist discourse in general as necessary and ironical repetitions of this fall. But, if Zola's naturalist descriptions ironically repeat the ahistorical space they describe, how can they historicize it? Are they not infected by the same ahistorical blindness they wish to cure? Despite Zola's historicist theories, *L'Oeuvre*'s characters pose critical questions about the contradictions that lie hidden in any historicist narrative of an irreversible fall into descriptive reversibility and ahistoricity. These questions temporalize the novel's fictionally spatialized present by questioning its descriptive presuppositions. They deconstruct the historicist narrative of how such a present came about and reintroduce the question, but only the question, of historicity.[60]

L'Oeuvre questions its spatialization of history in a culminating dialogue, at the moment of Claude's burial, between the successful painter Bongrand and the novelist Sandoz. Sandoz is writing a "série de bouquins" that is virtually identical to Zola's *Rougon-Macquart*. It centers on "une famille" in a "période historique déterminée, ce qui me donnera le milieu et les circonstances, un morceau d'histoire" (4: 162). The two creators meditate upon the consequences for future naturalist discourse of Claude's and his era's tragic fall into forgetting.[61] The question they implicitly ask is whether *L'Oeuvre* is, in the words of Michel Serres, "une œuvre qui ne dit rien que son propre fonctionnement": a modernist or postmodernist work that describes its own readable or unreadable descriptive nature.[62]

Sandoz and Bongrand interpret the relationship between Claude's and society's forgetting. His suicide is an allegory not only of his forgetting contemporary reality, but of his being forgotten by it:

> "Un travailleur héroïque, un observateur passionné dont le crâne s'était bourré de science ... Et il ne laisse rien."
>
> "Absolument rien, pas une toile ... Oui, c'est bien un mort, un mort tout entier que l'on va mettre dans la terre" [4: 356]!
>
> ...
>
> "Nous seuls l'aurons connu ... Plus rien, pas même un nom!" (4: 362)

Claude's tombstone is a memorial to the death of individual memory. The cemetery outside Paris in which it is erected memorializes the space of contemporary society that produces forgetting.[63] In the cemetery of this *fin-de-siècle* world, memory, even of forgetting, is soon consumed, replaced, and forgotten:

> [O]n apercevait de loin un gros tas de choses terreuses qui s'allumaient. Puis, on finit par comprendre. Cela se trouvait au bord d'un vaste carré, qu'on avait fouillé profondément de larges sillons parallèles, pour en arracher les bières, afin de rendre le sol à d'autres corps, de même que le paysan retourne un chaume avant de l'ensemencer de nouveau. (4: 358–59)

Since Paris's cemetery plots are in high demand, they are rented for a few years, after which the bones are removed, burned, and replaced by new bodies, the tombstones by new memorials, and the names by new names. Whereas the cemetery that culminates Balzac's *Le Père Goriot* represents the space society deliberately marginalizes and erases in its narrative struggle for power, Zola's cemetery is a spatialized metaphor for the temporality of history's own hidden and decentered self-erasure.[64] It constitutes history as a repeated alternation between inscribing and effacing the names, the memories, of society's members who, like Claude, forget their historical reality and are in turn forgotten. Zola's cemetery graphically illustrates the *Rougon-Macquart*'s representation of the consumer space of Second Empire France as an obsessive effacement and decentering of individual differences, and a consumption of products of its own forgetting, like Fagerolles's painting: its decadent consumption of signs of its own death.[65]

At first, Sandoz seems to accept Zola's historicist theory of a future cure for this decadence. He distinguishes between the present, in which discourse has the erasability of the cemetery's replaceable tombstones, and the future, in which it will be cured of its historically determined unreadability. The nineteenth century's early thirst for knowledge and memory, Sandoz argues, necessarily produced its own reversal, the *fin-de-siècle*'s desire for ignorance and forgetting: "C'était fatal," songea-t-il à demi-voix, "cet excès d'activité et d'orgueil dans le savoir devait nous rejeter au doute; ce siècle, qui a fait déjà tant de clarté, devait s'achever sous la menace d'un nouveau flot de ténèbres" (4: 359–60). But this forgetting will, in its turn, necessitate its own reversal, history's last reversal. As in Proust's later madeleine scenario, Zola's involuntary forgetting – here produced by historical and social determinism rather than individual neurosis – will be reversed by irreversible, involuntary remembering:[66] "Nous ne sommes pas une fin, mais une transition, un commencement d'autre chose ... nous marchons à la raison et à la solidité de la science ..." (4: 360); "[L]'homme naîtra, rien ne se perd, il faut bien que la lumière soit" (4: 359); "[C]'est la naissance d'une société nouvelle, et c'est nécessairement la poussée d'un nouvel art, dans ce nouveau terrain ..." (4: 162). A truly naturalist discourse, Sandoz fantasizes, will end society's involuntary forgetting. It will transform the apparent dead-end of *fin-de-siècle* society into "cette convulsion dernière du vieil effarement religieux," a transition (4: 360). By describing and remembering the historical cycle of forgetting and remembering, it will destroy this cycle, just as Victor Hugo's poet overcomes nature's forgetting through mental and poetic memory: "Nature au font serein, comme vous oubliez! ... Et là, dans cette nuit qu'aucun rayon n'étoile ... C'est toi qui dors dans l'ombre, ô sacré souvenir!"[67] Similarly, naturalist description for Zola will perform a linear narrative transformation of history from a determined cycle of death to a socially chosen cycle of birth in which "rien ne se perd," nothing is forgotten. Like the death of the seed, the death of Claude's memory will become an organic means of making the transition from death to life, ideal to real, old to new, forgetting to remembering.

Despite Zola's hatred for romantic idealism, the romantic heritage of his descriptive idealism is all too obvious. Sandoz can constitute a readable or mappable future only by means of an historicist tautology: history will produce a description ("l'homme naîtra") that will finally describe the natural course of history, and this description will produce the change in history that makes the descriptive possible:

> Il retomba sur le dos, il élargit les bras dans l'herbe, parut vouloir entrer dans la terre, riant, plaisantant.
>
> "Ah! bonne terre, prends-moi, toi qui est la mère commune, l'unique source de la vie! toi l'éternelle, l'immortelle, où circule l'âme du monde, cette sève épandue jusque dans les pierres, et qui fait des arbres nos grands frères immobiles ... Oui, je veux me perdre en toi ... c'est toi seule qui seras dans mon œuvre comme la force première, le moyen et le but, l'arche immense, où toutes les choses s'animent du souffle de tous les êtres!" (4: 162)

Nature, which nurtures the naturalist artist, is the cause of the descriptive. But, as Claude's story illustrates, nature must be cured, it must be made once again nurturing. It is thus also an effect of the descriptive. The descriptive becomes a perpetual motion machine.[68]

Sandoz seems totally unaware that his future reversal of historical reversibility – his transformation of the *fin-de-siècle* cemetery cycle of death into a post-*fin-de-siècle* cycle of birth – simply repeats Claude's facile "renversement de toutes les habitudes" that the novelist called mad (4: 248). Proust will parody Zola's love of reversal when he gives, as an example of the duchesse de Guermantes's superior social wit (not madness), her reversal of social expectations by exclaiming to her shocked anti-Dreyfusard guests: "Mais Zola n'est pas un réaliste, Madame! c'est un poète"![69]

L'Oeuvre provides considerable support for this historicist reading. It frequently gives its narrator's discourse an *effet de lisibilité* by making a careful distinction between Claude's pictorial blindness and Sandoz's or Zola's descriptive awareness of detail. The narrator distinguishes between Claude – who is impatient, has a jealous wife, and produces an art that fails to achieve public recognition – and Sandoz – who is patient, has a nurturing wife, and produces a naturalist art that, if for the moment incomplete, none the less achieves public recognition. As if he were predicting Sandoz's future completion of a naturalist description, the narrator indirectly describes his own post Second Empire descriptions which, unlike Claude's paintings, theoretically capture the essence of the real's metonymic detail:

> Les yeux vagues, Claude n'entendait pas. Il regardait dans le jardin. De sa place, il voyait le massif central, de grands palmiers qui se détachaient sur les draperies brunes, dont tout le pourtour était orné. Là, s'espaçait un cercle de statues: le dos d'une faunesse, à la croupe enfléé; le joli profil d'une étude de jeune fille, une rondeur de joue, une pointe de petit sein rigide...
>
> Mais Claude ne voyait rien, ce n'étaient que des taches grises dans le jour brouillé et verdi. Sa stupeur continuait, il eut une seule sensation, le grand luxe des toilettes. (4: 299)

By framing the narrator's long list of details of the milieu (which continues for another sixteen lines) within references to Claude's deafness and his looking without seeing, the narrator reinforces the impression that Zola is the future great man who has changed the course of history, the one whose future naturalist discourse has produced, and yet has been produced by, an historical return from Second Empire forgetting to remembering.

Were the *Rougon-Macquart* to be this idealized naturalist discourse, it would eliminate forgetting along with the forbidden sexual, narcissistic, and death drives that bring it about and that Zola attributes to an historical, rather than Freud's individual, unconscious: the desire to kill and be killed, the will to forget and be forgotten.[70] Rather than sublimate these aggressive desires by displacing them onto constructive work, Zola's naturalist discourse would make them visible, memorable, and conscious in order to eliminate them entirely.

Zola's fears provide support for this historicist reading. In Dr. Toulouse's published report of his analysis, he notes that the novelist doggedly tried not to be contaminated by received discourses (as was Claude), out of a real "crainte de se *déformer*."[71] The *Rougon-Macquart* is noteworthy for the absence of explicit literary allusion, as if Zola had learned to wipe his naturalist eyes (eyeglasses?) clean of any conventional spots that might deform his physiological perceptions, spontaneous reactions, or descriptive memories of the historical present.

But the elder Bongrand, whose experience has taught him that "je ne suis pas même mon maître" (4: 134), questions the young novelist's delusions of gaining power over history. Confronted by Claude's and the Second Empire's tragic fate, Sandoz is forced to agree. Together, they reinterpret *L'Oeuvre*, not as an overcoming of forgetting, but as a repetition. Moreover, they ask whether this repetition eliminates or reintroduces historical difference and differentiation into their own descriptive art.

Throughout *L'Oeuvre*, Sandoz increasingly shares Bongrand's fear that the novelist and the painter will inevitably repeat Claude's fate. Their final exchanges interpret his gradual forgetting as an allegory of *L'Oeuvre*'s forgetting of history. Like Hugo, Sandoz concludes that nature effaces, rather than nurtures, signs of the past. But, going a step further, he argues that it also makes the human mind forget: "Si les choses, qui ont l'éternité, oubliaient si vite, est ce qu'on pouvait compter une heure sur la mémoire des hommes?" (4: 320) If this is the case, then future naturalist discourse will forget reality and, like Claude's unpopular and Fagerolles's popular paintings, be forgotten:

Et s'il n'y avait pas plus de paradis pour l'artiste que pour le catholique, si les générations futures se trompaient comme les contemporains, continuaient le malentendu, préféraient aux œuvres fortes les petites bêtises aimables!... Ah! quelle duperie, hein? quelle existence de forçat, cloué au travail, pour une chimère!... L'immortalité ne serait donc qu'à la moyenne bourgeoisie, à ceux qu'on nous entre violemment dans le crâne, quand nous n'avons pas encore la force de nous défendre... (4: 320)

The possibility that his works will forget and be forgotten in the eternal cemetery of bourgeois society transforms writing into a "travail[] enfin sans espoir d'aucune sorte," a purely narcissistic means of making the writer feel he has power over discourse and over its effect on the public: "[L]'on arrive très bien à en mourir, avec l'illusion consolante qu'on sera aimé un jour..." (4: 263).[72] The birth of the novel, like the birth of Claude's paintings and of Mallarmé's poems, becomes an "enfant" which "me semble une horreur" (4: 263).[73] Writing, Sandoz says on the eve of the death of Claude's son, is the infernal repetition of an "idée fixe" (4: 262), an obsessive still birth of dead memories that "recommence; puis, ça recommencera toujours" (4: 264). The truth of naturalist writing is thus the suicide of memory and the will to forget:

"Au moins, en voilà un qui a été logique et brave," continua Sandoz. "Il a avoué son impuissance et il s'est tué."
"C'est vrai," dit Bongrand. "Si nous ne tenions pas si fort à nos peaux, nous ferions tous comme lui... N'est-ce pas?"
"Ma foi, oui. Puisque nous ne pouvons rien créer, puisque nous ne sommes que des reproducteurs débiles, autant vaudrait-il nous casser la tête tout de suite." (4: 363)

The end of the novel dramatizes the historically determined suicide of representational memory in the form of an accelerating train. It thus foreshadows the uncontrollable train of Second Empire society at the end of *La Bête humaine* published four years later (1890). The accelerating train of history destroys the observer's power to make spatial distinctions between individuals sitting in neighboring windows or to make temporal distinctions between those who go by before and those who go by after:

Quand le train roula, avec son fracas de tonnerre, on distingua nettement, comme sur un transparent d'ombres choinoises, les découpures des wagons, jusqu'aux gens assis dans les trous clairs des

fenêtres. Et la ligne redevint nette, un simple trait à l'encre coupant l'horizon; tandis que, sans relâche, au loin, d'autres coups de sifflet appelaient, se lamentaient, aigus de colère, rauques de souffrance, étranglés de détresse. Puis, une corne d'appel résonna, lugubre.
"*Revertitur in terram suam unde erat...*" (4: 361)

History becomes an accelerating process of reversal and effacement, a passage from dust to dust, forgetting to forgetting, that transforms all representational discourse into an unreadable black line, an inexorable effacement of spatial and temporal difference.

If *L'Oeuvre* is indeed describing its own writing and reading, if it is a forgetting, rather than a remembering, of the contemporary historical milieu, then Sandoz's attempts to distinguish between his nurturing wife and Claude's jealous wife, between nurturing nature and destructive nature, or between his naturalist writing and Claude's idealized painting, are only a self-serving means by which he and Zola's narrator make Claude the scapegoat for their descriptive forgetting. Only when Sandoz pessimistically "confesses" (4: 261–62), as in the passages quoted above, would they admit that their descriptions must repeat Claude's effacement of the real.

Were *L'Oeuvre* to culminate in Zola's indirect confession, through Sandoz, of the reversibility of its historical descriptions, then it would be the author's historicist allegory of how history rendered all description, and thus his naturalist project, impossible.[74] It would describe its own act of writing as a necessary deferral of naturalist description. Zola in fact periodically admitted that he could not rid his discourse of romantic rhetoric.[75] He also conceded that his experimental novel had not yet become a reality.[76] If *L'Oeuvre* is indeed Zola's indirect confession that he has lost the battle to forgetting, then it recounts his allegory of the tragic fall of the *Rougon-Macquart*'s discourse, either into narcissistically blaming Claude (Cézanne?) for its own descriptive illusion or into opportunistically selling repeated discourses and mnemonic illusion to *fin-de-siècle* society.[77] His later utopian novels would represent the moment when he, like society, bought this illusion and forgot his necessary forgetting.

But Sandoz's pessimistic historicist allegory of the fall of its descriptions into forgetting and impotence is as self-contradictory as his optimistic historicist allegory of the descriptive's recovery of memory and of the power to change history. By bringing this contradiction to the fore, *L'Oeuvre* questions all of its historicist masks, be they optimistic or pessimistic, comic or tragic. It does so by exploring the consequences of necessary forgetting for its own discourse on, and the author's consciousness of, history. At the very moment that the priest describes life as a transition from dust to dust, from forgetting to forgetting, a second train arrives. Rather than interpret this train, like the last one, as history's reversal of descriptive differences, Sandoz and Bongrand interpret it as history's alternation between perceiving and not perceiving the priest's words on life and death, his discourse on history:[78]

Mais on ne l'entendait plus, une grosse locomotive était arrivée en soufflant, et elle manœuvrait juste au-dessus de la cérémonie... Elle allait, venait, haletait, avec son profil de monstre lourd. Brusquement, elle lâcha sa vapeur, dans une haleine furieuse de tempête.

"*Requiescat in pace*," disait le prêtre.

"*Amen*," répondait l'enfant de chœur.

Et tout fut emporté, au milieu de cette détonation cinglante et assourdissante, qui se prolongeait avec une violence continue de fussillade.

Bongrand, exaspéré, se tournait vers la locomotive. Elle se tut, ce fut un soulagement... Et, là-haut, sur le talus, la locomotive avait repris ses manœuvres, reculait en hurlant, à chaque tour de roue, le foyer ouvert, incendiant le jour morne d'une pluie de braise." (4: 361–62)

Rather than dramatize history as an accelerating effacement of marks of history, this train alternately enables Claude's friends to perceive, then prevents them from perceiving, the words marking memory's death: "Plus rien, pas même un nom!" (4: 362). And, as the train drowns out the priest's words on death, the smoke from the fires blinds them to the flames consuming memory's skeletons: "... mais on ne voyait toujours pas les flammes, la fumée seule avait augmenté." (4: 363).

By erasing signs of society's forgetting, history is putting off the moment when society can abandon its belief in memory:

> [M]aintenant, il lui semblait qu'on allait mettre en terre sa jeunesse; c'était une part de lui-même, la meilleure, celle des illusions et des enthousiasmes, que les fossoyeurs enlevaient, pour la faire glisser au fond du trou. Mais, à cette minute terrible, un accident vint encore augmenter son chagrin. Il avait tellement plu, les jours précédents, et la terre était si molle, qu'un brusque éboulement se produisit. Un des fossoyeurs dut sauter dans la fosse, pour la vider à la pelle, d'un jet lent et rythmique. Cela n'en finissait pas, s'éternisait au milieu de l'impatience du prêtre et de l'intérêt des quatre voisins, qui avaient suivi jusqu'au bout, sans qu'on sût pourquoi. (4: 362)

Rain, which deferred consciousness of Paris's historical tragedy at the beginning of the novel, now defers the moment when the novelist can bury forever his naturalist belief in his youthful illusion of memory. By preventing him from saying, hearing, or seeing memory's death, history is putting off the act of describing naturalist discourse itself, the act of historicizing the present of writing and reading.

In the final pages of *L'Oeuvre*, history, the central character in the *Rougon-Macquart*, questions Sandoz's and Bongrand's post-modernist interpretation of the space of Second Empire life as a cemetery, a reversible passage from forgetting to forgetting. If the cemetery represents the historical present of discursive forgetting, then it too is forgotten by discourse. The concept of an historically determined forgetting produces only an absurd statement: history makes discourse necessarily forget whether or not history makes discourse forget. Rather than "sublimate" or displace the violence of forgetting, *L'Oeuvre*'s meta-discourse on its discourse on forgetting deconstructs the very possibility of saying that complete forgetting takes place at all.[79]

The act of witnessing Claude's fall into forgetting convinces neither Sandoz nor Bongrand that it is an allegory of history. Rather, Claude's example serves a cathartic role. It gets their hysterical fear of forgetting out of their system by making them realize that they cannot show that their fears are justified.

Just as Sandoz fails to constitute future naturalist discourse as a readable descriptive system of signs, one that periodically remembers reality's differences, so he fails to constitute it as an unreadable descriptive system of signs, one that methodically effaces these differences. He thus fails to show that discourse is structured by the imperfective aspect's reversibility or by its spatialization of time, in other words, that it is descriptive. By deconstructing the imperfective and spatial aspects of the descriptive, *L'Oeuvre* reintroduces the perfective aspect of narrative and history in the form of chronological time and the act of working:

> "Fichtre! onze heures!" dit Bongrand en tirant sa montre. "Il faut que je rentre."
>
> Sandoz eut une exclamation de surprise.
>
> "Comment! déjà onze heures!"
>
> Il promena sur les sépultures basses, sur le vaste champ fleuri de perles, si régulier et si froid, un long regard de désespoir, encore aveuglé de larmes. Puis, il ajouta:
>
> "Allons travailler." (4: 363)

Both Bongrand and Sandoz suddenly act as if time had an irreversible direction ("'Comment! déjà onze heures!'"), as if they could complete a description and make an historical difference. The artificial cemetery into which history has transformed Second Empire life turns against its own artificiality and takes on the appearance of nature. The pearls hung on the graves transform the cemetery into the "vaste champ fleuri" of hope.

This final reintroduction of the perfective aspect of change and action is not based on empirical evidence of memory; rather it is based on the impossibility of providing empirical evidence of necessary forgetting. It is not a scientific deduction derived from Claude's and society's present forgetting. Rather it represents the novel's realization that it cannot constitute itself descriptively, either as a readable naturalist description of present historical space – one that performs the act of changing history – or as an unreadable postmodernist description of present discursive space – one that ironically repeats society's pastiches and performs no act at all.

Any attempt to historicize the present as the product of a linear historical fall into incompleteness, reversibility, and spatiality necessarily states its own incompleteness, reversibility, and ahistoricity. The imperfective aspect of the descriptive puts itself into question and reintroduces the perfective aspect of temporal completeness. Zola's repeated effort to constitute the novel as a descriptive genre thus deconstructs the very concept of the descriptive and reintroduces signs of the narrative. This return of the narrative aspect does not mean that discourse is narrative rather than descriptive in nature, nor does it make the novel a narrative genre. Bongrand and Sandoz fully know that their acts may do nothing at all. It simply marks the text's discovery that it cannot constitute itself in the spatialized, ahistorical terms of the imperfective aspect without temporalizing itself, without becoming allegory. And allegory, "the tendency of the language toward narrative," necessarily reintroduces the question of historicity.[80]

L'Oeuvre thus recounts an allegory of discourse's deconstruction of the historicist illusion that discourse can be ironically reduced to the descriptive, and its deconstruction of the modernist illusion that discourse can ironically describe itself. This allegory reinterprets the gap between Claude's seeing of history's signs and his artistic doing. It marks an irreconcilable difference between Zola's theory of descriptive space and his temporalized practice of writing. The mark of this gap between descriptive theory and narrative practice is Sandoz's and Bongrand's seemingly arbitrary return to repeating the perfective aspect of narrative. Their repetition of narrative signs, like Frédéric's stories, signifies the failure of Zola's attempt to constitute history as an ironical reversal or a spatialization of time, in other words, as a market space in which all memory of history is ironically consumed. It allegorically undoes Zola's historicist irony.

Forgetting of the fear of forgetting and the necessary repetition of narrative take Sandoz and Bongrand beyond the *fin-de-siècle* and thus beyond the postmodernist repetition of Zola's historicist illusion.[81] This "beyond" exists only in the gap between their present, erroneously historicized descriptions of history as a necessary forgetting, and their undescribable future narrative acts of writing and painting. Such a "beyond" must take the form of what Kierkegaard calls the "organ for the historical": "It is clear, then, that the organ for the historical

... must have within itself the corresponding something by which in its certitude it continually annuls the incertitude that corresponds to the uncertainty of coming into existence ... This is precisely the nature of belief..."[82]

For Sandoz, the "beyond" of Kierkegaard's belief is only a reassuring habit which masks itself as, without necessarily becoming, a lie. His versions of present dystopia and future utopia are not unlike Frédéric's memories of an idealized Mme Arnoux he knows never existed. Historical discourse in the late nineteenth century is becoming a feigned, but unavoidable, anachronism. Perhaps deliberate anachronism is the only possible stance in a world that can succeed in being neither historical nor ahistorical, modern nor postmodern, and that cannot not pose the question of its historicity.[83] "Cela me calme, cela me fait du bien," Sandoz concludes, "de croire que nous marchons à la raison et à la solidité de la science." (4: 360).

Conclusion

In the realist novels of Balzac, Flaubert, and Zola, the characters' lying and forgetting raise crucial questions about the relationship between consciousness, memory, and discourse in the nineteenth-century novel as a whole, questions that are easily obscured by realist theory and the third-person narrator's omniscience. Balzac's and Zola's narrators often speak as if their discourse passively repeats memories, and as if their memories passively repeat objective perceptions of character types and places. So do their authors. Flaubert's narrator seems to remember, even when his characters forget, their minutest thoughts and perceptions. In the twentieth century, Proust's first-person, limited narrator will explicitly reverse this apparent derivation of the narrator's memory from consciousness and of his discourse from memory: "Les surfaces et les volumes sont en réalité indépendants des noms d'objets que notre mémoire leur impose quand nous les avons reconnus."[1] Rather than a passive imprint of an objective consciousness of the real, memory in Proust, and later in Beckett, will become an active process of producing consciousness, writing it, by repeating conventional discourses. The narrator's consciousness will be derived from memory and memory from discourse.

But this reversal of the apparent derivation of the narrator's discourse from memory and consciousness is already taking place on the level of Balzac's, Flaubert's, and Zola's characters. In their novels, narrators and characters meditate on whether the latters' words produce or efface conscious signs of the real. Proust's first-person narrator thus merely makes explicit the implications of the characters' lying and forgetting for the third-person narrator's discourse. It redefines his use of the *passé simple* tense as a mark of temporal aspect, not of time and memory.[2]

Balzac's and Flaubert's comparison of their characters' discourse to a lie is hardly new. But their use of lying to question the relations among consciousness, memory, and discourse is, at least in the novel, quite new. Over the course of the nineteenth century, memory increasingly becomes what voluntary memory will become for Proust: a mere repetition of conventional discourses that produces a false consciousness of the real.[3] Balzac, the traditional example of naive realism, makes this redefinition possible by giving consciousness a significant role in his early novels. His seemingly detachable descriptive passages representing place, physiognomy, and character are much more than means of deferring the action and constructing a fixed physical or social background, as in the novels of Walter Scott.[4] From German literature, he learned to foreground the implicit temporality of the descriptive, its imperfective aspect, and thus to construct and give temporal duration, not only to background and characters, but to a narrator's or character's consciousness observing them in time. The imperfective aspect of the descriptive makes possible the construction of a dynamic historical reality in which observed objects and observing subjects of consciousness exist together in time.

Although Balzac's observing consciousness does not explicitly reverse the priority of memory over discourse, it does take an important step in that direction by putting this priority into question. Balzac's observer is an objective consciousness, but of a social milieu that is producing a false consciousness of itself, one that is lying about itself. In Chabert's dilapidated appearance, which seems to identify a mad bum, Derville learns to decipher society's act of reducing its Napoleonic past to poverty, impotence, and madness in order to increase its wealth and power. But Balzac's "moteur social," at least theoretically, not only produces Chabert's degraded, and his wife's elegant, appearance, it generates a false consciousness of Restoration society as a whole, as if it were governed by fixed, rational hierarchies that distinguish the Napoleonic past's lies from the Restoration present's truth, poverty from wealth, and status from non-status. It masks (Chabert's) individual truth as lie and (his wife's) social lie as truth. Balzac's narrative teaches his observing characters to decipher society's lies about itself in order to become ironical accomplices in these lies. In this way it constitutes his observing narrator as a lucid consciousness of society's production of a false consciousness. It is a consciousness of a social world of lies. If Balzac's observing narrator attributes his memory and discourse to objective perceptions, therefore, the world of deceit he observes attributes consciousness to memory and discourse. Vautrin's prodigious memory of received discourses is a means of making his victims see the reality he wants them to see in order better to manipulate them.

This Balzacian consciousness of the milieu's lies is more subversive than it might appear. His knaves must repeatedly defend themselves against the ironical possibility that their objective awareness of society's lies is itself a lie, the possibility that they are deceiving themselves about their power over their own lies. Gaudissart and Vautrin must confront situations in which they are deceived by their own presupposition that they have the power to deceive or that they are in a social struggle to deceive. The characters' ironical complicity in deceit is thus subject to an irony of irony that puts their consciousness of lying into question. It indirectly threatens to reverse even the third-person narrator's priority of consciousness and memory over discourse.

Flaubert develops the full subversiveness of Balzac's observing consciousness by replacing the thematics of lying with the thematics of self-deception. The fictional consciousness of Flaubert's characters, as of Proust's narrator, is a product of the mind's self-deceived repetition of remembered discourses. By repeating romantic discourses of the self or Balzacian discourses of deceit, Frédéric deceives himself into believing that he is conscious of the world that these remembered discourses represent. He actively constructs a consciousness of reality that is by its very nature self-deceived. Balzac's observing character's consciousness of real acts of lying thus becomes in Flaubert the mental and discursive processes of writing consciousness. Flaubert's characters lie not only to others, but to themselves.

The resulting interiorization of reality is not a flight from exterior reality into interior fantasy, but a flight from the illusion of consciousness into an acceptance that society constitutes discursively what it calls exterior reality. Flaubert thus redefines consciousness as an effect rather than a cause of memory, and rewrites memory as an effect of discursive repetition.

By redefining consciousness as a product of self-deception, Flaubert appears to replace memory's passive descriptive function with an active narrative function, with the act of producing a self-deceived consciousness of an unknowable present. In a letter to Louis Bouilhet, he argues that "l'avenir nous tourmente et le passé nous retient. Voilà pourquoi le présent nous échappe."[5] Flaubert's dramatization of a self-deceived consciousness that is produced by discursive repetition raises the Nietzschean possibility that any memory of received discourses is an obstacle, rather than an aid as in Balzac, to increasing power. If all consciousness is self-deceived, perhaps power will be increased only by forgetting the discourses that produce this self-deception, and by choosing only those that increase individual power, regardless of their truth or falsity. Flaubert's most powerful liars, M. and Mme Dambreuse, methodically repress the knowledge that might decrease the effectiveness of their lies. They choose to be conscious only of the discourses that increase their power. But even this narrative consciousness of present performance ironically turns out, Frédéric realizes, to be self-deceived, as it was for Balzac's Gaudissart and Vautrin. It becomes a discursive mode of self-deception, of forgetting the real. Without direct access to the real, without any certainty of knowledge or power, individual consciousness is decentered in Flaubert and replaced by discursive repetition.[6]

Flaubert's deconstruction and decentering of individual consciousness does not lead to its replacement by a divine, a historical, or a linguistic unconscious that is producing individual self-deception and forgetting. Rather it culminates in a conscious acceptance of involuntary repetition that prevents characters from consciously knowing whether or not they remember or forget the real. The full transition from Balzac's thematics of lying and consciousness to a thematics of forgetting and unconsciousness takes place only in Zola's *Rougon-Macquart*. This transition does not constitute a progress in understanding discourse, but displaces Balzac's thematics of lying and power from the individual character onto a collective character called "history." *L'Oeuvre*'s thematics of individual and social forgetting seem to demonstrate an increasing nineteenth-century awareness of the unconscious structures of discursive repetition. But they also represent a fall into an historicist self-contradiction that has reappeared in some Neomarxist, postmodernist historicisms: the assertion that discourse can represent the historical forces that are effacing its power to represent history and are rendering it ahistorical.

The increasing belief over the first half of the nineteenth century that words and memory lie about the real, and the growing belief over the latter half that they forget the real are not presented as truths of discourse in the novels we have discussed; rather they are seductive and/or frightening illusions that they repeatedly go beyond. The illusions of discursive lying and forgetting would appear to be produced by a growing nineteenth-century need to represent discourse as an event in time and history, a need it attempted to satisfy by means of discourse's perfective aspect of irreversibility or its imperfective aspect of reversibility. If these novels are indeed representative (and that remains to be shown), then the realist novel tried and failed to constitute time either narratively – as in Balzac's subordination of bourgeois social space to individual acts of temporal change – or descriptively – as in Zola's subordination of historical change to ahistorical reversibility in a chaotic, bourgeois social space. But discourse and the novel are neither temporally irreversible nor temporally reversible, neither narrative nor descriptive, neither a sequence of lies nor a process of forgetting differences. Neither discourse nor the novel can be reduced to representations of time.

These nineteenth-century novels repeat narrative or descriptive illusions, they take on a narrative or descriptive aspect, purely in order to purge themselves of their tendency to constitute discourse temporally. The themes of lying and forgetting are the means by which they foreground their dominant temporal error: the illusory identification of discourse with narrative lying or with descriptive forgetting. These themes are also the means by which the novels disclose their discursive mode of going beyond this error: irony and allegory. Irony and allegory are not authentic rhetorics of temporality; rather they are means by which the text enacts its failure to constitute discourse as a temporal entity.[7]

The theme of lying foregrounds an ironical mode of discourse. Irony, Kierkegaard notes, resembles "dissemblance." But "dissemblance describes more than the objective act by which the disparity between essence and phenomenon is effected ..." It has "an external purpose foreign to dissemblance itself." Irony, by contrast, has a purpose that "is none other than irony itself."[8] Nietzschean ironical lies, those of Balzac's Vautrin or Flaubert's M. Dambreuse, combine lying and irony in an ironical complicity between liars by subordinating the reversibility of irony to the irreversibility of lies whose purpose (external to dissemblance) is power. They constitute discourse as a narrative sequence of acts of transformation in time, each of which has the irreversibility of the perfective aspect. At first glance, irony seems compatible with lying. Liar and accomplice can ironically negate the content of a lie or the conventional speech act it feigns to perform, while still performing a powerful act of transformation on discourse or on others.

Both Vautrin and Frédéric take lying to an extreme by not only making others ironical accomplices in their lying, but trying to seduce them with this complicity. Frédéric tells Mme Dambreuse that he does not expect her to believe either the content of his romantic words (which he has already spoken to Mme Arnoux) or their perlocutionary force as conventional speech acts (which have seduced Rosanette). He openly tells her, in other words, that he is lying to her, and he makes her an accomplice in his lies. He thus implicitly denies that either speaker or listener is deceived by the discursive conventions of meaning or speech action they repeat. Like Vautrin with Lucien, Frédéric creates the illusion that he and his wealthy lover are free from discursive conventions, as if they were among an elite group of individuals who can repeat discourse's conventions ironically, while freely doing what they want with words.

But irony ultimately undercuts the very basis of the Nietzschean ironical lie. It turns against itself, in the form of irony of irony, and negates the lie's claim to perform an irreversible act of transformation. Balzac and Flaubert dramatize this ironical reversal of the Nietzschean ironical lie by recounting a character's failed attempt to deceive and dominate another liar. Frédéric's efforts to subordinate irony to lying only reverse his claim to deceive, as do Vautrin's lies at the end of *Splendeurs et misères des courtisanes*. Rather than confirm that his lies are doing what he thinks they are doing, rather than substantiate his power over words or the power of words, he only helps Mme Dambreuse subordinate him, humiliate him, all the better. Similarly, the apparent victory of her lies over his lies is only pyrrhic, for she ultimately drives him away, thus disproving her power over him. Vautrin's and Frédéric's very attempts to constitute discourse as narrative acts of transformation, as ironical and irreversible Nietzschean lies, thus ironically give themselves the lie. They produce an irony of irony that states their own self-deception.

By rendering linear transformations reversible, irony of irony negates discourse's sequential temporality. Irony, de Man writes, tends towards being an "instantaneous process," towards a purely spatial juxtaposition of a false affirmation with its ironical denial.[9] Frédéric's ironical negation of his Balzacian stories of achieving power, and Vautrin's ironical submission in the name of mastery to the hierarchical space of the social order, render reversible the polarities with which they have tried to make their lives irreversible transformations. Power becomes indistinguishable from impotence, domination from subordination, pride from humility. Vautrin's and Frédéric's attempts to impose onto discourse the irreversibility of narrative's perfective aspect thus ironically make it tend towards the simultaneity and reversibility of the descriptive's imperfective aspect. By reversing all irreversible temporal transformations, irony of irony seems to subordinate time to the space of the enormous memory in which Balzac or Flaubert collect souvenirs of characters or clichés, just as Frédéric and Félicité collect souvenirs in their apartment or room. It spatializes time.

To deny that discourse is sequential is not logically equivalent to affirming that it is simultaneous and spatial. By negating sequentiality, irony only constructs an appearance of simultaneity in the reader's mind. This is why irony must constantly repeat itself, both within and between works. It is a becoming simultaneous, a becoming spatial, of discourse. Although irony of irony repeatedly plagues Balzac's characters, his characters refuse to renounce their hopes of dominating language, even when domination takes the form of subordination. Locked within repetition and reversal, the *Comédie humaine* repeats and ironically undercuts its allegory of a middle-class search for power. It is an irony of allegory which, over the time of its reading, creates the spatialized impression of a gallery of paintings. By contrast, in Flaubert's *L'Education sentimentale*, irony of irony not only creates, it also turns against, the notion that the text is ironical or spatial at all. Frédéric's inability to wield power over words without producing a sign of impotence leads him, unlike Vautrin, to redefine the present space of irony as a degraded repetition of an original past reversal when he and Deslauriers fled from the women in a brothel. This repetition reintroduces the question of change in the form of a fictional fall out of an ideal past. It recounts an allegorical deconstruction of irony.

Flaubert's allegorization of irony thus co-exists with his irony of allegory. In Zola, allegory of irony becomes a central discursive mode. Indeed, in *L'Oeuvre*, forgetting begins to constitute a major threat within discourse to discourse. The *Rougon-Macquart* repeatedly confronts and goes beyond a *fin-de-siècle* fear that historical time is effacing temporal differences and ironically spatializing time. *L'Oeuvre* unfolds this allegory of irony by recounting the thoughts of a character who strongly resembles Zola, the novelist Sandoz. History in this Second Empire is an unconscious destructive process that is rendering the natural differences between parts of the milieu and between its concrete signs of historical change ironically reversible. It is imposing an imperfective aspect of reversibility onto conscious and artistic signs of irreversible historical change. It thus transforms the mind's act of remembering history into an ironical revelation that it is forgetting history. Discourse's act of representing history discloses only its erasure of history. Destroying spatio-temporal differences, Zola's *fin-de-siècle* history is transforming Second Empire discourse into a space, not unlike the space of Freud's unconscious, in which all signs of history seem to be ironically reversible and ahistorical.

Balzac's attempt to constitute discourse as a temporal sequence of irreversible ironical lies ends up by reversing itself ironically. Conversely, Zola's efforts to constitute history as a space in which remembering is reversible generates the irreversible allegory of its deconstruction. If contemporary discourse on history is historically determined to have the imperfective aspect of reversibility, if it must culminate ironically in spatiality and ahistoricity, in a forgetting of history, then it must also have forgotten its own historical forgetting. Any historicist attempt to narrate history as a fall into ironical reversibility is "constitué par la menace ou l'angoisse de ... la disparition de sa disparition."[10]

Allegory arises out of discourse's failure to constitute itself descriptively as a spatial simultaneity of reversible signs, a failure that produces the "spreading out of an" irreversible "imaginary time."[11] It is produced by discourse's remembering that it has forgotten whether or not there was ever anything to forget in the first place. This forgetting of forgetting puts into question any transformation of discourse into a space of ironically reversible signs. It reintroduces the category of memory in the form of a "*repetition* (in the Kierkegaardian sense of the term) of a previous sign with which it can never coincide."[12] Hence Frédéric's final characterization of his life as the repetition of an unreadable, initial visit to a brothel with flowers from his mother's garden. Hence Sandoz's repetition of an original complete act of naturalist representation after he has concluded that he cannot distinguish between the completeness of memory or the incompleteness of forgetting. Since these allegories cannot establish a fixed relation to the past that they repeat, they are not narrative in nature. Rather they are "the tendency," but only the tendency, "of the language toward narrative."[13] They temporalize discursive space.

In the French realist novels that we have discussed, therefore, irony's spatialization of discursive time and allegory's temporalization of discursive space disclose a repeated failure of discourse to become an historical act of change in time or a spatial structure outside time. They mark the novel's going beyond its illusion that it is a narrative act of writing and reading signs in time or a descriptive text in space, the illusion that discourse is authentically temporal or spatial.

Irony and allegory go beyond the narrative aspect of time, and the descriptive aspect of space and time, by redefining them as repetitions of each other. Rastignac's rejection of society's marginal, like Goriot, and his choice of its powerful actors, like Vautrin, transform his descriptive rhetoric into an ironical repetition of an irreversible act of transformation. His words become deceitful acts of upward mobility with the perfective aspect of narrative. But Vautrin's discovery that society ironically reverses the individual's power to perform narrative acts of transformation redefines these acts as repetitions of the descriptive error they sought to overcome.

Frédéric's narrative of how he and Deslauriers, as adolescents, brought prostitutes flowers from his mother's garden, then ran away before they could present their gift, constitutes itself as an ironical repetition of a descriptive illusion: respect towards his (quite unmotherly) mother's love. But his conclusion that this failed act was the best moment in his life redefines the descriptive rhetoric with which he later glorified the quite maternal Mme Arnoux as a repetition of a narrative illusion of exchange in front of a brothel.

L'Oeuvre's central character, History, redefines naturalism's production of irreversible acts of historical change, its narrative aspect, as an ironical repetition of its reversible descriptive rhetoric. But Sandoz's realization that any discourse on History indirectly states its own error redefines the act of naturalist description as the repetition of an original, but fictional, lost narrative transformation: a return to work as if it necessarily brought about change.

By defining the descriptive and narrative aspects as repetitions of each other, irony and allegory break down their difference. They go beyond, or never arrive at, the difference between perfective irreversibility and imperfective reversibility. Discourse goes beyond, or never becomes, descriptive or narrative. Given that Frédéric experiences narrative irreversibility as a symbolic murder of Mme Arnoux ("comme s'il avait vu des corbeaux déchiquetant son cadavre") and Sandoz experiences descriptive reversibility as a suicide ("autant vaudrait-il nous casser la tête tout de suite"), irony's or allegory's negation of one aspect and their repetition of the other take the form of a Freudian sublimation of the death drive.[14] Each character methodically forgets one aspect of time as if it were a figure of his will to die, and repeatedly remembers the other as if it were a figure of his will to live. This sublimation is made possible by the character's allegorical or ironical redefinition of both aspects as repetitions of each other, a repetition that breaks down any distinction between signs of life and death. Whether a character ultimately chooses to remember the descriptive aspect of reversibility, as does Frédéric, or the narrative aspect of irreversibility, as does Sandoz, remembrance takes the form of a repetition, of a habit in Flaubert and Zola, that situates their discourses between temporal and spatial difference.[15]

By breaking down any distinction between the perfective temporal aspect of narrative and the imperfective temporal aspect of the descriptive, irony and allegory put into question whether the nineteenth-century French novels of Balzac, Flaubert, and Zola were about time at all. They situate their narrators' discourses in the interval between their fictions of time and space. Irony constitutes Balzac's narrator's discourse as what Jacques Derrida calls a becoming space of time. The ironical act of becoming spatial can appear to be the authentic temporality of writing and reading only to the extent that it indirectly states that it is ceasing to be temporal. Conversely, allegory constitutes Zola's narrator's discourse as a becoming time of space. This allegorical act of becoming temporal can appear to be the authentic temporality of writing and reading only to the extent that it indirectly defers completion of this act.[16]

What the novels of Proust and Beckett will change is not the centering and decentering of time, of time's aspects, or of its masks, lying and forgetting. Nor will the modes of going beyond them, irony and allegory, disappear. All that will change is the place where irony and allegory appear and disappear. Whether this displacement of irony and allegory from a character's to a first-person narrator's discourse performs a real historical change or merely continues an ongoing discourse on change is another story.

Notes

PREFACE

1 Roland Barthes, "L'Effet de réel," *Communications* 11 (1968): 84–89.

2 Cf. Paul de Man, *Allegories of Reading* (New Haven: Yale University Press, 1979) 204 and Ann Jefferson, *Reading Realism in Stendhal* (Cambridge: Cambridge University Press, 1988) xii.

3 See, for example, Martin Kanes, *Balzac's Comedy of Words* (Princeton: Princeton University Press, 1975).

4 Cf. Richard Terdiman, *Discourse/Counter-Discourse: The Theory and Practice of Symbolic Resistance in Nineteenth-Century France* (Ithaca: Cornell University Press, 1985).

5 This book does not pretend to be an exhaustive treatment of the French realist novel as a whole. Rather, it posits a method of reading realist discourse that could be applied to all realist novels, particularly those concerned with time.

INTRODUCTION

1 Friedrich Nietzsche, "On Truth and Lies in a Nonmoral Sense," *Philosophy and Truth*, trans. Daniel Breazeale (New Jersey: Humanities Press, 1979) 84, 96.

2 Sigmund Freud, *The Standard Edition of the Complete Psychological Works*, trans. James Strachey, vol. 6 (London: Hogarth Press, 1966–74) 134.

3 Umberto Eco, *A Theory of Semiotics* (Bloomington: Indiana University Press, 1976) 7. Eco's emphasis.

4 Eco, *Theory* 7.

5 Jacques Derrida, "Freud et la scène de l'écriture," *L'Ecriture et la différence* (Paris: Seuil, 1967) 339.

6 Marcel Proust, *A la recherche du temps perdu*, Bibliothèque de la Pléiade, vol. 3 (Paris: Gallimard, 1954) 191.

7 Proust, *Recherche* 1: 427.

8 Honoré de Balzac, *La Comédie humaine*, Bibliothèque de la Pléiade, vol. 3 (Paris: Gallimard, 1976–80) 116.
9 Balzac, *Comédie* 1: 15.
10 Balzac, *Comédie* 5: 695.
11 Emile Zola, *Les Rougon-Macquart*, Bibliothèque de la Pléiade, vol. 4 (Paris: Gallimard, 1960–67) 53.
12 Nietzsche, "Truth" 77–97, and "On the Uses and Disadvantages of History for Life," *Untimely Meditations*, trans. R. J. Hollingdale (Cambridge: Cambridge University Press, 1983) 57–123.
13 Nietzsche, "Truth" 88. Nietzsche's emphasis.
14 Nietzsche, "Truth" 88.
15 Nietzsche, "Truth" 84.
16 Nietzsche, "Truth" 89.
17 Nietzsche, "Truth" 89–90. These irreversible speech acts of transformation are not logical semiotic transformations. They are "guided by intuition rather than by concepts." Nietzsche, "Truth" 90.
18 Nietzsche, "Uses" 64.
19 Nietzsche, "Truth" 96. Richard Terdiman constitutes history in a manner quite similar to the way in which Nietzsche constitutes the individual, as necessary, irreversible, and deceitful acts of transformation or production. He too presupposes that discourse is capable of remembering these acts of transformation: "Since the memory crisis of the nineteenth century, cultural objects have carried the enigma of the past and of its determinations as a particularly stressful and mystified content. They bear these problematic meanings in the form of time become palpable, of the labor which determines it become material: as representations of the movement which, in separating the present from the past, produces the present as the past's representation." Richard Terdiman, "Deconstructing Memory: On Representing the Past and Theorizing Culture in France Since the Revolution," *Diacritics*, Winter (1985): 35.

Like Nietzsche, Terdiman recognizes that, in order to constitute discourse as a memory of past action, he must overcome forgetting, the product of "a massive disruption of traditional forms of memory" in the nineteenth century. "Deconstructing" 14. Terdiman overcomes forgetting by projecting it onto the content of "dominant discourses" and by reserving memory for the act of producing dominant discourses: "The discourses of domination, in their effort to stabilize the flux of social life and veil the violence by which such factitious order is established, ceaselessly attempt to erase the *difference* which marks this flow of time. But memory – of events, of institutions, of language itself – preserves precisely such difference." "Deconstructing" 35.

20 Freud, *Works* 21: 69. Repression, Freud argues, is only one of the opponents of psychoanalysis. These also include "isolation" and "undoing." For this reason, Freud later reintroduces the "concept of *defence*, which can cover all these processes that have the same purpose – namely, the protection of the ego against instinctual demands – and for subsuming repression under it as a special case." Freud, *Works* 20: 164. Freud's emphasis.

21 Freud, *Works* 19: 177. Repression for Freud signifies "a universal mental process in so far as it lies at the root of the constitution of the unconscious as a domain separate from the rest of the psyche." J. Laplanche and J.-B. Pontalis, *The Language of Psycho-Analysis*, trans. Donald Nicholson-Smith (New York: Norton, 1973) 390.

22 Freud, *Works* 21: 97.

23 Freud, *Works* 21: 123.

24 Freud, *Works* 21: 123.

25 Freud, *Works* 21: 133.

26 Freud, *Works* 21: 144.

27 Freud, *Works* 21: 135.

28 On the problem of the new in Freud, see Jean Laplanche, *Problématiques III: la sublimation* (Paris: Presses Universitaires de France, 1980) 251.

29 Freud, *Works* 20: 95.

30 Freud, *Works* 12: 150.

31 Derrida, "Freud" 317.

32 Derrida, "Freud" 322. Speaking about Freud's notion of the deferral ("retardement") of "la perception de la scène primitive," Derrida argues: "Cela devrait conduire sinon à la solution, du moins à une nouvelle position du redoutable problème de la temporalisation et de la dite 'intemporalité' de l'inconscient. Ici plus qu'ailleurs l'écart est sensible entre l'intuition et le concept freudiens. L'intemporalité de l'inconscient n'est sans doute déterminée que par opposition à un concept courant du temps, concept traditionnel, concept de la métaphysique, temps de la mécanique ou temps de la conscience. Il faudrait peut-être lire Freud comme Heideggar a lu Kant: comme le *je pense*, l'inconscient n'est sans doute intemporel qu'au regard d'un certain concept vulgaire du temps." Derrida, "Freud" 317–18. Derrida's emphasis.

On reversibility in Freud, see Laplanche, *Problématiques* 400: "Anna Freud classes reversal into the opposite and turning round upon the self among the mechanisms of defence and asks whether we ought not to view them as the most primitive of defensive processes... Certain passages in Freud tend to support this position."

33 Freud, *Works* 19: 231.

34 Freud, *Works* 14: 193.

35 Derrida, "Freud" 339.

36 See Paul de Man's essays on Nietzsche in *Allegories* 79–131. Freud constructs a very different story of civilization in other texts, one in which consciousness masters an unconscious that only periodically threatens it. According to this story, the unconscious "would ... be dethroned and overlaid by human reason, when that faculty came to be acquired, but ... in some people, perhaps in every one, [it] would retain the power of drawing down to it the higher mental processes." Freud 17: 120. See Jean Laplanche's comments on the ambivalent relationship between Freud's theories of sublimation and culture, which Laplanche interprets as both "renoncement au ça" and "appropriation du ça." *Problématiques* 194–95, 251.

37 Bernard Comrie, *Aspect: An Introduction to the Study of Verbal Aspect and Related Problems* (Cambridge: Cambridge University Press, 1976) 3.

38 Comrie 18; A. J. Greimas, *Sémiotique, dictionnaire raisonné de la théorie du langage*, vol. 2 (Paris: Hachette, 1986) 24.

39 Greimas, *Sémiotique* 21. "[L]'opposition imperfectivité/perfectivité ... relève ... de la catégorie cadentielle, dans la mesure où l'imperfectif s'identifie avec le réversible, et le perfectif avec l'irréversible."

40 Greimas, *Sémiotique* 21–22.

41 A. J. Greimas, *Semiotics and Language* (Bloomington: Indiana University Press, 1982) 350. For the relationship between the perfective aspect and narrative, see Claude Zilberberg's discussion of aspectualization in *Sémiotique*: "La *saillance* [prenant en charge les sèmes 'inchoativité' et 'terminativité'] renvoie à l'opération de *démarcation* dont les aboutissants sont les *limites* ... L'aspectualisation narrative, et par suite également discursive – familière au point qu'elle s'identifie au sens même – est *générale*, mais non *universelle*. Rien n'empêche d'imaginer une organisation du contenu qui ne problématiserait que la *saillance*, l'immédiation. Le récit, qui privilégie transformations et médiations, n'est qu'un possible." Greimas, *Sémiotique* 24.

Greimas repeatedly denies that he is identifying the narrative transformations he studies with discourse as a whole, but then ignores his own qualification: "If we conceive of narrative discourse – and perhaps discourse in general – as 'something that happens,' i.e., as a trajectory leading from an initial state to a final state, then a *transformation algorithm* should be able to account for this trajectory: discourse then appears as a string of transformations." Greimas, *Semiotics* 350.

42 For a critique of Greimas's presupposition that transformations are logical, see Paul Ricoeur, *Temps et Récit*, vol. 2 (Paris: Seuil, 1983–85) 89. Also see Søren Kierkegaard's critique of Hegel's presupposition that the category of transition is logical. *The Concept of Anxiety*, trans. Reidar Thomte (Princeton: Princeton University Press, 1980) 81–85.

43 Comrie, *Aspect* 24.

44 A. J. Greimas, *Du Sens* II, vol. 2 (Paris: Seuil, 1970–83) 144–45. The third chapter of this book will demonstrate that descriptive passages can be marked off by tenses other than the *passé simple* tense. These signify either a perfective aspect of completion or a perfect aspect of being completed.

45 See Harald Weinrich for a discussion of the French imperfect tense as a means of constructing background. *Le Temps*, trans. Michèle Lacoste (Paris: Seuil, 1973) 107–17. Weinrich's interpretation of the imperfect tense denies any significance to aspect. He spatializes the tense in the same way that tradition has spatialized descriptive discourse in general.

See also Richard Terdiman's distinction between active and synthetic narration, which he links to the distinction between the preterit and imperfect tenses in *The Dialectics of Isolation* (New Haven: Yale University Press, 1976) 71. Terdiman treats what he calls "active narration" as referential, as representing a real world of action, and what he calls "synthetic narration" as non-referential, as representing a fictional mental world.

46 See, for example, Gérard Genette, "Frontières du récit," *Figures* II (Paris: Seuil, 1969) 57. Genette imagines that a "texte[] purement descriptif[]" (of which he knows no example) would try to "représenter des objets dans leur seule existence spatiale, en dehors de tout événement et même toute dimension temporelle."

47 Greimas, *Sémiotique* 66.

48 Philippe Hamon, *Introduction à l'analyse du descriptif*, (Paris: Hachette, 1981) 42.

49 Philippe Hamon, *Le Personnel du roman: le système des personnages dans les* Rougon-Macquart *d'Emile Zola* (Geneva: Droz, 1983) 23.

50 Hamon, *Introduction* 48.

51 The descriptive's imperfective aspect thus presupposes, by negating it, the narrative's perfective aspect. The concept of permanence that it makes possible presupposes the concept of (deferred) change. Conversely, the concept of change presupposes the concept of (ended) permanence. Consequently, the descriptive cannot

have the "relative indépendance par rapport à toute 'syntaxe'" that Hamon posits and that allows him to imagine a purely descriptive text *Introduction* 45. The descriptive negation of completion is presupposed by, it is the deep structure of, the copulative, the surface syntax of the descriptive. It masks itself as a purely lexical discourse.

52 Hamon, *Personnel* 235.

53 Hamon, *Introduction* 254.

54 See Jean Ricardou on the "vertige de la description infinie" in the new novel, *Le Nouveau roman*, (Paris: Seuil, 1973) 125.

55 See Ricoeur's *Temps et récit*, in particular volume three, for a distinction between modes of representing time that has strong resemblances to the aspectual distinction made here. Whereas I derive the subject/object relation from the imperfective aspect, and chronological relationships from the perfective aspect, Ricoeur derives discourses on time from what he calls real subject/object and real chronological relations. He locates a non-chronological discourse on time in Augustine and Husserl, and states that its subject/object distinction arises out of the mind's real subjective perception of its own inner temporality. To this he opposes a chronological discourse on time in Aristotle and Kant which arises out of science's objective perception of outer time. Rather than distinguish between a narrative and descriptive mode of constituting time, Ricoeur calls both of his perceived times "narrative." He thus subordinates temporal simultaneity to temporal sequentiality. Although he does raise the possibility of a non-narrative, non-sequential discourse on time, *Temps* 3: 391, he puts off any discussion of what it might be or what relation it might have to his subjective, non-chronological, narrative time. He does not question the centrality of the category of time for discourse.

56 Paul de Man, "The Rhetoric of Temporality," in *Interpretations*, ed. Charles Singleton (Baltimore: Johns Hopkins University Press, 1970) 191–209.

57 "Rhetoric" 204.

58 *Allegories* 9–10.

59 *Allegories* 115.

60 "Irony is ... the undoing of the deconstructive allegory of all tropological cognitions." *Allegories* 301.

61 "Rhetoric" 203–24.

62 "Rhetoric" 206, 190.

63 "Rhetoric" 180, 182. De Man's examples of the symbolic are primarily derived from descriptive passages in Rousseau and Proust.

64 "Rhetoric" 191.

65 "Rhetoric" 205. For a discussion of forgetting in de Man, see Timothy Bahti, "Lessons of Remembering and Forgetting," *Reading de Man Reading*, eds. Lindsay Waters and Wlad Godzich (Minneapolis: University of Minnesota Press, 1989) 244–58.

66 "Rhetoric" 206.

67 "Rhetoric" 204. See Ann Jefferson's discussion of the roles of mimesis and irony in Stendhal, *Reading* 40–41.

1 BALZAC: THE POWER OF LYING AND THE IRONY OF POWER

1 Quoted by Kanes, *Comedy* 89. All references to the *Comédie humaine* in this chapter will be followed, in parentheses, by the title (when necessary), the volume, and the page numbers from the Pléiade edition.

2 See in particular, Georg Lukács, *Studies in European Realism* (New York: Grosset and Dunlap, 1964) 47–64; Shoshana Felman, "Honoré de Balzac: Madness, Ideology, and the Economy of Discourse," *Writing and Madness* (Ithaca: Cornell University Press, 1978) 101–15; and Kanes.

3 Kanes, *Comédie* 89.

4 See Kanes, *Comedy* 167–88 and Terdiman, *Discourse* 85–116.

5 On Balzac's contextual use of detail and its relation to Walter Scott, also see Maurice Bardèche, *Balzac romancier* (Paris: Plon, 1940) 34.

6 See Kanes, *Comedy* 122 on theoretical statements by Balzac that come close to demanding a contextual reading of all discourse.

7 See Michael Riffaterre, "Contraintes de lecture: l'humour balzacien," *L'Esprit créateur* 24:2 (1984): 22.

8 Quintilian, *Institutes of Oratory*, trans. John Selby Watson, vol. 2 (London: George Bell and Sons, 1888) 138. Also, see Rainer Warning's excellent discussion of irony, "Reading Irony in Flaubert," *Style* 19.3 (1985): 304–16.

9 Cf. Patrick Imbert, "Double texte et autoparodie dans *La Comédie humaine*," *Nineteenth-Century French Studies* 15.4 (1987): 371–75.

10 See Warning 306 and Søren Kierkegaard, *The Concept of Irony*, trans. Lee M. Capel (Bloomington: Indiana University Press, 1965) 341, for discussions of the pragmatic nature of ironic discourse.

11 Kanes, *Comedy* 89. This lie is inherent in, "intended by," language. It need not be intended by a speaker nor does it necessarily deceive a listener. Speaker and listener do retain the possibility of being ironical accomplices in language's lie.

12 Kanes, *Comedy* 205.

13 On the relationship between lying and irony see Harald Weinrich, *Linguistik der lüge*, 5th edn. (Heidelberg: Lambert-Schneider, 1966) and Kierkegaard, *Irony* 272–73: "[W]hereas dissemblance describes more the objective act by which the disparity between essence and phenomenon is effected, irony is also descriptive of a subjective satisfaction, for it is by means of irony that the subject emancipates himself from the constraint imposed upon him by the continuity of life, whence it may be said of the ironist that he 'cuts loose.' To this must be added that dissemblance, insofar as one wishes to relate it to the subject, has a purpose, an external purpose foreign to dissemblance itself. Irony, on the other hand, has no purpose, its purpose is immanent in itself, a metaphysical purpose. The purpose is none other than irony itself. When an ironist exhibits himself as other than he actually is, it might seem that his purpose were to induce others to believe this. His actual purpose, however, is merely to feel free, and this he is through irony."

14 Warning, *Irony* 306. Lying does not exclude, any more than it necessarily includes, the presence of an accomplice.

15 "Sans ses observations curieuses et l'adresse avec laquelle il sut se produire dans les salons de Paris, ce récit n'eût pas été coloré de[] tons vrais." (3: 56). See Sandy Petrey, *Realism and Revolution: Balzac, Stendhal, Zola and the Performances of History* (Ithaca: Cornell University Press, 1988) 83.

16 Hamon, *Introduction* 92–139.

17 Hamon, *Introduction* 140.

18 Roman Jakobson was the first to emphasize the importance of metonymy for the realist novel and, by implication, for the descriptive. See "Two Aspects of Language and Two Types of Aphasic Disturbances," *Selected Writings*, vol. 2 (The Hague: Mouton, 1971) 257–58.

19 "[L]a narration s'attache à des actions ou des événements considérés comme purs procès, et par là même elle met l'accent sur l'aspect temporel et dramatique du récit; la description au contraire, parce qu'elle s'attarde sur des objets et des êtres considérés dans leur simultanéité, et qu'elle envisage les procès eux-mêmes comme des spectacles, semble suspendre le cours du temps et contribue à étaler le récit dans l'espace." Genette, "Frontières du Récit," *Figures II* 59. Genette, unlike Hamon but like Lessing, considers written discourse to be fundamentally narrative, sequential, in nature. Gotthold Lessing, *Laocoön*, trans. Edward Allen McCormick (New York: Bobbs-Merrill, 1962) 78. The descriptive for Genette is thus a sub-category of the narrative

which can only create the illusion of the simultaneous and the spatial. *Figures II* 60. Unlike Lessing, however, he does not consider the descriptive to be an inferior mode of discourse that is appropriate only to painting. In an essay accompanying "Frontières du récit," however, "La Littérature et l'espace," *Figures II* 43–48, he, like Hamon, describes a spatiality of language, but he does not link this spatiality to a spatial mode of representing things. I wish to argue that the descriptive is language's mode of representing itself as if it were spatial, and that the descriptive and narrative are different means by which language represents itself as if it were temporal.

20 Hamon, *Personnel* 32.

21 Roland Barthes, *S/Z* (Paris: Seuil, 1970) 61.

22 See Hamon, *Introduction* 105: [L]a déclinaison d'un système descriptif sollicite davantage une reconnaissance de la part du lecteur qu'une compréhension ... [U]n système descriptif fait appel à un déjà-connu lexical plutôt qu'il ne construit un objet formel jamais-vu." Balzac's descriptive irony is just as much an active construction as a recognition. Hamon's important reminder that writing and reading involve the remembering of conventional lexical paradigms underestimates, in my opinion, the active component of discourse. See the second section of this chapter.

23 Hamon, *Introduction* 116, 215.

24 "[T]he art belonged to [ancient] rhetoric as a technique by which the orator could improve his memory, which would enable him to deliver long speeches from memory with unfailing accuracy ... The first step was to imprint on the memory a series of *loci* or places. The commonest, though not the only, type of mnemonic place system used was the architectural type ... The images by which the speech is to be remembered ... are then placed in imagination on places which have been memorised in the building." Frances Yates, *The Art of Memory* (Chicago: University of Chicago Press, 1966) 2–3. Also see Mary Carruthers, *The Book of Memory: A Study of Memory in Medieval Culture* (Cambridge: Cambridge University Press, 1990) 46, 71–75 and Hamon, *Introduction* 45.

25 Raymonde Debray-Genette, "La Pierre descriptive," *Revue de Théorie et d'Analyse Littéraires* 11:43 (1980): 293–304.

26 Auerbach, Erich, *Mimesis*, trans. Willard R. Trask. (Princeton: Princeton University Press, 1953) 473.

27 See Ann Banfield for a suggestive study of the relationship between the French imperfect tense and the construction of a character's consciousness, *Unspeakable Sentences: Narration and Representation in the Language of Fiction* (Boston: Routledge and Kegan Paul, 1982) 104. Banfield's presupposition – that only the imperfect tense and

not the *passé simple* tense can represent the NOW of consciousness – prevents her from paying attention to the temporal implications of the imperfect tense. For an early demonstration that the *passé simple* also serves to construct consciousness, if with a perfective aspect, see Marcel Proust, "A Propos du 'style' de Flaubert," *Contre Sainte-Beuve*, Bibliothèque de la Pléiade (Paris: Gallimard, 1971) 588–89. By restricting consciousness not only to the imperfect tense, but also to an atemporal instant, the "NOW," Banfield effectively excludes the question of the imperfective temporal aspect of the imperfect tense.

Banfield's disregard for the aspectual connotations of the imperfect tense arises out of the tendency of some linguists to reduce verb tense to a purely grammatical, rather than semiotic, category. It is reinforced by French grammar in particular, whose tense system tends to replace the aspectual distinction between different qualities of temporal duration with the spatial distinction between the outside (perfect tenses) and the inside (imperfect tense) of an event. See Roch Valin, "The Aspects of the French Verb," appendix to *Time, Aspect and the Verb* by W. H. Hirtle (Québec: Laval University Press, 1975) 136, 138. Whereas French grammar de-emphasizes the temporal distinction between imperfective and perfective duration, French nineteenth-century literature often re-emphasized it. It countered the spatial implications of the grammatical distinction between imperfect and perfect tenses by means of semantic references to time. It is a particularly valuable corpus on which to study the semiotic, rather than grammatical, function of aspect. This study has been receiving increasing attention from Greimassian semiotics.

28 Gérard Genette, "Discours du récit," *Figures III* (Paris: Seuil, 1972) 134.

29 Debray-Genette, "Pierre" 294–301.

30 Naomi Schor, *Reading in Detail: Aesthetics and the Feminine* (New York: Methuen, 1987) 142. Lessing, *Laocoön* 85–90.

31 Comrie defines the imperfective as "explicit reference to the internal temporal structure of a situation, viewing a situation from within." Comrie, *Aspect* 24. Also see Banfield's discussion of Kate Hamburger's theory that the novel makes PAST and NOW coincide such that the aorist does not signify a past at all. See also her comments on how the imperfect tense encourages this coincidence. Banfield, *Unspeakable* 154–57.

32 See Ricoeur, *Temps* 3: 37–144 for a discussion of philosophical commentaries on the subject in time, in particular St. Augustine, Husserl, Kant, and Heidegger. Ricoeur's presupposition that there *exists* a unique, subjective time sidesteps the question of how

language constitutes the fiction of a subject. See Banfield, *Unspeakable* 183–223 for a discussion of how the imperfect tense serves to represent a past SELF. Banfield argues that this SELF exists independently of the narrator's present discourse, thus avoiding the question of whether or not only the imperfect tense in particular but the imperfective aspect in general serve to constitute the fiction of an independent conscious subject outside time and language.

33 In his notes, the editor of the Pléiade edition identifies this as an allusion to "l'hôpital des Capucins ou des *Vénériens*, faubourg Saint-Jacques." Balzac, *Comedy* 3: 1224.

34 Not only does Balzac claim to be describing objects metonymically juxtaposed in space – a statue and a nearby hospital – his ironical grammar is based on a series of metonymic transfers of the antecedent of the relative clause ("qu'on guérit à quelques pas de là") from the body (venereal disease) to feeling ("amour") to discourse ("mythe").

35 J. W. Goethe, *Selected Verse*, (Middlesex: Penguin, 1964) 195–96.

36 See Michel Foucault, *Les Mots et les choses: une archéologie des sciences humaines* (Paris: Gallimard, 1966) 232, 264.

37 See Kanes, *Comedy* 195 for an excellent discussion of Balzac's attempt to describe the indescribable. Kanes does not associate the indescribable nature of identity with the temporal aspect of Balzacian description.

38 See also the description of the police spy, Cotenson: "Sur le costume, un observateur se fût dit: 'Voilà un homme infâme, il boit, il joue, il a des vices, mais il ne se soûle pas, mais il ne triche pas, ce n'est ni un voleur, ni un assassin.' Et Contenson était vraiment indéfinissable jusqu'à ce que le mot espion se fût venu dans la pensée," cited by Kanes, *Comedy* 169. Although powerful actors like Cotenson, unlike victims in the mould of Goriot, are agents of history, they none the less manifest their agency only by hiding it.

39 See Bardèche, *Balzac* 313 for an early critical intuition of this metonymic structure and its development in Balzac's early descriptions.

40 J. C. Lavater, *Essays of Physiognomy: for the Promotion of the Knowledge and the Love of Mankind*, trans. Thomas Holcroft, 3 vols. (London: C. G. T. and J. Robinson, 1789).

41 Unlike the description of the area around the Maison Vauquer in the later *Le Père Goriot*, this early description does not use active verbs to dramatize the process of temporal differentiation, nor does it explicitly represent the ongoing duration of this process with imperfect or present historical tenses. The imperfect tenses –

"était," "décrivait," "projetaient," "faisait ressortir," and "s'accordait" – explicitly construct the ongoing duration of Derville's act of observing Chabert, not of the process transforming the colonel. The imperfect tenses none the less imply the imperfective aspect of the object being "objectively" described during the time of observation. Balzac's narrator tells the reader that his description has an imperfective aspect by situating Derville in the middle of the duration of the process transforming the colonel. The imperfective aspect creates a fictional point of view in the middle rather than at the end of this transformation.

42 Hamon, *Introduction* 110.

43 As in Scott, Stendhal, and Hugo, the date, 1819, situates the NOW of Chabert's appearance at a particular historical moment. Balzac's description brings this historical NOW alive by giving it a dynamic aspect of ongoing change that is molding society as a whole.

44 See Paul Johnson, *The Birth of the Modern: World Society* 1815–1830 (New York: Harper Collins, 1991) 138–40.

45 See Jean Baudrillard, *For a Critique of the Political Economy of the Sign*, trans. Charles Levin (St. Louis: Telos, 1981) and Petrey's discussion of the demise of the proper name as a guarantee of the Restoration's political and social order and of the role of money as a guarantor of identity, *Realism* 91, 97–98.

46 Although Balzac dramatized the opportunism of all societies, he felt that Restoration society had been insufficiently opportunistic, and that it brought about its own downfall. See Pierre Barbéris, *Mythes Balzaciens* (Paris: Armand Colin, 1972) 18.

47 Only when Vautrin's wig is pulled off do others see the physical marks of his fated rise to power: "Chacun comprit tout Vautrin, son passé, son présent, son avenir." Balzac, *Comédie* 3: 218.

48 Cf. Sandy Petrey, "The Reality of Representation: Between Marx and Balzac," *Critical Inquiry* 14 (1988): 452–53.

49 Frank Kermode, *The Sense of an Ending, Studies in the Theory of Fiction*, (London: Oxford University Press, 1966). See Kermode's discussion of how the imminent ending of the Christian Apocalypse became, in Elizabethan tragedy, the immanent ending or crisis, what Paul Ricoeur calls a "transition sans fin." *Temps* 2: 41. Balzac dramatizes a similar crisis in the Restoration's acceleration and deferral of the aristocratic apocalypse. The aristocracy put off its replacement by the bourgeoisie only by provoking it politically, and by implicitly adopting its market values.

50 Martin Heidegger, *Being and Time*, trans. John Macquarrie and Edward Robinson (New York: Harper and Row, 1962) 474, 480, 483–84.

51 Ricoeur, *Temps* 3: 289. Ricoeur's emphasis.

52 See G. W. F. Hegel, *The Phenomenology of Mind*, trans. J. B. Baillie (New York: Harper and Row, 1967) 641, 644, for the relationship between the dissembling and revealing of knowledge. According to Kierkegaard, Hegel characterizes irony as an "infinite absolute negativity," but condemns it as "an abomination in his sight." *Irony* 271, 282.

53 Ricoeur, *Temps* 3: 288.

54 See de Man, "Rhetoric" 206–07 for a discussion of how irony renders the sequential simultaneous.

55 Stendhal, *Romans et nouvelles*, Bibliothèque de la Pléiade, vol. 1 (Paris: Gallimard, 1952) 220.

56 See Ann Jefferson's suggestive analysis of irony, ignorance, and passionate action in *Stendhal* 231–32.

57 Jefferson, *Stendhal* 118–33.

58 Hamon in *Introduction* argues that the realist novel is fundamentally descriptive in nature. Much, but not all, of Kanes's analysis also treats Balzac's novels in descriptive terms.

59 Paul Ricoeur makes a similar critique of the "caractère mixte" of Greimas's narrative model, which claims to ground irreversible narrative transformations with a perfective aspect in a descriptive origin, the semiotic square, whose spatial relationships are by definition temporally reversible and have an imperfective aspect. See *Temps* 2: 89–91 and Petrey, *Realism* 84–86.

60 Kanes shows that Balzac was skeptical about the reader's attaining the fleeting knowledge expressed in his descriptions, but he does not go beyond locating this absence within descriptive structures.

61 The descriptive thus implicitly puts into question its Hegelian mode of deriving time from space, and invites a derivation of space from time. As Heidegger discusses, Hegel derives time from space by interpreting time as the truth of space. Heidegger, *Being* 486. Space is the "indifferent subsistence of [the] differences" between its multiple points. Heidegger *Being* 482. Time is the process of thinking the being of space by negating the negations that constitute these points. It is a process of differentiating spatial differences from themselves which also transforms them. Heidegger, *Being* 482. But if the transformation of a spatial difference into a temporal difference negates, rather than affirms, the logic of the spatial, then it puts into question any logical link between them. It radically differentiates temporal from spatial differences. This gap between spatial and temporal differences, this radical differentiation, comes to the fore in Kierkegaard's critique of Hegel's concept of transition in *Anxiety* 81. It leads, in some of Hegel's critics, to a redefinition of time in terms of a narrative, rather than

a descriptive, logic of irreversible acts of transformation, a logic that Marx characterizes as historically necessary, and Nietzsche as arbitrary.

62 *Falthurne*, quoted in Kanes, *Comedy* 125.

63 Petrey, *Realism* 97.

64 J. L. Austin, *How to Do Things With Words*, 2nd edn. (Cambridge: Harvard University Press, 1975) 101.

65 Although Balzac treats her persecution ironically ("Voici sur quels faits la veuve Vauquer appuyait ses calomnies," Balzac, *Comédie* 3: 70), he mocks only her pettiness, not her use of words as speech acts. See Petrey, *Realism* 88 for a discussion of the devalorisation of paternal (and paternalistically political) authority in the derogatory use of "père."

66 Petrie, *Realism* 106.

67 See Terdiman *Discourse.* Whereas Terdiman argues that counter-discourses of individual power in the nineteenth century could not free themselves from historically determined dominant discourses, which masked themselves as discourses of knowledge, I argue that historically determined *and* individually chosen discourses of knowledge *and* power are both self-deceived.

68 See Jefferson, *Stendhal* 18–19.

69 Pierre Barbéris, "Dialectique du Prince et du Marchand," *Balzac: l'invention du roman*, Colloque de Cérisy (Paris: Belfond, 1982) 189.

70 Schor, *Reading* 144–47. Schor subordinates the narrative aspect of Balzac's "demonic figures" like Troubert to the descriptive aspect that hides and reveals their "sublime" power.

71 Speech action is being understood here in semiotic terms. "Une théorie conceptuelle de l'action ne se fonde pas sur la multiplicité discursive ou praxéologique des actions verbales, somatiques, techniques ou autres. Bien au contraire, ayant pour objet ce que J. Piaget appelle 'la coordination générale des actions,' elle relève du niveau sémio-narratif, c'est-à-dire des structures sémio-narratives profondes et de surface dans le parcours génératif. Ainsi seulement, une théorie conceptuelle de l'action peut déterminer la multiplicité des *formes* de l'agir, antérieures à leurs concrétisations dans l'univers spatio-temporel ... Le modèle de référence en vue de la construction de la forme ou de la coordination générale de l'action est le programme narratif entendu comme modèle de changement d'état. Le programme narratif, articulant une transformation hiérarchique entre un état initial et un état final, possède une dynamique intrinsèque" Greimas, *Sémiotique* 9–10. Greimas's emphasis.

72 Petrie, *Realism* 107. In his role as lawyer, Derville, like Vautrin, necessarily treats words as acts of transformation: "Monsieur,

reprit l'avoué, pendant le jour je ne suis pas trop avare de mon temps; mais au milieu de la nuit les minutes me sont précieuses. Ainsi, soyez bref et concis. Allez au fait sans digression" ("Chabert" 3: 323). But, when he begins to believe Chabert and feel pity for him, he subordinates his lawyer's discourse of power to the describer's discourse of knowledge.

73 D. A. Miller, "Balzac's Illusions Lost and Found," *Yale French Studies* 67 (1984): 179.

74 Petrey, *Realism* 107–08. Cf. Jean-François Lyotard, *Le Différend* (Paris: Minuit, 1983) 171.

75 The resemblances of Vautrin's historical theory to Nietzsche's construction of history are remarkable: "[K]nowledge of the past has at all times been desired only in the service of the future and the present and not for the weakening of the present or for depriving a vigorous future of its roots." "Uses" 77. Not only does Nietzsche subordinate knowledge of the past to present action, he subordinates any future goal to the present of acting by deconstructing the principle of causality: "The feeling that *post hoc* is *propter hoc* can easily be shown to be a misunderstanding." Friedrich Nietzsche, *The Will to Power*, trans. Walter Kaufmann and R. J. Hollingdale (New York: Vintage, 1967) 293. Nietzsche's emphasis. All that remains is a present of acting. This present of acting, in which knowledge is self-negating, must be carefully distinguished from the present of Spirit's becoming in Hegel, where action is a self-negating means to the end of disclosing absolute knowledge. Hegel, *Phenomenology* 111–14. Nietzsche recognized Balzac as a precursor: "What is *noble*? ... – Avoidance of petty honors and mistrust of all who praise readily: for whoever praises believes he understands what he praises: but to understand – Balzac, that typical man of ambition, has revealed it – *comprendre c'est égaler*," *Will* 496. Nietzsche's emphasis.

76 "[Nietzsche's] conception of historical representation has its own conceptual underpinnings; it presupposes a lexicon, a grammar, a syntax, and a semantic system by which the historical field can be provided with a number of possible meanings," Hayden White, *Metahistory: The Historical Imagination in Nineteenth-Century Europe* (Baltimore: Johns Hopkins University Press, 1973) 371.

77 "That immense framework and planking of concepts to which the needy man clings his whole life long in order to preserve himself is nothing but a scaffolding and toy for the most audacious feats of the liberated intellect. And when it smashes this framework to pieces, throws it into confusion, and puts it back together in an ironic fashion, pairing the most alien things and separating the closest, it is demonstrating that it has no need of these makeshifts

of indigence and that it will now be guided by intuitions rather than concepts." Nietzsche, "Truth" 79–97. In Nietzsche's later writing, this ironic reconstruction of concepts will be motivated less by the creative transformation of old into new metaphors, and more by the pure will to produce the feeling of power. See my essay, "Lying, Irony, and Deconstruction: Nietzsche and Proust," *Style*, 22.3 (1988): 467–78.

78 "Art. Necessary lies and voluntary lies." Nietzsche, "Truth" 96.

79 "'Changes' are only appearances (or sense processes for us)." Nietzsche, *Will* 293. Although both Vautrin's and Greimas's theories of speech acts describe transformations, Greimas, like Nietzsche, redefines perlocutionary, social effects in terms of the discursive transformations that may or may not produce them. *Sémiotique* 9.

80 "The term 'transition' is and remains a clever turn in logic. Transition belongs in the sphere of historical freedom, for transition is a *state* and it is actual," Kierkegaard, *Anxiety* 82. Kierkegaard's emphasis.

81 On Balzac's bracketing out of the question of the historical specificity of his era in his *Avant-propos*, see Françoise Gaillard, "La Science: modèle ou vérité: réflexions sur *l'avant-propos* à *La comédie humaine*," *Balzac: l'invention du roman*, Colloque de Cérisy (Paris: Belfond, 1982) 77.

82 Barbéris, *Mythes* 18. Barbéris notes that the Restoration, for Balzac, was obsessed with revenge, rather than power for its own sake. Like Mme Vauquer, it confused the process of confirming power at the expense of others, a politically and socially necessary evil, with a process of wreaking revenge upon them.

83 See Sharif Gemie, "Balzac and the Moral Crisis of the July Monarachy," *European History Quarterly* 19 (1989): 474 for a discussion of the new class of notables that blended the nobility and the bourgeoisie, yet resisted those who were gaining economic power. Balzac, in my opinion, attributed this blending to the avowed or unavowed search for economic power.

84 See "Balzac: Lost Illusions," in Lukács, *Studies* 47–64, for a discussion of *Lost Illusions* as a novel about capitalist society's economically necessary demystification of its own illusions, in particular his remarks on the commodification of words.

85 Terdiman, *Discourse* 105. For examples of this structure of initiation, which lies hidden in many of Balzac's novels, see among others *Eugénie Grandet*, *Sarrasine*, "Le Curé de Tours," *La Cousine Bette* and *Le Cousin Pons*.

86 Terdiman, *Discourse* 106.

87 Petrey, *Realism* 85.

88 "[S]aying 'I salute you' is no more describing my performance than is saying 'Salaam.' To do or to say these things is to make plain how the action is to be taken or understood, what action it is. As so it is with putting in the expression 'I promise that.' It is not a description, because (1) it could not be false, nor, therefore, true; (2) saying 'I promise that' (if happy, of course) *makes it* a promise, and *makes it* unambiguously a promise." Austin, *How* 70. Austin's emphasis.

Vautrin would certainly not agree with Austin that, within a prescribed situation, to say the words "I promise" "*makes it* unambiguously a promise." For Vautrin, the laws that dictate the situation in which these words act are arbitrary and subject to change according to who he is with and when he is with them. Only particular circumstances in space (the particular group of people) and time (the specific moment in history), not laws, can decide whether these words perform the act of promising. Whereas, from Austin's point of view, the explicit performative, "I promise," performs, but does not describe, the act of promising whenever a conventionally prescribed situation is present, from Vautrin's point of view, it does so only according to individual circumstances that cannot be prescribed.

89 De Man, *Allegories* 8.

90 Miller, "Illusions" 179. Balzac's defenders of the social order do not do so by deliberately forgetting facts of the past as will Nietzsche's powerful. Memory remains the best means of maximizing power over circumstances. By remembering what the honest want to hear, the powerful transform their blind belief in knowledge into a useful circumstance that enables them to dupe and overcome them.

91 Jefferson, *Stendhal* 124.

92 For a discussion of the increasingly narrative nature of Balzac's novels see Miller, "Illusions" 178.

93 "[C]'est en somme le *calcul* qui fait le plein de cette littérature." Barthes, *S/Z* 188. Barthes's emphasis.

94 Proust points to Balzac's vulgar pleasure in boasting about his power to manipulate others. He cites the following letter written by Balzac to his sister concerning his forthcoming marriage to Mme Hanska: "Va, Laure, c'est quelque chose à Paris que de pouvoir, quand on le veut, ouvrir son salon et y rassembler l'élite de la société, qui y trouve une femme polie, imposante comme une reine, d'une naissance illustre, alliée aux plus grandes familles, spirituelle, instruite et belle. Il y a là un grand moyen de domination." "Sainte-Beuve et Balzac," in *Contre* 263.

95 See Lynn R. Wilkinson, "Embodying the Crowd: Balzac's

L'Envers de l'histoire contemporaine and the Languages of Class Consciousness," *Symposium* 43 (1989): 127–37. Wilkinson discusses Balzac's reaction, during the 1840s, to a growing working-class consciousness. He reduced this consciousness to a retrograde guild consciousness and to a form of female hysteria, and he opposed it to superior and male modern individualism. She makes the interesting suggestion that Balzac's representation of victimized classes may have been a novelistic talking cure. If so, the providing of novelistic therapy and expression to the working classes was a means of making them accomplices in their own repression.

96 Johnson, *Modern* 880–83. Within Balzac's model of the text as narrative and social transformation, descriptive and narrative representations function only as obstacles or aids to the transformation being performed, whether this be to produce an "effet de réel historique," to satisfy the readers' desire to feel that they are accomplices in powerful actions, or to make the transformations arbitrarily chosen by Balzac appear necessary. Balzac's description of the visible evidence of fate branded into Chabert's body would be what Greimas calls a "mini-récit," a means of making the acts of repression performed by the colonel's wife appear to be necessary. But this narrative representation of her acts would simply mark, not describe, the act of linguistic and social transformation that Balzac is performing.

97 Miller, "Illusions" 178.

98 If Vautrin's reader, Lucien, were to truly become powerful and confirm his master's power, his gratitude for his master's benevolent teaching would also be deceptive. It would ironically serve to subordinate his master and thus disconfirm his power: "[S]i vous étiez ingrat avec moi, vous seriez alors un homme fort, et je plierais devant vous." Balzac, *Comédie* 5: 698. See Lyotard, *Différend* 174.

99 For examples of works where resentment plays this role, see Mlle Michonneau in *Le Père Goriot* and *Splendeurs et misères des courtisanes*. For an example of renunciation see the duchess in "La Duchesse de Langeais." M. Vernier in "L'Illustre Gaudissart" provides the most striking example of indifference, but one might also consider as a similar indifference Paquita's inability to understand the concept of possession or of the rivalry between sister and brother in "La Fille aux yeux d'or."

100 See Felman, *Writing* 101–15 for a discussion of the decentering of the ego's narcissistic illusion of power and Terdiman, *Discourse* for a discussion of the decentering of the bourgeois individual's illusion of power.

I owe a great debt in this discussion to Felman's chapter on

Gaudissart as I do to Terdiman's chapter on Balzac. Felman and Terdiman decenter the concept of power by denying it to the individual speaker, but they recenter it by attributing it to language and, in the case of Terdiman, to history. I will argue that language not only decenters the power of the individual, it decenters itself by deconstructing the very category upon which the power/impotence polarity is based: action. It demystifies the illusion that text, writing, or reading can be accurately characterized according to the category of power, any more than to the category of knowledge.

101 Along with Felman's and Terdiman's discussions of these relations, see Kanes, *Comedy* 174.

102 See Terdiman, *Discourse* 106, for the link between liberal capitalism and the belief that language provides the individual with power.

103 Felman, *Writing* 105.

104 Editors note, 3. Balzac crossed this comment out near the beginning of his manuscript.

105 Both Felman and Terdiman argue that Balzac constructs reality as a field of rival forces, in other words, as what the former calls the "free play of language," and the latter calls a "dialectic" of "social transformation."

106 Nietzsche's theory of speech acts, for example, asserts that knowledge is arbitrary and that there is no difference between a statement and its contrary: all affirmations are logically reversible. But, as Paul de Man shows, Nietzsche realizes in certain passages that his attempt to replace the reversibility of knowledge with the description of irreversible speech acts, a replacement that also takes place in speech act theory and Greimassian narrative semiotics, ironically states the reversibility of this description and of the knowledge about speech acts that it claims to provide, *Allegories* 119–31.

107 Felman, *Writing* 113.

108 See De Man, "Promises (Social Contract)" in *Allegories* 246–77.

109 Balzac's emphasis. Balzac's own father was victimized by a similar false written guarantee. See Barbéris, Pierre, ed., Balzac, *Comédie* 4: 1347.

110 Austin, *How* 14–15.

111 Austin, *How* 70.

112 Felman, *Writing* 111. Felman discusses reversibility in "L'Illustre Gaudissart," although she is specifically speaking about the reversibility of logical categories (madness/reason), not of narrative transformations. She interprets logical reversibility in the

same way that I have interpreted the reversibility of Balzac's descriptions: as a negation of knowledge. Like Gaudissart, however, she concludes that this negation is equivalent to an affirmation that language is constituted by speech acts.

113 See Terdiman's definition of nineteenth-century "counter-discourse" in *Discourse* 86.

114 Even the act of producing profit for the provincial is unproductive of anything new: "Pour tout négoce nous tâchons *bonifacement* de vendre les choses plus cher qu'elles ne coûtent. Nous resterons dans cette ornière-là sans que ni Dieu ni diable puisse nous en sortir" (4: 581).

115 James Gleick, *Chaos*: *Making a New Science* (New York: Penguin, 1987) 41. "Balzac may have been moving toward a recognition of the role that the novel could play, as a form of social therapy which could bring to expression suppressed and excluded voices." Wilkinson, "Crowd" 136–37.

116 Balzac had a bust of Napoleon in his apartment.

117 Felman, *Writing* 105.

118 Terdiman, *Discourse* 110–12.

119 Cf. Christopher Prendergast, *The Order of Mimesis*: *Balzac, Stendhal, Nerval, Flaubert* (Cambridge: Cambridge University Press, 1986) 83.

120 Thus it is impossible for a protégé to describe Vautrin as a powerful liar without indirectly describing his own description as a misrepresentation. As long as Lucien remains Vautrin's marionette, his slavish servitude, as Hegel explained, cannot confirm his master's power. It can only prove this master's impotence to make himself or his slave powerful. When Lucien truthfully denounces Vautrin as a liar and seducer, he appears to achieve Vautrin's ideal. He acts as if he were exercising real power over Vautrin, but he does so at the expense of destroying any possibility of his own future power over society. He really disconfirms Vautrin's power to make his protégé powerful.

121 If a linguistic proposition about what words do is true – for example, "Je suis ou je serai plus puissant que jamais" (6: 929) – it cannot be proved to be true without providing evidence that the contrary proposition is also true. This is a law of propositional logic which dictates the inability of closed systems to confirm their own consistency or completeness and which was enunciated by Gödel: "Gödel made the remarkable discovery that each of the systems which he investigated had the property that there was a proposition p such that the proposition $p = \sim p$ [P is true if and only if I do not believe P to be true] was provable in the system

... Here we have a proposition p equivalent to its own non-provability in the system!" Raymond Smullyan, *Forever Undecided: A Puzzle Guide to Gödel* (New York: Knopf, 1987) 109.

122 See James Smith Allen, "Obedience, Struggle and Revolt: The Historical Vision of Balzac's *Father Goriot*," *Clio*, 16.2 (1987) 109. Allen refers to Vidocq's memoirs as a possible source for Vautrin, citing François Vidocq, *Histoire de Vodocq, chef de la police de surêté* ..., 4 vols. (Paris: Tenon, 1828–29).

123 Balzac would have preferred that this unifying role be played by a monarch. But the failure of the Restoration and the growing power of upper middle-class bankers and industrialists in French politics made this solution impossible. See Barbéris, *Mythes* 12–13 and Balzac, *Comédie* 1: 13.

124 Cf. Miller, "Illusions" 176–77.

125 See Terdiman for the argument that Lucien is a reflection of the individual's impotence in the face of historical determinism, *Discourse* 112. Also see Felman for the argument that the madman is a reflection of "the play of language in and for itself" which "produces its own space," language's pure autonomy and power, *Writing* 110.

126 Barbéris, "Dialectique" 212. Also see Miller, "Illusions" 172, 176–77 and Prendgergast, *Order* 112–118.

127 Auerbach, *Mimesis* 23.

128 For the argument that discourse in Balzac is reversible, see Felman, *Writing* 111–12. For the argument that history makes discourse in Balzac irreversible see Terdiman, *Discourse* 116.

129 See Lucien Dällenbach, "Le Tout en morceaux (*La Comédie humaine* et l'opération de lecture II)," *Poétique* 42 (1980): 156–69 for an argument that the *Comédie humaine* is, rather than appears, fragmented.

2 DESCRIPTIVE AND NARRATIVE SELF-DECEPTION: FLAUBERT'S ALLEGORY OF PARODY

1 For a definition of parody, see Graham Falconer, "L'Effet parodie chez Flaubert," *Etudes littéraires*, 19.1 (1986): 109. I presuppose that parody is a form of irony which negates, by repeating it, a recognizable, conventional discourse. Flaubert parodies the conventional novelistic discourses that create a narrative or descriptive effect: the false impression that the novel is narrative or descriptive in nature.

2 See Ross Chambers, *Mélancolie et opposition: Les débuts du modernisme en France* (Paris: Corti, 1987) 223–34.

3 "Such a work as *L'Education sentimentale* radically deconstructs the very forces and systems that function in the creation of meaning in the Balzacian or Jamesian novel." Peter Brooks, *The Melodramatic Imagination: Balzac, Henry James, Melodrama, and the Mode of Excess* (New Haven: Yale University Press, 1976) 198.

4 Flaubert, *Oeuvres*, Bibliothèque de la Pléiade, 2 vols. (Paris: Gallimard, 1951–52). All references to Flaubert's prose in this chapter will be followed, in parentheses, by the title (when necessary), the volume, and the page numbers from the Pléiade edition.

5 "Beyond events, beyond psychology, time gives [Flaubert's characters] the essential quality of their existence." Georg Lukács, *The Theory of the Novel: A Historico-Philosophical Essay on the Forms of Great Epic Literature* (Cambridge: MIT Press, 1971) 125. Flaubert is "the first major novelist to understand that the novel is essentially an experience *in time*." Victor Brombert, *The Novels of Flaubert* (Princeton: Princeton University Press, 1966) 179. I will argue that temporalization is only one aspect of Flaubert's texts. For general theoretical remarks about the imperfective/perfective difference, see the Introduction.

6 Eric Auerbach has argued that Flaubert's narrator does not adopt an interior point of view since many of his utterances represent a character's thought with words that the character would never use or know. Auerbach confuses discourse with identifiable lexical items or syntactical structures. My thesis is not that the narrator pretends to be repeating the character's exact words or linguistic structures, but rather that he is repeating their attempt to impose a descriptive or narrative aspect onto discourse and conscious reality. The narrator can create semiotically the same discursive illusion as the character's mind, he can repeat it without using the same words. Cf. Auerbach, *Mimesis* 485 and Banfield, *Unspeakable* 187–89.

It might be objected that many of the narrator's utterances appear to be attributed to no point of view. I will argue that moments of interiorized discourse are indirect means of representing discourse in general, including those of the narrator's utterances that do not construct the fiction of an interior point of view.

7 Hamon, *Introduction* 54.

8 "[L]es hommes ... dans cette vision continue, homogène, ne sont pas plus que les choses, mais pas moins, 'une illusion à décrire.'" Proust, "A Propos du 'Style' de Flaubert," *Contre* 589.

9 A. J. Greimas, *Sémantique structurale* (Paris: Larousse, 1966) 178–80.

10 See Terdiman's distinction between "synthetic" and "active"

narration, where the first is based on the imperfect tense, the latter on the preterite. *Dialectics* 71. Terdiman interprets the imperfect as interiorizing and rendering passive, and he interprets the preterite as exteriorizing and rendering active. Although these are tendencies of both tenses, they can express interiorization because they are signs of the imperfective and perfective discursive aspects, which enable the minds of Flaubert's characters to construct the fictions of interior/exterior, passive/active.

11 Jefferson, *Stendhal* 126.

12 Proust, *Contre* 588–89. Proust discusses how Flaubert uses inanimate objects as the subjects of active verbs. This use, he shows, interiorizes the act signified by the *passé simple* tense. Such interiorization refutes the recent attempt by grammarians to eliminate the perfective aspect from the aorist in order to exclude it from the representation of thought. Ann Banfield has asserted that grammatical distinctions between the *passé simple* and imperfect tenses represent conceptual distinctions between action and thought. The *passé simple*, she contends, signifies only temporal anteriority in relation to the present of narration. It does not signify the perfective aspect of past time and thus is not contrasted to the imperfective aspect of time signified by the imperfect tense. However, French grammarians have long realized that the *passé simple*/imperfect distinction, particularly in prose fiction, is an aspectual distinction that brackets out the chronological relation to the present of narration. Only the aspectual interpretation of the *passé simple* can explain Proust's reading of passé simple tenses, like "filèrent," as subjective perceptions of change. Banfield does make a convincing case, however, that the concept of consciousness in the novel presupposes the imperfect tense, but this presupposition is based on the tense's imperfective aspect. These problems would appear to disappear if it is posited that the imperfective aspect constitutes the subject of consciousness as a point of view within a duration. But the object of consciousness can be constituted either as something passing by, by means of the imperfective aspect, or as a complete change, by means of the perfective aspect. See Banfield, *Unspeakable* 104; and J. P. Vinay and J. Darbelnet, *Stylistique comparée du français et de l'anglais* (Paris: Didier, 1958) 132.

13 Proust, *Contre* 588.

14 Greimas, *Semiotics* 93.

15 See Paul De Man, "Semiology and Rhetoric," *Allegories* 3–19, 16 in particular.

16 The representation of mental time as a process of forgetting, rather

than remembering, distinctions between the temporal and the non-temporal, indeed, as a breaking down of distinctions between the temporal and the spatial, is also occurring in nineteenth-century poetry. See, for example, the end of Baudelaire's "Le Voyage":

> Faut-il partir? rester? Si tu peux rester, reste;
> Pars, s'il le faut. L'un court, et l'autre se tapit
> Pour tromper l'ennemi vigilant et funeste,
> Le Temps! Il est, hélas! des coureurs sans répit
> ...
> Nous nous embarquerons sur la mer des Ténèbres
> Avec le cœur joyeux d'un jeune passager.
> Entendez-vous ces voix, charmantes et funèbres,
> qui chantent: "Par ici!" vous qui voulez manger
> Le Lotus parfumé!...

Les Fleurs du Mal, Classiques Garniers (Paris: Gallimard, 1961) 155–60. The redefinition of remembering as a forgetting will be discussed at the end of this chapter and in Chapter III.

17 The notion of a mental text lies implicit in Proust's reading of Flaubert. It becomes explicit in *Le Temps retrouvé*: "Quant au livre intérieur de signes inconnus (de signes en relief, semblait-il, que mon attention, explorant mon inconscient, allait chercher, heurtait, contournait, comme un plongeur qui sonde), pour la lecture desquels personne ne pouvait m'aider d'aucune règle, cette lecture consistait en un acte de création." (3: 879).

18 As Proust noted, in order to create the fiction of continuous thought, Flaubert, who is generally quite sloppy about rules of syntax, becomes highly rigorous, precisely because syntax enables him to create the impression of erasing spaces between representational signs: "[D]ans cette deuxième page de l'*Education*, s'il s'agit de relier deux paragraphes pour qu'une vision ne soit pas interrompue, alors le pronom personnel, à renversement pour ainsi dire, est employé avec une rigueur grammaticale, parce que la liaison des parties du tableau, le rythme régulier particulier à Flaubert, sont en jeu..." Proust is referring to a passage that we have already quoted ("il en surgit une autre, plus proche sur la rive opposée. Des arbres la couronnaient"). Flaubert, he argues, chooses "il en surgit une autre" in order to eliminate some of the distance on the page between "autre" and the direct object, "la," in the next sentence and paragraph. *Contre* 588. This grammatical continuity is encouraged by the French language which, unlike English, tends to create as many syntactical links as possible within and between sentences. See Vinay, *Stylistique* 220–23. The overall

effect of Flaubert's syntactical manipulation is to reinforce verbally the impression of a continuous rhythm of thought, the fiction of a continuous mental reality. This is not the continuity of an unmediated or unreflected perception, but that of thought's unending repetition and alternation between discourse's two temporal aspects, its two means of constituting itself temporally.

19 The rhetorical nature of Flaubert's text methodically negates the assertion that there exist grammatical markers of a character's (or a narrator's) point of view, as argued by Banfield, *Unspeakable* 68–70. Flaubert does use grammar to construct deceptive points of view, but as Proust's article demonstrates, he does so in order to demonstrate the rhetorical reversibility of such grammatical structures and thus the deceptiveness of the fictional "views" they construct, of the consciousness or focal "point" of his characters' minds. See Henry H. Weinberg, "Centers of Consciousness Reconsidered", *Poetics Today*, 5.4 (1984) 771.

20 Jean-Jacques Rousseau, *Les Rêveries du promeneur solitaire* (Paris: Garnier-Flammarion, 1964) 102.

21 Rousseau, *Rêveries* 100.

22 See Jacques Derrida's comments on "auto-affection" in Rousseau, in *De la grammatologie* (Paris: Minuit, 1967) 221.

23 Rousseau, *Rêveries* 102.

24 I do not wish to suggest that Rousseau is unaware of the precariousness of this self-consciousness. The construction of his self-consciousness in the "Fifth Promenade" is framed by repeated reminders that society has alienated him from this state, exiling it to a past or redefining it as a fleeting repetition. Moreover, approaching death progressively destroys his mind's ability to construct this state. However, unlike Flaubert, he does not, I believe, present it as a fiction of time, but as a reality threatened by time.

25 Jonathan Culler, *Flaubert: The Uses of Uncertainty*, Revised Edition (Ithaca: Cornell University Press, 1985) 156. For an argument that *Mme Bovary* is an "expression mélancolique" with a "pathos du manque" that marks it as a modernist rather than post-modernist text, see Chambers, *Mélancolie* 224–25. Also see Chamber's comparison of Flaubert's discourse to a "degré zéro" of discourse in "Simplicité de cœur et duplicité textuelle. Etude d'*Un cœur simple*," *Modern Language Notes*, 96 (1981): 772.

26 I use the word "allegory" according to what I believe to be Paul de Man's implicit use of the term: a process of writing and reading that temporalizes spatial conceptions of rhetoric, a becoming time of rhetorical space. See "Rhetoric" 205–06.

27 For a different reading of parody in Flaubert, one that grounds it in the affirmation or denial of historical reality, see Richard Terdiman, "Counter-humorists: Strategies of Resistance in Marx and Flaubert," *Discourse* 198–226.

28 Hamon, *Introduction* 40, 98. Like Hamon, I do not believe that discourse is descriptive or narrative. But whereas Hamon argues, in synecdochal terms, that all texts are partially constituted by the structures of both, with some having the "descriptif comme une dominante," others the narrative, I argue that neither exists as a part or whole of discourse. The descriptive and the narrative are pure appearances, "aspects." Certain texts create the illusion of being dominated by the descriptive aspect by denying that they are narrative, others create the illusion of being dominated by the narrative aspect by denying that they are descriptive, but no text can become descriptive or narrative, in part or in its entirety.

29 For a discussion and deconstruction of the narrative aspect of romantic discourse, see Nathaniel Wing, *The Limits of Narrative: Essays on Baudelaire, Flaubert, Rimbaud and Mallarmé* (Cambridge: Cambridge University Press, 1986) 75–77.

30 The parody of Félicité's self-deception in *Un cœur simple* is much less evident, although just as present. The parody of Emma's self-deception in *Mme Bovary* is sometimes hidden behind the tragic aspect of the narrative, but well documented. Parody is much more evident in *L'Education sentimentale*, where Frédéric's self-deception often appears burlesque, and he a clown.

31 See Rensselaer W. Lee, *Ut Pictura Poesis: The Humanistic Theory of Painting*, (New York: Norton, 1967).

32 Flaubert mocks Lamartine in *Mme Bovary* and in his *Correspondance*. See Françoise Martin-Berthet, "La Perception de la parodie du romantisme dans *Madame de Bovary* et *L'Education sentimentale*," *Burlesque et formes parodiques dans la littérature et les arts*, eds. Isabelle Landy-Houillon and Maurice Ménard (Seattle-Tubingen: Wolfgang Leiner, 1987) 590.

33 For a discussion of romantic ambivalence over the relationship between imagination and perception, see de Man, "Rhetoric" 181–84.

34 Flaubert's discussion of descriptive illusion deconstructs the Hegelian dialectic between the sublime particular detail and the general idea. He interprets the particular, the present, as he interprets the universal. They are both fictional products of the generality of signs, of linguistic absence. Since the particular is a fictional product of general signs, there can be no true "details" in Flaubert, only characters, like Félicité, who create the fetishistic

illusion of detail. For a discussion of Hegel's discourse on the detail and its relationship to Barthes, see Naomi Schor, *Reading* 23–41, 94–97.

35 Paul De Man, "The Rhetoric of Blindness: Jacques Derrida's Reading of Rousseau," *Blindness and Insight: Essays in the Rhetoric of Contemporary Criticism*, (New York: Oxford University Press, 1971) 102–41.

36 For a discussion of romantic discourse's lack of distinction between people and things, see Wing, *Limits* 70.

37 For an argument that the realist text remembers past discourses of knowledge, see Philippe Hamon, *Introduction* 51–54.

38 Cf. Terdiman, "Deconstructing" 13–36.

39 For a discussion of irony and speech acts, see Warning, "Reading" 304–16. For suggestions on the relationship between irony and fetishism, see Naomi Schor, "Fetishism and its Ironies," *Nineteenth-Century French Studies*, 17.1–2 (1988–89): 89–97.

40 For a psychoanalytic discussion of the implicit aggression in Frédéric's romantic discourse and in his ironical repetition of it, see Vaheed K. Ramazani, "Lacan/Flaubert: Towards a Psychopoetics of Irony," *Romanic Review*, 80.4 (1989): 553.

41 Greimas interprets the descriptive in the same way, as the surface manifestation of a narrative act of transformation, a referential lie. An introductory passage describing the market day in Maupassant's "La Ficelle" is thus for Greimas the surface manifestation of a profound narrative structure "à la base des relations sociales, et qui consiste *à tromper et à ne pas se laisser tromper* dans un monde où la vérité n'est que le masque du mensonge." The descriptive illusion of reference hides and reveals the reality of a narrative transformation and seduction that is "*dépourvu de sens*" and that acts out the "auto-destruction des valeurs péniblement acquises." It destroys the hierarchical illusion of the descriptive. *Du Sens* II 151–53. Greimas's emphasis.

42 See Victor Brombert's discussion of the role of the prostitute in *L'Education sentimentale*, *Novels* 125–39.

43 See René Girard, *Mensonge romantique et vérité romanesque* (Paris: Grasset, 1961) and Michal Peled Ginsburg, *Flaubert Writing: A Study in Narrative Strategies* (Stanford: Stanford University Press, 1986) 140–47.

44 The many Parises that Frédéric and the revolution of 1848 discursively construct throughout the rest of the novel are only projections of their immediate preconceptions of their needs. None for Flaubert constitute accurate representations of the center of Parisian life. See P. M. Wetherill, "Paris dans *L'Education senti-*

mentale," *Flaubert: la femme, la ville* (Paris: Presses universitaires de France, 1982) 130.

45 See Terdiman, *Discourse* 198–226, for an argument that "counter-discourses" in Flaubert, such as Frédéric's and the revolution's models of exchange, are determined by social history rather than language.

46 Fredric Jameson, *Postmodernism: or, the Cultural Logic of Late Capitalism* (Durham: Duke University Press, 1991) 410.

47 T. J. Clark, *The Absolute Bourgeois: Artists and Politics in France 1848–1851* (Princeton: Princeton University Press, 1982) 67.

48 Cf. Michel Crouzet, "Passion et politique dans *L'Education sentimentale, Flaubert, la femme, la ville* (Paris: Presses universitaires de France, 1982) 51–57.

49 Clark, *Absolute* 21.

50 Jameson, *Postmodernism* 410–11.

51 See Lynne Layton, "Flaubert's *L'Education sentimentale*: A Tragedy of Mind," *French Forum* 11.3 (1986) 343, for remarks on the relationship between Rosanette and masochism. Also see Crouzet, *Passion* 57, for a discussion of the self-destructiveness of the Second Republic.

52 Dambreuse is totally impervious to love. Balzac's Nucingen is not. See Balzac, *Splendeurs* 6: 684.

53 Prendergast, *Order* 210.

54 For comments on the relationship between lying and forgetting in Flaubert's early "Mémoires d'un fou," see Felman, *Writing* 100.

55 On forgetting in the nineteenth century, see Terdiman, "Deconstructing" 16–17.

56 Friedrich Nietzsche, "Uses" 57–123.

57 For a similar statement about the heart of a man, see Flaubert's description of Rodolphe's letters in *Mme Bovary, Oeuvres* 1: 509.

58 See Terdiman, *Discourse* 25–81, for a determinist point of view on counter-discourses in general.

59 "Flaubert is in fact depicting a society in which more and more people appear to have power within their reach and more and more people are aware of power (through newspapers, urbanization, etc.), but in which fewer and fewer people are actually allowed to attain it," Layton, "Tragedy" 347.

60 See chapter 1 above.

61 See both Culler, *Uses* 195 and Pierre Bergounioux, "Flaubert et l'autre," *Communications* 19 (1972): 50 for discussions of what the latter calls "le caractère parataxique du 'style' flaubertien."

62 Proust, *Contre* 595.

63 Flaubert's use of the *passé simple* tense to construct a character's

memory of repeated past actions, a memory situated after that repetition is completed, foreshadows Proust's use of the *passé composé*, in the first sentence of his novel, of a narrator's memory of the repeated act of remembering, also situated, perhaps, after this repetition is completed: "Longtemps, je me suis couché de bonne heure," *Recherche* 1: 3. Both authors, I would argue, use the perfective to frame remembering as a repetition within a forgetting and a rewriting of the past.

64 Falconer, "Effet" 109.

65 This illusion of forgetting is not a Nietzschean forgetting, one whose purpose is to increase power over discourse. Frédéric has rejected such a forgetting as self-defeating and self-deceived. Rather, it resembles a Freudian sublimation which economizes energy by resigning itself to the inability to repeat discourse without being repeated by it. On the complex question of whether Freudian sublimation reduces or produces energy, see Laplanche, *Problématiques* 215–24.

66 Frédéric's and French society's resignation to being repeated by, as well as to repeating, discourse must be distinguished from Sartre's interpretation, in *L'Idiot de la famille*, of the reification process in which, in Layton's words, "humans and their products come to be experienced as the result of forces outside of human control." Layton, "Tragedy" 335. Flaubert's is not a "black humanism" or a "tragedy of mind," but a renunciation of the power to make the black/white, tragic/comic, power/impotence distinctions, a renunciation necessitated or made possible only by the nature of discourse.

67 Jacques Derrida, "La différance," *Marges de la philosophie* (Paris: Editions de Minuit, 1972) 1–29.

68 Meile Steele, "*L'Education sentimentale* and the *Bildungsroman*: Reading Frédéric Moreau," *Romanic Review*, 78.1 (1987): 101.

69 Cf. Steele, "*Bildungsroman*" 87.

70 Cf. Girard, *Mensonge* and Eric Gans, "Flaubert's Scenes of Origin," *Romanic Review* 81.2 (1990): 199.

71 Ramazani, "Psychopoetics" 559. See also Shoshana Felman, "Illusion réaliste et répétition romanesque," *La Critique générative*, ed. Jean Paris (Paris: Sehers, 1973): 193–48.

72 See Martin-Berthet, "Perception" 597 for a fascinating evocation of the slippage of Flaubert's novels out of pastiche over the history of their reading. Also see Prendergast, *Order* 200–04.

73 de Man, *Rhetoric* 190.

74 Cf. Culler, *Uses* 226.

75 Georges Poulet, *Etudes sur le temps humain* (Paris: Plon, 1949) 317.

76 Charles Carlut, *La Correspondance de Flaubert: étude et répertoire critique* (Columbus: Ohio State University Press, 1968) 389. Flaubert's emphasis. For a discussion of the text as spatial form, see Joseph Frank, *The Widening Gyre* (New Brunswick: Rutgers University Press, 1963), Hamon, *Personnel* 32, and W. J. T Mitchell, "Spatial Form in Literature: Toward a General Theory," *Critical Inquiry*, 6 (1980): 539–67. On the relation between the space of Paris and the novel's action, see Wetherill, "Paris" 123–35.

77 This is perhaps what Derrida means by "espacement." See Derrida, *Grammatologie* 99, Culler, *Uses* 151. and Falconer, "Effet" 121.

78 Carlut, *Correspondance* 390. Jameson calls such a spatial juxtaposition of parodied (he would say pastiched) discourses "postmodern." See *Postmodernism* 412–18.

79 Weinberg, "Centers" 772.

80 Cf. Chambers, *Mélancolie* 216. Also Fredric Jameson's conclusion that the *Trois Contes* "emits a message about art language, only in order thereby to free some deeper fantasy about history itself." "Flaubert's Libidinal Historicism: *Trois Contes*," in *Flaubert and Postmodernism*, eds. Naomi Schor and Henry F. Majewski (Lincoln: University of Nebraska Press, 1984) 83. In Flaubert, however, time is constantly reborn out of the spatiality of form, if in the form of fictional narratives of which Jameson's "history" is a modern version.

81 Carnivalization is one, but only one, form that temporalization takes in Flaubert's texts. See Dominick LaCapra, Madame Bovary *on Trial* (Ithaca: Cornell University Press, 1982) 118.

82 Cf. Falconer, Effet 109.

83 de Man, "Rhetoric" 205.

3 FORGETTING AND BEYOND: ZOLA AND ALLEGORY

1 David Quint, *Origin and Originality in Renaissance Literature: Versions of the Source* (New Haven: Yale University Press, 1983) 3.

2 See chapter 3 above, Terdiman, "Deconstructing" 14, Yates, *Art* and Carruthers, *Book*.

3 On the proliferation of memory in Flaubert, see LaCapra, *Trial* 65–117.

4 Friedrich Nietzsche, "Uses" 64.

5 Jon Whitman, "From the Textual to the Temporal: Early Christian 'Allegory' and Early Romantic 'Symbol,'" *New Literary History* 22.1 (1991) 161; Susan K. Hagen, *Allegorical Remembrance: A Study of* The Pilgrimage of the Life of Man *as a Medieval Treatise*

on Seeing and Remembering (Athens: University of Georgia Press, 1990) 68.

6 See Terdiman, "Deconstructing" 14 on the crisis of memory, Jameson, "Postmodernism" 6, on the crisis of historicity, and Denis Hollier, "How to Not Take Pleasure in Talking about Sex," *Enclitic* 8:1–2 (1984) 88, on Zola and sublimation.

7 This and all subsequent quotations from Zola's *Rougon-Macquart* will be followed, in parentheses, by the volume and page numbers from the Pléaide edition.

8 Proust, *Recherche* 1: 3. Claude's wife, Christine, later compares his blindness to sleeping. He begins to paint with "des yeux élargis de somnambule" (4: 342) and she later cries: "'Réveille-toi, ouvre les yeux, rentre dans l'existence'" (4: 347). Similarly, the narrator characterizes Claude's return from his flight into the countryside, where he tries to escape the tragic reality of Paris, as "comme réveillé d'un long sommeil" (4: 193). See Jacques Derrida's discussion of Freud's "Note on the 'Mystic Writing Pad,'" in "Freud" 334.

9 See chapter 2 above.

10 Ann Banfield's theory of the relation between imperfect and *passé simple* tenses and the representation of consciousness is useful in studying Zola precisely because it presupposes the fixed reality of a subject/object distinction. See chapter 2, note 12 above.

11 On the relation between description and intention, see Richard J. Bernstein, *Praxis and Action* (Philadelphia: University of Pennsylvania Press, 1971) 271–73.

12 Gilles Deleuze, "Zola et la fêlure," Preface, *La Bête humaine*, by Emile Zola, Folio (Paris: Gallimard, 1977) 7–24.

13 On the unconscious destructive power that Nana wields over men, see Naomi Schor, *Zola's Crowds* (Baltimore: Johns Hopkins University Press, 1978) 167–68.

14 See the Introduction to this study for a discussion of Freud's description of the mind as an alternation between consciousness and unconsciousness.

15 For Zola, the ability to see details is far from universal, being limited to those whose eyes are physiologically endowed with "[l]e sens du réel." Some people have "des yeux qui ne voient rien du tout. Ils ont sans doute quelque lésion, le nerf qui les relie au cerveau éprouve une paralysie que la science n'a pu encore déterminer." Emile Zola, *Le Roman expérimental* (Paris: Garnier-Flammarion, 1971) 215.

16 Henri Mitterand, "Le regard d'Emile Zola," *Europe*, April-May (1968): 197.

17 William J. Berg, "*L'œuvre*: Naturalism and Impressionism," *L'Esprit créateur*, 25:4 (1985) 45.
18 Schor, *Zola's* 175.
19 See Schor's discussion of the ambivalent status of the sacred in the *Rougon-Macquart*, *Zola's* 19–21.
20 Austin, *How* 67–82.
21 Proust, *Recherche* 1 : 3.
22 Hegel, *Phenomenology* 250.
23 Zola, *Expérimental* 79.
24 Zola, *Expérimental* 231. Also see Hilda Olrik and Marianne Marcussen, "Le Réel chez Zola et les peintres impressionistes: perception et représentation," *Revue d'histoire littéraire de la France*, 80.6 (1980) 972.
25 Zola, *Expérimental* 66.
26 Zola, *Expérimental* 232. Cf. Petrey, *Realism* 174–75.
27 Zola, *Expérimental* 214.
28 Zola, *Expérimental* 77
29 Zola, *Expérimental* 78.
30 Zola, *Expérimental* 79.
31 Cited in Hamon, *Introduction* 225.
32 Jameson, *Postmodernism* 25.
33 Jameson, *Postmodernism* 418. I am writing here only of Jameson's historicist definition of the postmodern. There are quite different definitions, the most interesting of which are ironical and anti-historicist, since they deconstruct the distinction between the modern and the postmodern. For an introduction to the history of the term "postmodernist," see many of the fine essays on the postmodern in Ingeborg Hoesterey ed., *Zeitgeist in Babel: The Postmodernist Controversy* (Bloomington: Indiana University Press, 1991).
34 Hamon, *Personnel* 321; Jameson 413.
35 Hamon, *Personnel* 32–38 and *Introduction* 225–26, 241–54.
36 See Hamon's discussion of a readable description, *Introduction* 153.
37 Balzac, *Comédie* 10: 436.
38 "[L]'art prétendu réaliste... ne serait pas si mensonger si nous n'avions pris dans la vie l'habitude de donner à ce que nous sentons une expression qui en diffère tellement, et que nous prenons au bout de peu de temps pour la réalité même." *Recherche* 3: 881.
39 Zola, *Expérimental* 213–18.
40 Zola contrasts Claude's choice of Christine, a woman who encourages his self-destructive desires, "[l]a femme dévastatrice, la femme qui tue l'artiste, lui broie le cœur et lui mange le cerveau," with Sandoz's choice of a wife who encourages his

constructive desires: "Lui, d'ailleurs, avait le besoin d'une affection gardienne de sa tranquillité, d'un intérieur de tendresse où il pût se cloîtrer, afin de consacrer sa vie entière à l'œuvre énorme dont il promenait le rêve" (4: 160).

41 See Hamon, *Personnel* 318–19 and Henri Mitterand, "Pour une poétique de l'espace romanesque: l'exemple de Zola," *Zola and the Craft of Fiction* (*Essays in Honour of F. W. J. Hemmings*), eds. Robert Lethbridge and Terry Keefe (Leicester: Leicester University Press, 1990) 80–88.

42 See Schor, *Zola's* 171, also 121 on Zola's criticism of wasting sperm, birth control, and abortion in *Fécondité.*

43 Samuel Beckett, *En attendant Godot* (Paris: Minuit, 1952), 156; Jameson, *Postmodernism* 364.

44 Zola, *Expérimental* 219–23.

45 Hamon, *Personnel* 321–23.

46 "Se peindre" becomes the equivalent of "se pendre."

47 Jameson, *Postmodernism* 276.

48 Jameson, *Postmodernism* 206.

49 Cf. Jameson, *Postmodernism* 382–83 for an unconvincing attempt (in my opinion) to distinguish his postmodern art from *fin-de-siècle* decadence. Zola's self-destructing, decadent monopoly capitalism takes on all the attributes that Jameson attributes to a postmodernist, world market capitalism.

50 Jameson, *Postmodernism* 412.

51 Michel Serres, *Feux et signaux de brume* (Paris: Grasset, 1975) 342.

52 See the discussion of the imperfective aspect in the Introduction and the meditation on reversible descriptions in *Chabert* and *L'Education sentimentale* in chapter's 1 and 2.

53 "[L]a modalité du pouvoir apparaît toujours fortement régie et surmodalisée par les modalités du vouloir, et surtout, du savoir ..." Hamon, *Personnel* 272. The descriptive, Hamon argues, structures the text as a cyclical movement of hiding and revealing. *Personnel* 235. But the knowledge this movement periodically reveals, I believe, is a paradoxical knowledge of the descriptive's forgetting and deceitfulness, a knowledge of its unreadability that is marked by Christine's final inability to read or write: "[E]lle en était venue à oublier jusqu'à son orthographe" (4: 355).

54 De Man, *Allegories* 8. De Man defines "grammatical patterns" as a "consistent link between sign and meaning."

55 "This inclination of the naturalist novelist towards a position of complete exteriority, which is in the end nothing more than the critical moment of Romantic individualism, the moment in which its insufficiencies become blatantly obvious, will soon make him opaque even to himself. Obliged to recognize that despite his

differences, he is one of these people, he will be devoured, as it were, by the quality of absolute strangeness he has attributed to them." Michel Butor, *Répertoire II* (Paris: Editions de Minuit, 1964) 82–83. Cited in Schor, *Zola's* 132. Schor's translation.

56 "La 'bande,' chez Zola, n'est souvent que l'actant collectif-chœur qui fait et défait le personnage..." Hamon, *Personnel* 322.

57 Cf. Petrey, *Realism* 181 on *Germinal*'s "acceptance of a natural paradigm" that "condemns its proletarian characters to a future that will repeat their brutal past." This natural paradigm is produced by the reversibility of the descriptive's imperfective aspect.

58 Warning, *Irony* 314–15.

59 Jameson, *Postmodernism* 258–59.

60 For a brief history of the word "historicism" and a critical interpretation of its contemporary use and relation to historicity, see Jonathan Rée, "The Vanity of Historicism," *New Literary History*, 22:4 (1991) 962.

61 Zola repeatedly identified Sandoz as himself. Patrick Brady, "*L'œuvre*" *de Emile Zola* (Geneva: Droz, 1967) 258.

62 Serres, *Feux* 351.

63 On the cemetery images of death, fire, and blood not only at the beginning of the *Rougon-Macquart*, but at the end as well, *La Débâcle*, see Schor, *Zola's* 175.

64 Balzac *Comédie*, 3: 289–90.

65 Schor, *Zola's* 71.

66 Despite the strong differences between Zola's theories of realist representation and Proust's redefinition of realist representation as a lie, there are important formal similarities between their modes of dramatizing the interplay between the consciousness and the unconscious, remembering and forgetting. Moreover, on the level of Proust's narrator and on that of his characters (as in Zola), the inevitability of forgetting raises serious questions about the possibility of novelistic representation. See, for example, the narrator's comparison, at the end of *A la recherche du temps perdu*, between novels like his future novel and an unmarked cemetery: "l'herbe drue des œuvres fécondes, sur laquelle les générations viendront faire gaîment, sans souci de ceux qui dorment en dessous, leur 'déjeuner sur l'herbe.'" *Recherche* 1038. Much could be said about this passage as Proust's reinterpretation of Zola's naturalist pastiche of Manet's painting, Claude's "Plein air."

67 Victor Hugo, *Oeuvres poétiques*, Bibliothèque de la Pleiade (Paris: Gallimard, 1964) 1093–98.

68 See Serres, *Feux* 65.

69 Proust, *Recherche* 2: 499.

70 Deleuze, *Zola* 22.

71 Edouard Toulouse, *Emile Zola* (Paris: Société d'editions scientifiques, 1896) 258. (Toulouse's underlining). When Toulouse asked him to identify the styles of well-known authors, his answers were outrageously off, the doctor says.

72 Zola reinforces this comparison between Claude's forgetting and his own forgetting by his very choice of a name for his surrogate, Sandoz. This name includes not only part of Zola's own name "oz," as has been often pointed out, but the entire name of Georges Sand, his prime example of a novelist who is guilty of repeating Romantic clichés. See *Expérimental* 214. If we make the further guess that "oz" recalls "œil," precisely that which Sand's romanticism blinds, then Zola's history is throwing romantic sand into Claude's, Sandoz's, and his own eyes. For an interpretation of Sandoz's name as a sign of historical reversibility, see Schor, *Zola's* 179–80. All interpretations of Sandoz's name obviously depend upon discourse's power to mirror its own functioning, precisely what Zola's novels, I will argue, put into question.

73 See Stephane Mallarmé, "Don du poème," *Poésies*, Collection poésie (Paris: Gallimard, 1952) 44. "O la berceuse, avec ta fille et l'innocence / De vos pieds froids, accueille une horrible naissance ..."

74 Schor, *Zola's* 69–70.

75 There are many discussions of Zola's romantic heritage, one of the best being in Schor's *Zola's Crowds*. See also Brady, "*L'œuvre*" 364.

76 Aimé Guedj, Préface, *Expérimental* 18.

77 See Jack Lindsay, "Cézanne and Zola," *Arts and Artists*, Sept. (1969): 23–27, and Henri Mitterand, "Etudes, notes et variantes," Zola, *Rougon* 4: 1385–86.

78 One must carefully distinguish between Zola's multiple interpretations of the train here and in *La Bête humaine*. In some cases, he dramatizes it as history's destruction of individuality. In others, he dramatizes it as history's destruction of the power to see and describe what history is making individuals do. I develop this difference in a reading of *La Bête humaine* in "Writing History as Temporality: the *Rougon-Macquart*," *Naturalism in the European Novel: Modern Essays in Criticism*, ed. Brian Nelson (Oxford: Berg, 1992) 80–95.

79 Sandoz implicitly recognizes the possibility of Eugen Weber's conclusion that the apocalyptic mentality in some *fin-de-siècle* literature, including Zola's, did not reflect the reality of everyday life. Eugen Weber, *France: Fin de Siècle* (Cambridge: Harvard University Press, 1986) 9–26.

80 de Man, *Rhetoric* 206.
81 Cf. Jameson, *Postmodernism* 382–83.
82 Søren Kierkegaard, *Philosophical Fragments*, trans. Howard V. Hong and Edna H. Hong (Princeton: Princeton University Press, 1985) 81.
83 Rée, "Vanity" 978–80.

CONCLUSION

1 Proust, *Recherche* 2: 419.
2 Cf. Kate Hamburger, *The Logic of Literature*, trans. Marilynn Rose (Bloomington: Indiana University Press, 1973).
3 See Terdiman, "Deconstructing" 14–17: "[T]he functioning of memory itself, the institution of memory and thereby of history, became a critical preoccupation of the effort to think through the present."
4 Debray-Genette, "Pierre" 293.
5 Gustave Flaubert, letter to Louis Bouilhet, 19 December 1850, cited by Terdiman, "Deconstructing" 15.
6 Flaubert deconstructs the basis of the Neomarxist, historicist argument that nineteenth-century discourse remembers "its long production within a network of cultural struggle, the *difference* which marks this flow of time." Terdiman, "Deconstructing"' 13, 35. For Flaubert, any consciousness of an irreversible historical act or difference is a self-deceived discursive construct.
7 De Man, "Rhetoric" 207. The critique and decentering of speech act theory in de Man's *Allegories of Reading* deconstruct the centrality that his earlier "The Rhetoric of Temporality" appeared to give to the temporality of writing and reading. See "Reading (Proust)" and "Rhetoric of Persuasion," *Allegories* 77–78 and 119–31.
8 Kierkegaard, *Irony* 272–73.
9 de Man, "Rhetoric" 193.
10 Derrida, "Freud" 339.
11 de Man, "Rhetoric" 206.
12 de Man, "Rhetoric" 190.
13 de Man, "Rhetoric" 206.
14 Flaubert, *Oeuvres* 2: 443; Zola, *Rougon* 4: 363.
15 Laplanche's discussion of sublimation, it seems to me, traces a similar breakdown of contraries, such as between the sexual and the non-sexual or "énergie non-liée" and "énergie liée." See in particular *Sublimation* 249–51.
16 Jacques Derrida, *Grammatologie* 99.

Bibliography

Allen, James Smith. "Obedience, Struggle and Revolt: The Historical Vision of Balzac's *Father Goriot.*" *Clio* 16.2 (1987): 103–19.

Aristotle. *Poetics*. Trans. S. H. Butcher. New York: Hill and Wang, 1961.

Auerbach, Eric. *Mimesis*. Princeton: Princeton University Press, 1953.

Austin, J. L. *How to Do Things With Words*. 2nd edn. Cambridge: Harvard University Press, 1975.

Bahti, Timothy. "Lessons of Remembering and Forgetting." *Reading de Man Reading*. Eds. Lindsay Waters and Wlad Godzich. Minneapolis: University of Minnesota Press, 1989. 244–58.

Bal, Mieke. "Théorie de la description: l'exemple de *Madame Bovary*." *Flaubert: la dimension du texte*. Ed. P. M. Wetherill. Manchester: Manchester University Press, 1982. 175–236.

Balzac, Honoré de. *La Comédie humaine*. Bibliothèque de la Pléiade. 11 vols. Paris: Gallimard, 1976–80.

Banfield, Ann. *Unspeakable Sentences: Narration and Representation in the Language of Fiction*. Boston: Routledge and Kegan Paul, 1982.

Barbéris, Pierre. "Dialectique du Prince et du Marchand." *Balzac: l'invention du roman*. Colloque de Cérisy. Paris: Belfond, 1982. 181–212.

Mythes Balzaciens. Paris: Armand Colin, 1972.

Bardèche, Maurice. *Balzac Romancier*. Paris: Plon, 1940.

Barthes, Roland. "L'Effet de réel." *Communications* 11 (1968): 84–89.

S/Z. Paris: Seuil, 1970.

Baudelaire, Charles. *Les Fleurs du Mal*. Classiques Garnier. Paris: Gallimard, 1961.

Baudrillard, Jean. *For a Critique of the Political Economy of the Sign*. Trans. Charles Levin. St. Louis: Telos, 1981.

Beaujour, Michel. "Some Paradoxes of Description." *Yale French Studies* 61 (1981): 27–59.

Beckett, Samuel. *En attendant Godot*. Paris: Seuil, 1952.

Beizer, Janet L. *Family Plots: Balzac's Narrative Generations*. New Haven: Yale University Press, 1986.

Benveniste, Emile. *Problems in General Linguistics*. Trans. Mary Elizabeth Meek. Coral Gables: Miami University Press, 1971.

Berg, William J. "*L'œuvre*: Naturalism and Impressionism." *L'Esprit créateur* 25.4 (1985): 42–50.

Bergounioux, Pierre. "Flaubert et l'autre." *Communications* 19 (1972): 40–50.

Bernstein, Richard J. *Praxis and Action*. Philadelphia: University of Pennsylvania Press, 1971.

Borie, Jean. *Zola et les mythes ou de la nausée au salut*. Paris: Seuil, 1971.

Brady, Patrick. "*L'œuvre*" *de Emile Zola*. Geneva: Droz, 1968.

Brombert, Victor. "*L'Education sentimentale*: articulations et polyvalence." *La Production du sens chez Flaubert*. Paris: 10/18, 1975. 55–69.

"Flaubert and the Temptation of the Subject.' *Nineteenth Century French Studies* 12.3 (1984): 280–96.

The Novels of Flaubert. Princeton: Princeton University Press, 1966.

Brooks, Peter. *The Melodramatic Imagination: Balzac, Henry James, Melodrama, and the Mode of Excess*. New Haven: Yale University Press, 1976.

"Narrative Transaction and Transference (Unburying *Le Colonel Chabert*)." *Novel* 15.2 (1982): 101–10.

Reading for the Plot. New York: Knopf, 1984.

Butor, Michel. *Répertoire II*. Paris: Editions de Minuit, 1964.

Carlut, Charles. *La Correspondance de Flaubert: étude et répertoire critique*. Columbus: Ohio State University Press, 1968.

Carruthers, Mary. *The Book of Memory: A Study of Memory in Medieval Culture*. Cambridge: Cambridge University Press, 1990.

Chambers, Ross. *Meaning and Meaningfulness: Studies in the Analysis and Interpretation of texts*. Lexington: French Forum, 1979.

Mélancolie et opposition: Les débuts du modernisme en France. Paris: Corti, 1987.

"Simplicité de cœur et duplicité textuelle. Etude d'*Un cœur simple*." *Modern Language Notes* 96 (1981): 771–91.

Clark, T. J. *The Absolute Bourgeois: Artists and Politics in France* 1848–51. Princeton: Princeton University Press, 1982.

Comrie, Bernard. *Aspect: An Introduction to the Study of Verbal Aspect and Related Problems*. Cambridge: Cambridge University Press, 1976.

Crouzet, Michel. "Passion et politique dans *L'Education sentimentale*." *Flaubert, la femme, la ville*. Paris: Presses universitaires de France, 1982. 39–71.

Culler, Jonathan. *Flaubert: The Uses of Uncertainty*. Revised Edition. Ithica: Cornell University Press, 1985.

Dällenbach, Lucien. "Du fragment au cosmos (*La Comédie humaine* et l'opération de lecture I)." *Poétique* 40 (1979): 420–31

"Le Tout en morceaux: (*La Comédie humaine* et l'opération de lecture, II)." *Poétique* 42 (1980): 156–69.

Debray-Genette, Raymonde. "La Pierre descriptive." *Revue de Théorie et d'Analyse Littéraires* 11.43 (1980): 293–304.

"Some Functions of Figures in Novelistic Description." *Poetics Today* 5.4 (1984): 677–88.

Deleuze, Gilles. "Zola et la fêlure." Preface. *La Bête humaine*. By Emile Zola. Folio. Paris: Gallimard, 1977. 7–24.

De Man, Paul. *Allegories of Reading*. New Haven: Yale University Press, 1979.

Blindness and Insight: Essays in the Rhetoric of Contemporary Criticism. New York: Oxford University Press, 1971.

"The Rhetoric of Temporality." *Interpretations*, Ed. Charles Singleton. Baltimore: Johns Hopkins University Press, 1970. 173–209.

Derrida, Jacques. "Freud et la scène de l'écriture." *L'Ecriture et la différence*. Paris: Seuil, 1967. 293–340.

De la grammatologie. Paris: Editions de Minuit, 1967.

Marges de la philosophie. Paris: Editions de Minuit, 1972.

Diaz, Jose-Luis. "Balzac-Oxymore: logiques balzaciennes de la contradiction." *Revues des Sciences Humaines* 175 (1979): 33–47.

Eco, Umberto. *A Theory of Semiotics*. Bloomington: Indiana University Press, 1976.

Falconer, Graham. "L'Effet parodie chez Flaubert." *Etudes littéraires* 19.1 (1986): 103–24.

Felman, Shoshana. *La Folie et la chose littéraire*. Paris: Seuil, 1978.

"Illusion réaliste et répétition romanesque." *La Critique générative*. Ed. Jean Paris. Paris: Sehers, 1973. 293–348.

Writing and Madness. Ithaca: Cornell University Press, 1978.

Flaubert, Gustave. *Oeuvres*. 2 vols. Bibliothèque de la Pléiade. Paris: Gallimard, 1951–52.

Foucault, Michel. *Les Mots et les choses: une archéologie des sciences humaines*. Paris: Gallimard, 1966.

Frank, Joseph. *The Widening Gyre*. New Brunswick: Rutgers University Press, 1963.

Frappier-Mazur, Lucienne. "La description mnémonique dans le roman romantique." *Littérature* 38 (1980): 3–26.

"Sémiotique du corps malade dans *la Comédie Humaine*." *Balzac: L'Invention du roman*. Colloque de Cerisy. Paris: Belfond, 1982. 15–41.

Freud, Sigmund. *The Standard Edition of the Complete Psychological Works.* Trans. James Strachey. 24 vols. London: Hogarth Press, 1966–74.

Gaillard, Françoise. "L'En-signement du réel." *La Production du sens chez Flaubert.* Paris: 10/18, 1975. 197–219.

"The Great Illusion of Realism, or the Real as Representation." *Poetics Today* 5.5 (1984): 753–66.

"La Science: Modèle ou Vérité: Réflexions sur l'avant-propos à *La comédie humaine.*" *Balzac: l'invention du roman.* Colloque de Cérisy. Paris: Belfond, 1982. 57–83.

Gans, Eric. "Flaubert's Scenes of Origin." *Romanic Review* 81.2 (1990): 189–202.

Gemie, Sharif. "Balzac and the Moral Crisis of the July Monarchy." *European History Quarterly* 19 (1989): 469–94.

Genette, Gérard. *Figures II.* Paris: Seuil, 1969. 49–69.

Figures III. Paris: Seuil, 1972. 41–63.

Ginsburg, Michal Peled. *Flaubert Writing: A Study in Narrative Strategies.* Stanford: Stanford University Press, 1986.

Girard, René. *Mensonge romantique et vérité romanesque.* Paris: Grasset, 1961.

Gleick, James. *Chaos: Making a New Science.* New York: Penguin, 1987.

Goethe, J. W. *Selected Verse,* Middlesex: Penguin, 1964. 195–96.

Greimas, A. J. *Sémantique structurale.* Paris: Larousse, 1966.

Sémiotique, dictionnaire raisonné de la théorie du langage. 2 vols. Paris: Hachette, 1986.

Semiotics and Language. Bloomington: Indiana University Press, 1982.

Du Sens II. 2 vols. Paris: Seuil, 1970–83.

Hagen, Susan K. *Allegorical Remembrance: A Study of* The Pilgrimage of the Life of Man *as a Medieval Treatise on Seeing and Remembering.* Athens: University of Georgia Press, 1990.

Hamburger, Kate. *The Logic of Literature.* Trans. Marilynn Rose. Bloomington: Indiana University Press, 1973.

Hamon, Philippe. "Un discours contraint." *Poetique* 16 (1973): 411–45.

Introduction à l'analyse du descriptif. Paris: Hachette, 1981.

Le Personnel du roman: le système des personnages dans les Rougon-Macquart *d'Emile Zola.* Geneva: Droz, 1983.

Hegel, G. W. F. *The Phenomenology of Mind.* Trans. J. B. Baillie. New York: Harper and Row, 1967.

Philosophy of History. Trans. J. Sibree. New York: Dover, 1956.

Heidegger, Martin. *Being and Time.* Trans. John Macquarrie and Edward Robinson. New York: Harper and Row, 1962.

Hochberg, Julian. "The Repesentation of Things and People." *Art, Perception, and Reality*. Baltimore: Johns Hopkins University Press, 1970. 47–94.

Hoesterey, Ingeborg. Ed. *Zeitgeist in Babel: The Postmodernist Controversy*. Bloomington: Indiana University Press, 1991.

Hofmann, Carol. *Forgetting and Marguerite Duras*. Niwot: University Press of Colorado, 1991.

Hollier, Denis. "How to Not Take Pleasure in Talking about Sex." *Enclitic* 8:1–2 (1984): 84–93.

Hugo, Victor. *Oeuvres poétiques*. Bibliothèque de la Pléiade. Paris: Gallimard, 1964.

Imbert, Patrick. "Double texte et autoparodie dans *La Comédie humaine*." *Nineteenth-Century French Studies* 15.4 (1987): 365–75.

Jakobson, Roman. "Two Aspects of Language and Two Types of Aphasic Disturbances." *Selected Writings*. Vol. 2. The Hague: Mouton, 1971. 239–59.

Jameson, Fredric. "Flaubert's Libidinal Historicism: *Trois Contes*." *Flaubert and Postmodernism*. Lincoln: University of Nebraska Press, 1984. 76–83.

Postmodernism: or, the Cultural Logic of Late Capitalism. Durham: Duke University Press, 1991.

Jefferson, Ann. *Reading Realism in Stendhal*. Cambridge: Cambridge University Press, 1988.

Johnson, Paul. *The Birth of the Modern: World Society* 1815–1830. New York: Harper Collins, 1991.

Kanes, Martin. *Balzac's Comedy of Words*. Princeton: Princeton University Press, 1975.

Kermode, Frank. *The Sense of an Ending, Studies in the Theory of Fiction*. London: Oxford University Press, 1966.

Kierkegaard, Søren. *The Concept of Anxiety*. Trans. Reidar Thomte. Princeton: Princeton University Press, 1980.

The Concept of Irony. Trans. Lee M. Capel. Bloomington: Indiana University Press, 1965.

Philosophical Fragments. Trans. Howard V. Hong and Edna H. Hong. Princeton: Princeton University Press, 1985.

LaCapra, Dominick. Madame Bovary *on Trial*. Ithaca: Cornell University Press, 1982.

Laplanche, Jean. *Problématiques III: la sublimation*. Paris: Presses Universitaires de France, 1980.

Laplanche, J., and Pontalis, J.-B. *The Language of Psycho-Analysis*. Trans. Donald Nicholson-Smith. New York: Norton, 1973.

Lavater, J. C. *Essays of Physiognomy: for the Promotion of the Knowledge and the Love of Mankind*. Trans. Thomas Holcroft. 3 vols. London: C. G. T. and J. Robinson, 1789.

Layton, Lynne. "Flaubert's *L'Education sentimentale*: A Tragedy of Mind." *French Forum* 11.3 (1986): 335–51.

Lee, Rensselaer, W. *Ut Pictura Poesis: The Humanistic Theory of Painting*. New York: Norton, 1967.

Le Huenen, Roland, and Perron, Paul. "Reflections on Balzacian Models of Representation." *Poetics Today* 5.4 (1984): 711–28.

Lessing, Gotthold. *Laocoön*. Trans. Edward Allen McCormick. New York: Bobbs-Merrill, 1962.

Lindsay, Jack. "Cézanne and Zola." *Arts and Artists* Sept. (1969): 23–27.

Lukács, Georg. *Studies in European Realism*. New York: Grosset and Dunlap, 1964.

The Theory of the Novel: A Historico-Philosophical Essay on the Forms of Great Epic Literature. Cambridge: MIT Press, 1971.

Lyotard, Jean-François. *Le Différend*. Paris: Minuit, 1983.

Mallarmé, Stephane. "Don du poème." *Poésies*. Collection poésies. Paris: Gallimard, 1952.

Martin-Berthet, Françoise. "La Perception de la parodie du romantisme dans *Madame de Bovary* et *L'Education sentimentale*." *Burlesque et formes parodiques dans la littérature et les arts*. Eds. Isabelle Landy-Houillon and Maurice Ménard. Seattle-Tubingen: Wolfgang Leiner, 1987. 587–97.

Miller, D. A. "Balzac's Illusions Lost and Found." *Yale French Studies* 67 (1984): 164–81.

Mitchell, W. J. T. "Spatial Form in Literature: Toward a General Theory." *Critical Inquiry* 6 (1980): 539–67.

Mitterand, Henri. "Le regard d'Emile Zola." *Europe* April-May (1968): 182–99.

"Pour une poétique de l'espace romanesque: l'exemple de Zola." *Zola and the Craft of Fiction (Essays in Honour of F. W. J. Hemmings)*. Eds. Robert Lethbridge and Terry Keefe. Leicester: Leicester University Press, 1990. 80–88.

Neefs, Jacques. "*Illusions perdues*: Représentation de l'acte romanesque." *Le Roman de Balzac*. Eds. Roland Le Huenen and Paul Perron. Montreal: Didier, 1980. 119–30.

Niess, Robert J. *Zola, Cézanne, and Manet: A Study of L'œuvre*. Ann Arbor: Michigan University Press, 1969.

Nietzsche, Friedrich. "On the Uses and Disadvantages of History for Life." *Untimely Meditations*. Trans. R. J. Hollingdale. Cambridge: Cambridge University Press, 1983. 57–123.

"On Truth and Lies in a Nonmoral Sense." *Philosophy and Truth*. Trans. Daniel Breazeale. New Jersey: Humanities Press, 1979. 79–97.

The Will to Power. Trans. Walter Kaufmann and R. J. Hollingdale. New York: Vintage, 1967.

Olrik, Hilda, and Marianne Marcussen. "Le Réel chez Zola et les peintres impressionistes: perception et représentation." *Revue d'histoire littéraire de la France* 80.6 (1980): 965–77.

Petrey, Sandy. *Realism and Revolution: Balzac, Stendhal, Zola, and the Performances of History*. Ithaca: Cornell University Press, 1988.

"The Reality of Representation: Between Marx and Balzac." *Critical Inquiry* 14 (1988): 448–68.

Poulet, Georges. *Etudes sur le temps humain*. Paris: Plon, 1949.

Prendergast, Christopher. *The Order of Mimesis: Balzac, Stendhal, Nerval, Flaubert*. Cambridge: Cambridge University Press, 1986.

Proust, Marcel. *A la recherche du temps perdu*. Bibliothèque de la Pléiade. 3 vols. Paris: Gallimard, 1954.

Contre Sainte-Beuve. Bibliothèque de la Pléiade. Paris: Gallimard, 1971.

Quint, David. *Origin and Originality in Renaissance Literature: Versions of the Source*. New Haven: Yale University Press, 1983.

Quintilian. *Institutes of Oratory*. 2 vols. London: George Bell and Sons, 1888.

Ramazani, Vaheed K. "Lacan/Flaubert: Towards a Psychopoetics of Irony." *Romanic Review* 80.4 (1989): 548–59.

Rée, Jonathan. "The Vanity of Historicism." *New Literary History* 22.4 (1991): 961–83.

Reid, James. "Lying, Irony, and Deconstruction; Nietzsche and Proust." *Style* 22.3 (1988): 467–78.

"Writing History as Temporality: the Rougon-Macquart." *Naturalism in the European Novel: Modern Essays in Criticism*. Ed. Brian Nelson. Oxford: Berg, 1992: 80–95.

Ricardou, Jean. *Le Nouveau Roman*. Paris: Seuil, 1973.

Ricoeur, Paul. *Temps et Récit*. 3 vols. Paris: Seuil, 1983–85.

Riffaterre, Michael. "Contraintes de lecture: l'humour balzacien." *L'Esprit créateur* 24:2 (1984): 12–22.

Rousseau, Jean-Jacques. *Les Rêveries du promeneur solitaire*. Paris: Garnier-Flammarion, 1964.

Schor, Naomi. "Fetishism and its Ironies." *Nineteenth-Century French Studies* 17.1–2 (1988–89): 89–97.

Reading in Detail: Aesthetics and the Feminine. New York: Methuen, 1987.

Zola's Crowds. Baltimore: Johns Hopkins University Press, 1978.

Serres, Michel. *Feux et signaux de brume*. Paris: Grasset, 1975.

Smullyan, Raymond. *Forever Undecided: A Puzzle Guide to Gödel*. New York: Knopf, 1987.

Steele, Meile. "*L'Education sentimentale* and the *Bildungsroman*: Reading Frédéric Moreau." *Romanic Review* 78.1 (1987): 84–101.

Stendhal. *Romans et nouvelles*. Bibliothèque de la Pléiade. Vol. 1. Paris: Gallimard, 1952.

Terdiman, Richard. "Deconstructing Memory: On Representing the Past and Theorizing Culture in France Since the Revolution." *Diacritics* Winter (1985): 13–36.

The Dialectics of Isolation. New Haven: Yale University Press, 1976.

Discourse/Counter-Discourse: The Theory and Practice of Symbolic Resistance in Nineteenth-Century France. Ithaca: Cornell University Press, 1985.

Thibaudet, Albert. *Gustave Flaubert*. Paris: Gallimard, 1935.

Toulouse, Edouard. *Emile Zola*. Paris: Société d'éditions scientifiques, 1896.

Valin, Roch. "The Aspects of the French Verb." Appendix to *Time, Aspect and the Verb*. By Hirtle, W. H. Québec: Laval University Press, 1975. 131–45.

Vannier, Bernard. *L'Inscription du corps: pour une sémiotique du portrait balzacien*. Paris: Klincksieck, 1972.

Van Rossum-Guyon, Françoise. "Aspects et fonctions de la description chez Balzac." Année Balzacienne (1980): 111–36.

ed. *Balzac: Illusions perdues: "l'œuvre capitale dans l'œuvre"*. Paris: Crin, 1988.

Vidocq, François. *Histoire de Vodocq, chef de la police de surêté*. 4 vols. Paris: Tenon, 1828–29.

Vinay, J. P., and J. Darbelnet. *Stylistique comparée du français et de l'anglais*. Paris: Didier, 1958.

Warning, Rainer. "Reading Irony in Flaubert." *Style* 19 (1985): 304–16.

Waters, Lindsay, and Wlad Godzich, eds. *Reading de Man Reading*. Minneapolis: University of Minnesota Press, 1989.

Weber, Eugen. *France: Fin de Siècle*. Cambridge: Harvard University Press, 1986.

Weinberg, Henry H. "Irony and 'Style Indirect Libre' in *Madame Bovary*." *Canadian Review of Comparative Literature* 8.1 (1981): 1–9.

"Centers of Consciousness Reconsidered." *Poetics Today*. 5.4 (1984): 767–73.

Weinrich, Harald. *Linguistik der Lüge*. 5th edn. Heidelberg: Lambert Schneider, 1974.

Le Temps. Trans. Michèle Lacoste Paris: Seuil, 1973.

Wetherill, P. M. "Paris dans *L'Education sentimentale*." *Flaubert: la femme, la ville*. Paris: Presses universitaires de France, 1982. 123–35.

White, Hayden. *Metahistory: The Historical Imagination in Nineteenth-Century Europe*. Baltimore: Johns Hopkins University Press, 1973.

Whitman, Jon. "From the Textual to the Temporal: Early Christian 'Allegory' and Early Romantic 'Symbol.'" *New Literary History* 22.1 (1991): 161–76.

Wilkinson, Lynn R. "Embodying the Crowd: Balzac's *L'Envers de l'histoire contemporaine* and the Languages of Class Consciousness," *Symposium* 43 (1989): 127–37.

Wing, Nathaniel. *The Limits of Narrative: Essays on Baudelaire, Flaubert, Rimbaud and Mallarmé*. Cambridge: Cambridge University Press, 1986.

Yates, Frances A. *The Art of Memory*. Chicago: University of Chicago Press, 1966.

Zola, Emile. *Le Roman expérimental*. Paris: Garnier-Flammarion, 1971.

Les Rougon-Macquart. Bibliothèque de la Pléiade. 5 vols. Paris: Gallimard, 1960–67.

Index

CAMBRIDGE STUDIES IN FRENCH

Also in the series (* denotes titles now out of print)

1. J. M. Cocking
Proust: Collected Essays on the Writer and his Art
2. Leo Bersani
The Death of Stéphane Mallarmé
*3. Marian Hobson
The Object of Art: The Theory of Illusion in Eighteenth-Century France
4. Leo Spitzer, translated and edited by David Bellos
Essays on Seventeenth-Century French Literature
5. Norman Bryson
Tradition and Desire: From David to Delacroix
6. Ann Moss
Poetry and Fable: Studies in Mythological Narrative in Sixteenth-Century France
7. Rhiannon Goldthorpe
Sartre: Literature and Theory
8. Diana Knight
Flaubert's Characters: The Language of Illusion
9. Andrew Martin
The Knowledge of Ignorance: From Genesis to Jules Verne
10. Geoffrey Bennington
Sententiousness and the Novel: Laying Down the Law in Eighteenth-Century French Fiction
*11. Penny Florence
Mallarmé, Manet and Redon: Visual and Aural Signs and the Generation of Meaning
12. Christopher Prendergast
The Order of Mimesis: Balzac, Stendhal, Nerval, and Flaubert
13. Naomi Segal
The Unintended Reader: Feminism and Manon Lescaut

14. CLIVE SCOTT
A Question of Syllables: Essays in Nineteenth-Century French Verse
15. STIRLING HAIG
Flaubert and the Gift of Speech: Dialogue and Discourse in Four 'Modern' Novels
*16. NATHANIEL WING
The Limits of Narrative: Essays on Baudelaire, Flaubert, Rimbaud and Mallarmé
17. MITCHELL GREENBERG
Corneille, Classicism and the Ruses of Symmetry
*18. HOWARD DAVIES
Sartre and 'Les Temps Modernes'
19. ROBERT GREER COHN
Mallarmé's Prose Poems: A Critical Study
20. CELIA BRITTON
Claude Simon: Writing the Visible
21. DAVID SCOTT
Pictorialist Poetics: Poetry and the Visual Arts in Nineteenth-Century France
22. ANN JEFFERSON
Reading Realism in Stendhal
23. DALIA JUDOVITZ
Subjectivity and Representation in Descartes: The Origins of Modernity
24. RICHARD D. E. BURTON
Baudelaire in 1859
25. MICHAEL MORIARTY
Taste and Ideology in Seventeenth-Century France
26. JOHN FORRESTER
The Seductions of Psychoanalysis: Freud, Lacan and Derrida
27. JEROME SCHWARTZ
Irony and Ideology in Rabelais: Structures of Subversion
28. DAVID BAGULEY
Naturalist Fiction: The Entropic Vision
29. LESLIE HILL
Beckett's Fiction: In Different Words
30. F. W. LEAKEY
Baudelaire: Collected Essays, 1953–1988
31. SARAH KAY
Subjectivity in Troubadour Poetry
32. GILLIAN JONDORF
French Renaissance Tragedy: The Dramatic Word

33. Lawrence D. Kritzman
The Rhetoric of Sexuality and the Literature of the French Renaissance
34. Jerry C. Nash
The Love Aesthetics of Maurice Scève: Poetry and Struggle
35. Peter France
Politeness and its Discontents: Problems in French Classical Culture
36. Mitchell Greenberg
Subjectivity and Subjugation in Seventeenth-Century Drama and Prose: The Family Romance of French Classicism
37. Tom Conley
The Graphic Unconcious in Early Modern French Writing
38. Margery Evans
Baudelaire and Intertextuality: Poetry at the Crossroads
39. Judith Still
Justice and Difference in the Works of Rousseau: *Bienfaisance* and *Pudeur*
40. Christopher Johnson
System and Writing in the Philosophy of Jacques Derrida
41. Carol A. Mossman
Politics and Narratives of Birth: Gynocolonization from Rousseau to Zola
42. Daniel Brewer
The Discourse of Enlightenment in Eighteenth-Century France: Diderot and the Art of Philosophizing
43. Roberta L. Krueger
Women Readers and the Ideology of Gender in Old French Verse Romance